# The Healthcare Executive's Simple Guide to FMV

Edited by
# Jen Johnson, CFA
VMG Health

# The Healthcare Executive's Simple Guide to FMV

## For Attorneys, C-Suite, Compliance, and Physicians

AMERICAN BAR ASSOCIATION
Health Law Section

Cover design by Elmarie Jara/ABA Design

Printed in the United States of America.

21 20 19 18 17 5 4 3 2 1

Library of Congress Cataloging-in-Publication Data

Names: Johnson, Jen, editor. | American Bar Association. Health Law Section, editor.
Title: The healthcare executive's simple guide to FMV : for attorneys, C-Suite, compliance, and physicians / Edited by Jen Johnson, Health Law Section, American Bar Association.
Description: Chicago : American Bar Association, 2017.
Identifiers: LCCN 2017004507 (print) | LCCN 2017004580 (ebook)
| ISBN 9781634256964 | ISBN 9781634256971 (ebook)
Subjects: LCSH: Medical fees—Law and legislation—United States. | Medical care, Cost of—United States. | Compensation management—United States.
| Compensation (Law)—United States. | Medical personnel—Salaries, etc.—United States. | Health insurance—Law and legislation—United States.
Classification: LCC KF2907.F3 H43 2017 (print) | LCC KF2907.F3 (ebook) | DDC 344.7304/1—dc23
LC record available at https://lccn.loc.gov/2017004507

Discounts are available for books ordered in bulk. Special consideration is given to state bars, CLE programs, and other bar-related organizations. Inquire at Book Publishing, ABA Publishing, American Bar Association, 321 N. Clark Street, Chicago, Illinois 60654-7598.

www.shopABA.org

# *Dedication*

Special thanks to the entire Managing Director Team of VMG Health for quality reviewing and providing valuable input to the book.

# Contents

# *Introduction*

This guide is meant to both educate and save time for healthcare attorneys and executives who are tasked with reviewing a Fair Market Value (FMV) Opinion or any analysis related to the FMV standard within healthcare.

*****

As a result of the changing healthcare environment, the number of transactions and new models for healthcare reimbursement are multiplying. As the economics of healthcare change, so do the valuations of transactions, compensation arrangements, real estate, and fixed assets. This challenge, coupled with increased regulatory scrutiny on cost and referral relationships, has prompted healthcare executives to need more guidance related to the FMV standard.

Many healthcare attorneys, executives, and physicians have limited financial background, but are being asked to carefully review valuations for business and compliance purposes. This guide has been developed to provide basic information on nearly every type of transaction or compensation arrangement that must adhere to the FMV standard.

## ORGANIZATION OF THIS GUIDE

**The Overview Section** of this Guide is meant to be a reference source in order to understand the regulations surrounding FMV and provide general tips to assist in determining if an FMV report is sound and defensible. An appendix is included to provide an easily accessible FMV checklist for readers.

**The Business Valuation Section** provides an overview of the types of entities being valued in today's market. This overview also includes a thorough explanation of the three standard approaches to value (cost, income, market). These three approaches are addressed in most every business valuation analysis or report. Therefore, each chapter is formatted so that these three standard approaches and the nuances associated with each type of entity is addressed. This layout allows the reader to easily reference specific valuation guidelines when reviewing a report related to any entity type.

**The Compensation Arrangement Section** first provides an overview of the types of arrangements in today's market. Each chapter then provides a description of the service and an overview of the type of structures for each type of compensation arrangement. Lastly, value drivers for compensation and key considerations when reviewing each type of compensation FMV analysis are outlined.

**The Real Estate and Capital Asset Section** provide separate chapters for each and includes an additional chapter related to timeshares. Based on the uniqueness of these valuations, these chapters stand alone. Both real estate and capital assets may be leased or purchased, therefore valuation indicators and guidance associated with each are addressed as it relates to these types of valuations specifically.

VMG Health has contributed to this guide based on more than 20 years of experience focused solely on providing healthcare valuations. The overview and valuation methodologies described are not to be construed as legal, tax, consulting, or valuation advice. The following are only guidelines. Should a valuation apply different judgment, it does not indicate the valuation is unsupportable. Understanding regulatory guidance and the reasoning behind selected methods is important when assessing any opinion or analysis.

# Contributors

**Don Barbo, CPA/ABV**

Don Barbo is a Managing Director with VMG Health. He specializes in healthcare business valuations involving mergers and acquisitions, divestitures, partnership transactions, leasing arrangements, divorces, commercial damages, and financial reporting. His extensive healthcare valuation engagements have included hospitals, physician practices, ambulatory surgery centers, diagnostic imaging centers, cardiac catheter labs, pathology and clinical labs, cancer treatment centers, and dialysis centers. Mr. Barbo has also performed engagements for various contracts between hospitals and physicians.

Mr. Barbo has spoken extensively to various legal and valuation organizations and has published articles regarding business valuation issues. He also serves as an expert witness in litigated matters for his clients, including testifying before the U.S. Tax Court. Mr. Barbo is a CPA, holds the Accreditation in Business Valuation from the AICPA, is a member of the Medical Group Management Association (MGMA), and a member of the Healthcare Financial Management Association (HFMA). He also serves on the Technical Advisory Board for the AICPA's Forensics and Valuation Section Consulting Digest. He holds a BBA in Accounting from Texas Tech University, and an MBA from the Cox School of Business, Southern Methodist University.

**Sean Dowd**

Sean Dowd is a Senior Analyst in the Professional Services Agreements Division at VMG Health and is based in the Dallas office. He provides valuation and consulting services for professional service arrangements within the healthcare services industry with a focus on valuations related to management, billing, marketing, co-management, and other administrative services. Prior to joining VMG, he worked as a high school math teacher with Teach for America at the Dallas Independent School District.

Mr. Dowd graduated summa cum laude from the University of Massachusetts Amherst with a double major in finance and political science. He is currently a JD-MBA candidate at Northwestern University's Pritzker School of Law and Kellogg School of Management.

### Silas Eldredge

Silas Eldredge is a Senior Analyst working with the Business Valuation and Research Divisions at VMG Health's Dallas office. Mr. Eldredge has been with VMG Health for two and one-half years and has primarily focused on dialysis, acute-care hospital, specialty hospital, freestanding emergency room, ambulatory surgery, and rehabilitation valuations, in addition to developing benchmarking and transaction databases for a range of healthcare entities. Mr. Eldredge graduated magna cum laude with his bachelor's degree in business from the Bill and Vieve Gore School of Business at Westminster College. Additionally, Mr. Eldredge is also a Level II Candidate in the CFA Program.

### Mary Fan, CVA

Mary Fan is a Senior Analyst in the Professional Services Agreements Division at VMG Health and is based in the Dallas office. She provides valuation and consulting services for professional service arrangements within the healthcare services industry. She has particular expertise in valuations related to telemedicine/telehealth, clinical compensation, on-call coverage, subsidy coverage, and administrative compensation. In addition, she has written on the topics of telemedicine, primary care regulatory guidance, and hospital-based coverage in various healthcare publications.

Ms. Fan graduated summa cum laude and holds a bachelor of business administration degree in finance (with a specialization in alternative assets) from the Edwin L. Cox School of Business at Southern Methodist University. She is currently designated as a Certified Valuation Analyst (CVA) and is also in the process of becoming certified by the American Society of Appraisers.

### Kevin M. Florenz, ASA

Kevin M. Florenz is a Managing Director at VMG Health and oversees the Capital Asset Services Division. Mr. Florenz has more than 25 years of experience providing valuations for domestic and international transactions, such as mergers and acquisitions, and other financial reporting requirements, which include goodwill impairment and long-lived asset impairment. He has performed valuations for federal and international tax purposes, including purchase price allocations, international tax strategies, and debt forgiveness. Mr. Florenz has also performed valuation engagements for due diligence purposes, secured lending transactions, leasing transactions, property tax appeal, litigation and bankruptcy proceedings, insurance, and property records management.

Prior to joining VMG Health, Mr. Florenz held senior leadership positions with CBIZ Valuation Group; American Appraisal; Peritus Valuation Advisory Services; DoveBid Valuation Services, Inc; and KPMG LLP. Mr. Florenz began his career with the CIT Group in its Equipment Management Group and also spent three years at Ernst & Young LLP in the Valuation Group. He graduated with a bachelor of business administration degree in finance from St. Bonaventure University. He has completed several equipment leasing association programs, including an introduction to equipment leasing and the basics of residual forecasting. Mr. Florenz is an Accredited Senior Appraiser (ASA) with the American Society of Appraisers.

### Clinton Flume, CVA

Clinton Flume is a Director at VMG Health in the Dallas office. His focus has been on developing client relationships and providing valuation, transaction advisory, and operational consulting services in the healthcare services industry. He has significant experience with the physician practice, inpatient rehabilitation, cancer treatment, ambulatory surgery center, and diagnostic imaging segments. Mr. Flume's clients include for-profit and not-for-profit health systems, ancillary services providers, development companies across several healthcare industry sub-specialties, and other publicly owned and privately held healthcare entities.

Mr. Flume received a bachelor of arts degree in communication from the Texas Christian University and a master's in business administration from the Mays Business School at Texas A&M University. He has achieved the Certified Valuation Analyst designation from the National Association of Certified Valuators and Analysts and is actively pursuing the Chartered Financial Analyst designation from the CFA

Institute. Mr. Flume has also attended multiple business valuation courses offered by the American Society of Appraisers.

### Jonathan Helm, CVA

Jonathan Helm is a Managing Director in the Professional Service Agreements Division at VMG Health and is based in the Dallas office. His focus includes valuation and consulting services for professional service arrangements within the healthcare services industry. Specifically, he has valued compensation for professional services that include call coverage, clinical coverage, medical directorships, physician consulting, clinical co-management, administrative management, billing/collection, and development. Clients include for-profit and not-for-profit health systems and other publicly owned and privately held healthcare entities.

Mr. Helm serves as a contributor to VMG Health's FMV Tools,™ which allows users to quickly establish compensation levels for employed and independent contractor physicians in various roles based on systematic and unbiased guidelines. He holds a bachelor of business administration degree in financial consulting from Southern Methodist University and a master of business administration degree in finance from the University of Texas at Dallas. He is designated as a Certified Valuation Analyst (CVA) through the National Association of Certified Valuators and Analysts.

### Alexandra Higgins

Alexandra Higgins is a Director in the Professional Services Agreement Division of VMG Health. She specializes in the valuation of a wide variety of agreements and agreement structures, including management fees, billing and collection fees, physician and non-physician executive compensation, co-management compensation, and shared savings arrangements.

Ms. Higgins dedicates a large portion of her practice to consulting and valuation services related to co-management, pay-for-performance payment models, and shared savings distributions for clinical integration networks. She has valued hundreds of arrangements with pay-for-performance components. Other recent experience includes the valuation of post-transaction joint venture management, billing and collection, and managed care contracting fees for a variety of medical facilities, including free-standing emergency departments, urgent care centers, wound care centers, imaging centers, and cancer centers. Alex graduated magna cum laude from Texas Christian University with a Bachelor of Science in International Economics. She has recently written for *HFM Magazine*, *Health Care Compliance Today*, *Becker's Hospital Review*, and *ImagingBiz* and has made multiple presentations on co-management at national healthcare conferences.

### Mallorie Holguin

Mallorie Holguin is an Analyst in the Professional Services Agreement Division in VMG Health's Dallas office. Ms. Holguin joined VMG Health two years ago, and her primary focus has been on valuations related to hospital-based coverage arrangements and physician-group practice models. Prior to joining VMG Health, Ms. Holguin earned a bachelor of science in economics and a master of science in finance from Southern Methodist University.

### Jen Johnson, CFA

Jen Johnson is a Managing Director with VMG Health and has led the Professional Service Agreements Division for over ten years. Her expertise is related to determining Fair Market Value and understanding regulatory guidelines associated with valuing professional service and compensation arrangements. Mrs. Johnson has valued nearly every type of arrangement in the healthcare market and is a thought leader related to valuing pay for performance arrangements. She has also been integral in developing internal compensation tools for some of the largest health systems in the country. Her accomplishments also include providing expert witness testimony related to fair market value and serving as a peer review editor for the Journal of Hospital Administration. She earned her BBA and MBA in Finance, as well as the Chartered Financial Analyst designation, and served as a finance professor for the University of North Texas.

### David LaMonte, CFA

David LaMonte is a Manager in the Business Valuation Services Division at VMG Health in the Dallas office. He primarily works to assist both not-for-profit and for-profit clients with transaction-related valuation, financial, and consulting services. Specifically, Mr. LaMonte has extensive experience working with dialysis centers, acute care hospitals, diagnostic imaging centers, and ambulatory surgery centers. Additionally, he has broad experience providing valuation and consulting services for most other types of businesses in the healthcare industry.

Mr. LaMonte graduated summa cum laude from Texas Christian University with a bachelor of business administration in finance and a bachelor of science in economics. He also holds the Chartered Financial Analyst designation.

### Britt Martin, CVA

Britt Martin is a Manager in the Professional Services Agreement of VMG Health and is based in the Dallas office. She specializes in a wide variety of agreements and agreement structures, including clinical compensation, on-call coverage compensation, medical director/physician executive compensation, management fees, billing and collection fees, and quality incentive compensation.

Ms. Martin graduated from the Dedman College of Humanities and Sciences at Southern Methodist University with a bachelor of arts degree in economics. Ms. Martin is a Certified Valuation Analyst through the National Association of Certified Valuators and Analysts, is pursuing the Accredited Senior Appraiser designation through the American Society of Appraisers, and is currently a Level II Candidate in the CFA Program.

### Victor McConnell, MAI

Victor McConnell, MAI, is a Director in VMG Health's Real Estate Valuation Services department. His real property valuation experience spans the healthcare sector, including acute care and specialty hospitals, MOBs, ASCs, LTACHs, IRFs, imaging centers, cancer clinics, and other specialty facilities. His expertise includes in-depth knowledge of the regulatory issues unique to the valuation of healthcare real estate. Mr. McConnell has provided fair market value and fair market rent analyses to for-profit and not-for-profit health systems across the United States, as well physician groups, REITs, and private equity groups. He has served clients in 40 of the United States.

## Colin M. McDermott, CFA, CPA/ABV

Colin McDermott, CFA, CPA/ABV, is a Managing Director with VMG Health and is based in the Dallas office. He specializes in providing financial, valuation, and transaction advisory services to clients in the healthcare industry. His clients have included hospitals, hospital systems, ambulatory surgery centers, imaging centers, laboratories, physician groups, and other healthcare entities. Mr. McDermott leads the accounting-related valuation services team. He McDermott has assisted numerous nonprofit and for-profit clients with valuation analysis related to ASC 805 Business Combinations and has issued valuation opinions on the fair value of intellectual property and other intangible assets acquired as a result of the acquisition of acute care hospitals, ambulatory surgery centers, rehabilitation hospitals, and multi-specialty physician groups. Additionally, Mr. McDermott has assisted numerous health care clients with their annual impairment testing process as required by ASC 350 Intangibles—Goodwill and Other.

Mr. McDermott received a bachelor of business administration in accounting and a master of science in finance from Texas A&M University. He is a licensed Certified Public Accountant (CPA) in the state of Texas and holds the Chartered Financial Analyst (CFA) designation.

## Kevin McDonough, CFA

Kevin McDonough is a Managing Director at VMG Health and is based out of the Dallas office. During his tenure at VMG, Mr. McDonough has provided valuation, transaction advisory, feasibility, and operational consulting services to the firm's healthcare clients. His clients include acute care hospitals and health systems, ambulatory surgery centers, surgical hospitals, oncology centers, diagnostic imaging centers, dialysis centers, home health agencies, physicians groups, physical and occupational therapy centers, long-term care facilities, and numerous other ancillary healthcare service businesses. In addition, Mr. McDonough helps to lead the firm's life sciences practice, providing valuation services related to many forms of medical device and pharmaceutical consulting arrangements. Finally, he has served as a consultant in the formation and development of numerous physician-hospital joint venture initiatives.

Mr. McDonough graduated cum laude and holds a degree in finance from the McCombs School of Business at the University of Texas at Austin. Additionally, Mr. McDonough is a Chartered Financial Analyst (CFA).

### Nikolaus Melder

Nikolaus Melder is a Manager at VMG Health in the Dallas office and provides financial, valuation, and transaction advisory services to VMG Health's clients. Mr. Melder's experience includes acute care hospitals, ambulatory surgery centers, cancer treatment centers, diagnostic imaging centers, emergency transport companies, home health agencies, physicians groups, physical and occupational therapy centers, urgent care centers, and other ancillary healthcare service businesses. Additionally, Mr. Melder served as a consultant in assisting a publicly held company develop three-way joint ventures for ambulatory surgery centers.

Mr. Melder received a bachelor of business administration in finance from Virginia Commonwealth University and is currently pursuing the Chartered Financial Analyst designation from the CFA Institute and the Accredited Senior Appraiser designation from the American Society of Appraisers. Mr. Melder has collaborated in the development and publication of the Intellimarker Multi-Specialty ASC Benchmarking Study published annually by VMG Health and has been published in Becker's *ASC Review* and *ImagingBiz*.

### Aaron Murski, CVA

Aaron Murski is a Managing Director at VMG Health, where he focuses on providing valuation, transaction advisory, and consulting services to healthcare businesses and healthcare investors across the United States. His experience includes working with for-profit and not-for-profit organizations large and small, in support of the planning and execution of mergers and acquisitions, service line spin-offs, joint ventures, syndications, de novo projects, professional services arrangements, and other business transactions. His experience with healthcare business segments includes everything from primary and specialty care clinics, surgical and ancillary services, diagnostic services, acute and post-acute care, and health plan and other risk-bearing entities and networks associated with population health management.

Mr. Murski also leads the development and publication of the *Intellimarker Multi-Specialty ASC Benchmarking Study,* published annually by VMG Health. Mr. Murski received a bachelor of business administration in finance from the Mays Business School at Texas A&M University. He is also a member of the Healthcare Financial Management Association (HFMA) Lone Star Chapter and the National Association of Certified Valuators and Analysts (NACVA). He maintains the Certified Valuation Analyst (CVA) credential issued by NACVA.

## Taryn Nasr

Taryn Nasr is a Manager in the Business Valuation Services division at VMG Health and is based in the Dallas office. Her focus is on providing financial, valuation, and consulting services for business within the healthcare services industry. She has particular expertise in valuations relating to ambulatory surgery centers, surgical hospitals, oncology centers, diagnostic imaging centers, physician practices, and other ancillary healthcare service businesses.

Mrs. Nasr received a bachelor of business administration in corporate finance with a minor in Accounting from the McCombs School of Business at the University of Texas at Austin. She is currently pursuing the Accredited Senior Appraiser designation from the American Society of Appraisers (ASA).

## Corey Palasota, CFA

Corey Palasota is a Director at VMG Health in the Dallas office. In addition to providing valuation and transaction advisory services, Mr. Palasota is also involved in the firm's proprietary research and management consulting initiatives. Mr. Palasota's valuation and consulting experience spans numerous sub-industries within healthcare, including the valuation of complex multi-billion dollar enterprises. Since joining VMG, he has been involved in over 200 transactions comprised of acute-care hospitals, ambulatory surgery centers, diagnostic imaging centers, urgent care centers, freestanding emergency rooms, physician practices, diagnostic laboratories, inpatient rehabilitation facilities, long-term acute care hospitals, home health agencies, management companies, and assisted living facilities amongst various other healthcare entities.

Mr. Palasota received a bachelor of business administration in finance and Business Honors from the University of Texas at Austin. He has obtained the Chartered Financial Analyst designation from the CFA Institute and has also published numerous articles regarding valuation complexities within the healthcare industry.

### Zachary Sadau

Zachary Sadau is a Manager in the Business Valuation Services Division at the VMG Health Dallas office. He focuses on providing financial, valuation, and transaction advisory services to the firm's healthcare clients. His valuation experience extends across various healthcare sub-industries, including ambulatory surgery centers, cancer treatment centers, diagnostic imaging centers, emergency transport companies, home health agencies, physicians groups, urgent care centers, and other ancillary healthcare businesses.

Mr. Sadau received a bachelor of business administration degree in finance from Oklahoma State University and a master of business administration degree from the University of Dallas. He is currently pursuing the Accredited Senior Appraiser designation from the American Society of Appraisers (ASA).

### Nick Shannon, ASA

Nick Shannon is a Director with VMG Health in the Capital Asset Services Division. Mr. Shannon has extensive experience providing tangible asset valuation services and consulting for tax and financial reporting requirements including purchase price allocation and goodwill impairment, mergers and acquisitions, corporate conversions, fresh start accounting and other purposes. He has served clients across many different industries including healthcare and life sciences, consumer and industrial manufacturing, aerospace and defense, oil and gas, semiconductor manufacturing, and others.

Healthcare clients served by Mr. Shannon have included valuation engagements for hospitals, physician practices, ambulatory surgery centers, catheterization laboratories, and imaging centers. In addition, Mr. Shannon has performed valuation engagements for life sciences clients, including pharmaceutical companies, manufacturers of certified reference standards and materials, and biomanufacturing testing companies. Mr. Shannon graduated with a bachelor of science in industrial distribution from the college of engineering at Texas A&M

University. He is actively pursuing an Accredited Senior Appraiser (ASA) designation with the American Society of Appraisers.

### Chance Sherer, CVA

Chance Sherer is a Director at VMG Health and is based in the Dallas office. He specializes in providing financial, valuation, and transaction advisory services to the firm's healthcare clients. His clients include health systems, ambulatory surgery centers, surgical hospitals, oncology centers, diagnostic imaging centers, dialysis centers, physicians groups, and numerous other ancillary healthcare service businesses. In addition to extensive valuation experience for transaction planning and financial reporting purposes, he has consulted on numerous development, feasibility, and recapitalization analyses for joint venture, restructuring, and de novo business development purposes.

Mr. Sherer is also a research associate and collaborator in the development and publication of the *Intellimarker Multi-Specialty ASC Benchmarking Study*, published annually by VMG Health. Mr. Sherer received a bachelor of business administration in finance from the Cox School of Business at Southern Methodist University and is currently a member of the National Association of Certified Valuation Analysts.

### William Teague, CFA

William Teague is a Director based in the Nashville VMG Health office. Mr. Teague specializes in providing valuation, transaction advisory, and consulting services to the healthcare Industry. He has experience working with acute care hospitals, healthcare technology companies, ambulatory surgery centers, diagnostic imaging facilities, physician practices, and numerous other ancillary service businesses. In addition, Mr. Teague has performed valuations of financial derivatives, such as warrants, options, and other contracts, as well as specific intangible assets, including health system trade names. He also has an extensive background in physician compensation arrangements.

Mr. Teague graduated summa cum laude and holds a bachelor of science in finance and economics from the University of Tennessee at Knoxville. He holds the Chartered Financial Analyst (CFA) designation and is currently pursuing the Certified Valuation Analyst (CVA) designation.

## James Tekippe

James Tekippe is a Senior Analyst in the Professional Services Agreements Division at VMG Health and is based in the Dallas office. His focus is on providing valuation and consulting services for professional services arrangements within the healthcare services industry. He has particular expertise in valuations related to professional and technical reimbursement splits, clinical compensation, on-call compensation, subsidy coverage, and administrative compensation.

Mr. Tekippe graduated with a bachelor of arts in economics from Tulane University and a master of science in finance from the Edwin L. Cox School of Business at Southern Methodist University. In addition to his academic degrees, Mr. Tekippe is currently a Level III Candidate in the CFA Program.

## John S. Trabold, MAI

John S.Trabold has experience in the valuation of commercial, industrial, and investment grade properties to estimate market value and fair market value for ad valorem purposes, allocation of purchase price, financing, Stark law compliance, and investment decisions. Industries served include medical, banking, hospitality, manufacturing, and financial services.

Mr. Trabold has extensive experience in the valuation of complex healthcare properties including hospitals, medical office buildings, surgery centers, imaging centers, and long-term acute care hospitals. Clients include Glacier Hospital, Capella Healthcare, Wise County Regional Health System, Texoma Medical Center, Reliant Hospital Partners, HCA, Saint Peter's Healthcare System, Henry Ford Health System, Cirrus Health, Saint Joseph Healthcare, University General Hospital, MultiCare Health System, Baylor Health Care System, HMA, LifeCare Hospitals, USPI, CHRISTUS Spohn Health System, CHS, Kutak Rock, LLP, HealthSouth, Emerus, BayCare Health System, Shore Medical Center, Butler, Snow, O'Mara, Stevens & Cannada, PLLC, 21st Century Oncology, Citrus County Hospital, Jones Day, and Hunton & Williams, LLP.

## Bridget Triepke, CPA

Bridget Triepke is a Director with VMG Health and is based in the Dallas office. She has ten years of experience performing valuation, transaction advisory, and consulting services for the purposes of financial reporting compliance, tax planning, and merger and acquisition planning. Mrs. Triepke's clients include for-profit and not-for-profit hospital systems, ancillary service providers, and physician practices.

Mrs. Triepke is a part of VMG Health's financial reporting valuation team. She has performed numerous valuations related to acquisitions and affiliations as required by ASC 805, Business Combinations and ASC 958, Not-For-Profit Entities. Mrs. Triepke is a licensed Certified Public Accountant (CPA) in the state of Texas and holds a bachelor of business administration in accounting and a master of science in finance from Texas A&M University. Mrs. Triepke is a member of the American Institute of Certified Public Accountants and the Healthcare Financial Management Association.

### Ben Ulrich, CVA

Ben Ulrich is a Director in the Professional Service Agreements Division at VMG Health and is based in the Dallas office. His focus is on providing valuation and consulting services for professional service arrangements within the healthcare services industry. He has particular expertise in valuations relating to on-call coverage, physician administrative and executive services, clinical compensation, subsidy coverage, management, billing, development, and quality initiatives.

Prior to joining the Professional Service Agreements Division, Mr. Ulrich worked in VMG Health's Business Valuation division where he provided valuation services related to hospitals, specialty/surgical hospitals, ambulatory surgical centers, diagnostic imaging centers, and single and multi-specialty physician practices, among others. Mr. Ulrich graduated summa cum laude and holds a bachelor of business administration degree in financial consulting from the Edwin L. Cox School of Business at Southern Methodist University. Mr. Ulrich is currently designated as a Certified Valuation Analyst (CVA) and is a member of the National Association of Certified Valuation Analysts.

# *Part One:*
## *Overview*

# Fair Market Value in the Healthcare Regulatory Landscape

**1**

## Introduction

Federal and state governments have enacted complex laws and regulations to regulate the affairs of businesses. Where regulators once required individuals and businesses who inadvertently violated regulations to implement corrective measures, it's now commonplace for them to deploy the full range of potential sanctions against wrongdoers, including administrative, civil, and criminal measures.[1] The healthcare laws and regulations that physicians, hospitals, and other healthcare providers must obey when providing services to patients in this country have become so intrusive and sometimes counterintuitive that what seems to be a good business opportunity to the uninitiated often will be problematic.[2] Consequently, it's not unusual for

---

1. Adapted from Michael E. Clark, *Government Enforcement Risk Areas Facing In-House and Outside Business Counsel*, materials from the ABA Section of Business Law program "Keeping the Government Outside the Boardroom," ABA Annual Meeting (Aug. 9, 2002).

2. One federal court observed that the healthcare laws, "are among the most completely impenetrable texts within human experience" and that, while they are "dense reading of the most tortuous

healthcare clients to be informed that what makes good business sense may run afoul of these laws. This book offers a valuable tool designed to help minimize these risks.

So how did the healthcare industry get so complex and dangerous? For one thing, Congress and regulators have reacted to perceived program vulnerabilities by, respectively, enacting statutes and promulgating regulations to address these issues. Because of the money involved, healthcare providers can be expected to take advantage of available pathways that allow them to maximize their reimbursement for services they provide. In addition, most healthcare service consumers don't understand or fully appreciate the true costs being spent on healthcare services because they are cushioned from that shock by the prevalence of insurance coverage. Simply put, most healthcare consumers only focus on their insurance copayments and applicable deductibles.

The various coding and nomenclature regimens for identifying the places, types, and complexity of services provided add further complexity to the healthcare payment and reimbursement systems. Moreover, in response to perceived program vulnerabilities in the Medicare and Medicaid[3] programs, the Center for Medicare and Medicaid

---

kind, [] Congress also revisits the area frequently, generously cutting and pruning in the process and making any solid grasp of the matters addressed merely a passing phase." Rehabilitation Association of Virginia, Inc. v. Kozlowski, 42 F.3d 1444, 1450 (4th Cir. 1994) (Ervin, C.J.).

3. President Johnson signed the legislation into law that established the Medicare and Medicaid programs on July 30, 1965. *See* CMS, "Medicare & Medicaid 50th Anniversary," at https://www.cms.gov/Outreach-and-Education/ Look-Up-Topics/50th-Anniversary/Medicare-and-Medicaid-50th-Anniversary.html. Medicare is an aged-based program that provides health insurance for U.S. citizens 65 years of age or older (except that some people who suffer from certain disabilities, such as end-stage renal disease, are not subject to the age restrictions), while Medicaid is a jointly administered and needs-based federal and state program that helps to pay for the medical costs incurred by some people with limited income and resources. While Medicaid may cover services that Medicare does not (such as long-term care and personal care services), states have different rules about Medicaid eligibility. *See* "What is the difference between Medicare and Medicaid?" U.S. Dep't of Health & Human Services (June 2015), *available at* http://www.hhs.gov/answers/medicare-and-medicaid/what-is-the-difference-between-medicare-medicaid/index.html.

Services (CMS),[4] the agency within the U.S. Department of Health and Human Services (HHS) that oversees the Medicare program, continues to revise the requirements for payment and reimbursement to physicians and other participating providers. More recently, CMS has hired specialized fraud contractors that use data analytics to identify patterns that indicate possible wrongdoing.

Finally, Congress and state governments have enacted (and continue to add to) a patchwork quilt of statutes, rules, and regulations—collectively known as the "fraud and abuse laws"—that are designed to prevent fraud and to punish wrongdoers. Federal and state regulators also have, in turn, promulgated increasingly intrusive rules and regulations to deter and punish wrongdoers.

While the fraud and abuse laws are discussed in greater depth, *infra*, the key *federal* statutes worth noting here are the civil False Claims Act (FCA),[5] the Anti-Kickback Statute (AKS),[6] and the Ethics in Patient Referrals Act of 1989,[7] more commonly known as the Stark law (after former U.S. Rep. Fortney "Pete" Stark, (D-CA)).[8] Many states have enacted analogous measures (some of which are even *broader* than their federal counterparts), to address Medicaid fraud and, in some instances, private payor fraud.[9] The common goal in these statutes is

---

4. CMS was formerly known as the Health Care Financing Administration (HCFA).

5. The False Claims Act is codified, as amended, at 31 U.S.C. §§ 3729 et seq.

6. The federal Anti-Kickback Statute is codified, as amended, at 42 U.S.C. § 1320a-7b. "Since 1972, [it] . . . has prohibited the offering, solicitation, or receipt of kickbacks, bribes, or rebates in exchange for referrals of patients for items or services for which payment may be made under Medicare or a state health care program, which includes Medicaid state plans as well as programs receiving funds under Titles V, XX, and XXI of the Social Security Act." Robert Wanerman, et al., "Avoiding Fraud and Abuse Penalties and Sanctions," Cha. 6, p. 354, PHARMACEUTICAL LAW: REGULATION OF RESEARCH, DEVELOPMENT, AND MARKETING (Michael E. Clark, ed., BNA 2007).

7. The Stark law is codified, as amended, at 42 U.S.C. 1395nn.

8. *See generally*, "Pete Stark, Health Policy Warrior, Leaves a Long Legacy," Morning Edition, National Public Radio (Jan. 2, 2013) (describing Stark's accomplishments during 40 years in Congress), *available at* http://www.npr.org/sections/health-shots/2013/01/02/168133216/pete-stark-health-policy-warrior-leaves-a-long-legacy.

9. For example, the State of Texas enacted an anti-solicitation statute that broadly applies to ALL payors, which is codified as amended at TEX. OCC. CODE §§ 102.001, 102.003, and 102.011.

to prevent or reduce the types of improper financial incentives that may interfere with the independence of medical judgment-making decisions by physicians and other professionals for their patients.

In general, the fraud and abuse laws *significantly* impact how businesses and operations in the healthcare industry must be structured in order to be compliant. Underlying the fraud and abuse laws are concerns by Congress and regulators about how different business ventures and referral relationships otherwise may be structured to disguise the payment or receipt of improper financial incentives.

By requiring the healthcare industry to use "fair market value" (FMV) and other prophylactic measures in structuring business ventures and referral relationships, regulators hope to thereby minimize or eliminate what they consider to be perverse financial incentives that otherwise may affect medical decision-making by physicians and other providers. This chapter examines this key concept and the importance of obtaining appropriate valuations as a best practice for protecting clients from the substantial costs, sanctions, and the negative publicity associated with whistleblower and enforcement actions.

## Requirements for Healthcare Valuations

The Office of Inspector General (OIG) of the HHS doesn't mandate that "a party use an independent valuation consultant for any given arrangement when other appropriate valuation methods are available."[10] While there are many different formulations of FMV available to be used,[11] and having a valuation report will help to substantiate the parties' good faith in the underlying transaction if later questioned, such a report will not be dispositive on the issue of the parties' intent to the regulators. Rather, "[w]hile good faith reliance on a proper valuation may be relevant and persuasive evidence of a party's intent, it does not establish the ultimate issue of the accuracy of the valuation figure itself."[12]

---

10. Todd Kelly, *Physician Alignment*, seminar materials for HFMA Texas State Conference (March 24-26, 2013).

11. *See* Jerry M. Chang & R. Terry Heath, *Current Valuation Topics in Healthcare Transactions from Legal and Financial Perspectives*, 20130325 AHLA Seminar Papers 17 (April 25, 2013) (noting that fair market value definitions are provided under the Stark law, under IRS law, as to Fair Value for Dissenting Shareholders, by the FASB, etc.).

12. 69 Fed. Reg. 16107 (March 26, 2004).

Generally, there are three basic approaches used in valuation: (1) a Cost Approach, (2) an Income Approach, and (3) a Market Approach.[13] Each approach has its own inherent shortcomings.[14] Whatever methods are used, it is critical for the valuation report to describe the approaches that were considered, and to document each factor that was used in the process selected to arrive at the determinations made.

## Overview of Transactions and Contractual Arrangements Requiring Fair Market Value Studies

As discussed below, transactions involving parties who are in positions to influence the services for which federal healthcare benefit programs will be billed are subject to exacting scrutiny from regulators and to ruinous civil and criminal penalties for violations. Because these fraud and abuse laws are broad and so exacting in what they require in order to be compliant, fair market studies should be an essential part of proactive compliance measures.

In general, unless something is documented the agencies will not be willing to presume that the parties acted appropriately. Documentation is key when it comes to assessing FMV, and obtaining independent valuation reports from qualified individuals is a best practice in this industry. In addition, the approach should be one that can be "corroborated by a valid, secondary methodology."[15]

## *Overview of Major Legal Concerns*

As addressed in greater detail *infra*, the U.S. Department of Justice (DOJ) actively coordinates with private individuals who have *original knowledge* about alleged wrongdoing in the submission of reimbursement requests for services provided to federal program beneficiaries. By doing so, the DOJ not only seeks to recover monies siphoned from

---

13. *See* Andrew Demetriou, Terese Farhat, & Albert "Chip" Hutzler, *Anatomy of a Valuation Opinion*, webinar materials, ABA Health Law Section (May 14, 2014), at slide 12.

14. *See id.* at slide 12 (noting that the Income Approach may consider the income from referrals, the Market Approach may be limited and therefore include transactions between parties who are in positions to make referrals among one another, and the Cost Approach may not be practical to use since book or replacement value may understate the true value involved).

15. Chang & Heath, *Current Valuation Topics in Healthcare Transactions from Legal and Financial Perspectives*, at 2.

the federal FISC that should go to federal healthcare benefit programs (Medicare, Medicaid, and TriCare), but it also hopes to deter others from wrongdoing, and to punish those wrongdoers who get caught—by imposing large penalties, fines, and possible Medicare exclusion.[16]

## Stark Law

The Stark law is a very detailed and difficult statute. In theory, the Stark law was to provide a bright line separating appropriate physician business arrangements from inappropriate ones so that physicians and those who deal with them could conform their relationships accordingly. In application, however, the Stark law, is anything but a bright line. Rather, it is needlessly arcane, very nuanced, somewhat counterintuitive, and poses traps for the unwary.

In general, the Stark law prohibits a *physician* who has a *financial relationship* with an entity (i.e., an *ownership or investment interest* or a *compensation arrangement*) from making a *referral* for any of 11 *designated health services* (DHS)[17] *unless one or more exceptions* apply.[18]

---

16. The exclusion authority for the HHS OIG is set out at Section 1128(b)(7) of the Social Security Act, codified as amended at 42 U.S.C. § 1320a-7. An Anti-Kickback Statute conviction requires a *mandatory* exclusion from participation in Medicare of the provider, while a finding of Stark law or False Claims Act liability provides a *permissive* basis for exclusion to be imposed. The OIG also enforces the federal Civil Monetary Penalty provisions codified in 42 U.S.C. § 1320a-7a.

The effects of exclusion are incredibly far reaching. *See* HHS OIG, "Special Advisory Bulletin on the Effect of Exclusion from Participation in Federal Health Care Programs" (May 8, 2013) (observing, inter alia, that "the effect of an OIG exclusion is that no Federal health care program payment may be made for any items or services furnished (1) by an excluded person or (2) at the medical direction or on the prescription of an excluded person."); *available at https://oig.hhs.gov/exclusions/files/sab-05092013.pdf.*

17. DHS includes clinical laboratory services; physical therapy services; occupational therapy and speech-language pathology services; radiology and certain other imaging services; radiation therapy services and supplies; durable medical equipment and supplies; parenteral and enteral nutrients, equipment and supplies; prosthetics, orthotics, and prosthetic devices and supplies; home health services; outpatient prescription drugs; and inpatient and outpatient hospital services. 42 C.F.R. § 411.351. An entity that furnishes DHS is an entity or person that bills the Medicare program for DHS. 42 C.F.R. § 411.351. CMS has expanded the definition to include persons or entities who perform DHS, even if another person bills for the DHS. *Id.*

18. As noted, the Stark law is codified 42 U.S.C. § 1395nn. Its implementing

The Stark law is a *strict liability* civil statute. Fortunately, it in-cludes many available exceptions[19] that can be used to protect a busi-ness arrangement between a physician and an entity that provides a DHS from violating its prohibitions. Yet the Stark law's exceptions are quite exacting and not always easy to fully meet. Moreover, because the Stark law is a strict liability regime, the effect of not being able to fully meet an exception is catastrophic because, for liability purposes, a near miss is a complete miss. It is critical therefore to be familiar with the Stark law's many exceptions and their common features, such as the requirement of FMV. Moreover, it is also important to be familiar with the Stark law's many defined terms to assess whether a business arrangement is problematic or not.

Under the Stark law, the term *physician* broadly means an M.D., a D.O., a D.D.S., a podiatrist, a doctor of optometry, or a chiropractor.[20] The term also includes a physician's *immediate family members*,[21] such

---

regulations are set out at 42 C.F.R. §§ 411.350 through 411.389. 42 U.S.C. § 1395nn provides, in relevant part, that

> (1) In general. Except as provided in subsection (b) of this section, if a physician (or an immediate family member of such physician) has a financial relationship with an entity specified in paragraph (2), then—
>> (A) the physician may not make a referral to the entity for the furnishing of designated health services for which payment other-wise may be made under this subchapter, and
>> (B) the entity may not present or cause to be presented a claim under this subchapter or bill to any individual, third party payor, or other entity for designated health services furnished pursuant to a referral prohibited under subparagraph (A).

19. In addition to the definitional exceptions, the Stark law has over 30 ex-ceptions that may permit an otherwise prohibited referral to pass muster. There are three types of exceptions: (1) the general, service-based, exceptions apply to *all* financial relationships, while some exceptions only apply to (2) ownership/ investment interests, and others (3) apply only to compensation interests.

20. *See* 42 U.S.C. § 1395x(r), which provides the definition of a physician— as cross-referenced in 42 U.S.C. § 1395nn(b)(1) ("physician services").

21. "The operative language states that if a physician (or immediate family member) has a financial relationship with a DHS entity, the physician may not make a referral to the entity for the furnishing of any Medicare- or Medicaid-reimbursable DHS, and the entity may not present or cause to be presented a Medicare or Medicaid claim or bill to either program or any individual, third-party payor, or other party for such referred or ordered services." Massachusetts Medical Society, *Making Sense of the Stark Law: Compliance for the Medical Practice*, at p.6 (2005).

as a spouse, a natural or adoptive parent, a child, a sibling, an in-law, or a grandparent.

The term *designated health service* (DHS) means one of 11 specified services.[22] Yet excluded from the definition of a DHS are those services reimbursed by Medicare as a composite rate.[23]

A *referral* means a physician's request for the ordering of any DHS, or the certifying or recertifying of the need for any DHS, including the request for a consultation with another physician and any test or procedure ordered by or to be performed by (or under the supervision of) the other physician.[24] Significantly, however, the term referral *does not include* a *DHS that is personally performed* by the referring physician.[25]

A *financial relationship* includes both *compensation arrangements* and *ownership and investment interests* between the physician and the entity.[26] A *compensation arrangement* includes any financial arrangement involving remuneration.[27] *Remuneration* means any remuneration, direct or indirect, overt or covert, in cash or in kind.[28]

An *ownership and investment interest* can be acquired using debt, equity, or other means, and includes an interest in an entity that provides a DHS.[29] *Ownership interests* include, among other things, stock, partnership and membership interests, and loans and bonds.[30]

---

22. *See* 42 C.F.R. § 411.351 ("Definitions") DHS means clinical laboratory services; physical therapy services; occupational therapy and speech-language pathology services; radiology and certain other imaging services; radiation therapy services and supplies; durable medical equipment and supplies; parenteral and enteral nutrients, equipment and supplies; prosthetics, orthotics, and prosthetic devices and supplies; home health services; outpatient prescription drugs; and inpatient and outpatient hospital services

23. *See id.* This would include, for example, Skilled Nursing Facility Medicare Part A payments or Ambulatory Surgical Center services identified at 42 C.F.R. § 416.164(a) with some limitations. *Id.*

24. 42 U.S.C. § 1395nn(h)(5).

25. 42 CFR 411.351. But the regulation goes on to explain that "a designated health service is *not personally performed or provided* by the referring physician if it is performed or provided by any other person including, but not limited to, the referring physician's employees, independent contractors, or group practice members" (emphasis added).

26. 42 U.S.C. § 1395nn(a)(2).

27. 42 U.S.C. § 1395nn(h)(1); 42 C.F.R. § 411.354(c).

28. 42 U.S.C. § 1395nn(h)(1)(B).

29. 42 U.S.C. § 1395nn(a)(2)(b).

30. 42 C.F.R. § 411.354(b).

In order to assess if a business structure or arrangement is problematic, it is advisable to use a decision tree approach and carefully work through these definitions step by step. *The first step is to ascertain if the Stark law even applies to the facts in question.* Sometimes it does not: the Stark law *isn't applicable unless* (1) a physician is involved; (2) a DHS is involved; (3) there's a referral; and (4) a financial relationship is involved. Only then will further analysis need to be performed to determine if an applicable exception protects the structure or transaction in question.

As noted, many exceptions to the Stark law can be used to shelter otherwise actionable conduct. A few of these exceptions are known as "general" exceptions, meaning that they protect *both ownership/investment interests* and *compensation arrangements.*[31] The rest are "limited" exceptions, meaning that they only protect one prong of exposure under the Stark law or the other. Importantly, because a business transaction may involve both ownership/investment interests *and* a compensation arrangement, then, unless a general exception applies, an exception for each prong is needed in order to be fully protected.

Since the focus of this book is on valuation issues, we note some common key features underlying the exceptions, of which the key feature at issue in a valuation report is the requirement of FMV being used in the underlying transaction. The Stark law defines the term *fair market value* in the applicable regulations to mean:

> . . . the value in *arm's length transactions, consistent with the general market value,* and, with respect to rentals or leases, the value of rental property for general commercial purposes (not taking into account its intended use) and, in the case of a lease of space, not adjusted to reflect the additional value the prospective lessee or lessor would attribute to the proximity or

---

31. As noted, the Stark law provides many statutory exceptions, a few of which cover both *ownership* and *compensation arrangements,* including physician's services when personally provided or provided under the physician's supervision; in-office ancillary services; prepaid plans; and a catch-all exception for other financial relationships specified in regulations that don't pose a risk of program/patient abuse). 42 U.S.C. § 1395nn(b)(1)-(4). Electronic prescribing is also a general exception.

convenience to the lessor where the lessor is a potential source of patient referrals to the lessee.[32]
(Emphasis added.)

While there are several ways to determine FMV, as will be discussed *infra* and in subsequent chapters, practically speaking it is best to consider the question from the perspectives of highly suspicious regulators or bounty-seeking plaintiffs. In short, unless the fair market valuation is memorialized in writing, along with how it was determined, it will likely be rejected or viewed with considerable skepticism. If a contract only includes a provision that recites the "parties hereby represent that the agreed-upon price reflects fair market value," that provision will likely be viewed as self-serving. For this reason, a best practice is to use an independent and qualified source for the valuation issue.

## Anti-Kickback Statute

Although the Anti-Kickback Statute (AKS) is primarily an intent-based criminal statute,[33] it has also provided for civil money penalties since 1997.[34] The AKS prohibits the *knowing and willful* solicitation or receipt of *any* remuneration for referring patients to a person for the furnishing of items or services for which payment may be made by Medicare or Medicaid. In the Patient Protection and Affordability Act of 2010 (PPACA),[35] Congress amended the AKS to make it simpler to prove an AKS violation by making it easier to prove the requisite intent: "With respect to violations of this section, a person need not have actual knowledge of this section or specific intent to commit a viola-

---

32. 42 C.F.R. § 411.351.

33. "Violation of the Anti-Kickback Statute is a felony punishable by a maximum fine of $25,000, imprisonment up to 5 years, or both. Conviction will also lead to automatic exclusion from Medicare, Medicaid, and other federally funded health care programs. . ... In addition, under the . . . [BBA], violations . . . are also subject to CMPs of up to $50,000 and damages of up to three times the amount of the illegal kickback." BAUMANN, LINDA A., ED., HEALTH CARE FRAUD AND ABUSE: PRACTICAL PERSPECTIVES, ch. 1.II.A.1, ABA Health Law Section (BNA Publisher 2002).

34. The civil monetary penalties provisions were added by the Balanced Budget Act of 1997, PUB. L. 105-33, 111 Stat. 251 (Aug. 5, 1997).

35. PPACA, PUB. L. 111-148 (Mar. 23, 2010).

tion of this section."[36] This means that, in order to violate the law, a person need not know that he or she was specifically violating the AKS but, rather, was doing something he or she generally understood to be unlawful.

An AKS violation is committed if just *one purpose* underlying the payment of remuneration was to induce referrals of items or services paid for by federal or state healthcare programs.[37] The AKS is broader than the Stark law, since it doesn't require the involvement of a physician in order to be actionable. But, since the AKS is an intent-based regime (unlike the Stark law), the government must prove beyond a reasonable doubt (in a criminal action), or by a preponderance of the evidence (in a civil action), that the alleged acts were committed with the requisite intent.

After the AKS was enacted, Congress recognized that its potential reach was so broad that even socially appropriate conduct could be actionable, so it amended the statute to include various exceptions and also instructed HHS-OIG to develop regulatory safe harbors that providers could use for structuring their conduct in order to be protected.[38] Notably, because these exceptions and safe harbors aren't co-extensive with those offered by the Stark law, a separate analysis is required under each law, which adds to the confusion and complexity. While safe harbor protection under the AKS is afforded only to those arrangements that meet all of the required conditions, the failure to do so will not automatically trigger an AKS violation because it is an intent-based regime (unlike the Stark law). Like the Stark law's exceptions, many of the AKS's safe harbors and exceptions require that FMV be used in structuring the transactions in issue. But, unlike the Stark law, the AKS does not define what constitutes an FMV as that term is meant to be used under the act.

## False Claims Act/Qui Tam Litigation

The federal False Claims Act (FCA), which is codified as amended at 31 U.S.C. § 3729 *et seq.*, is the federal government's primary enforce-

---

36. PPACA § 6402(f)(2).

37. *See* United States v. Greber, 760 F.2d 68 (3d Cir.), *cert. denied*, 474 U.S. 988 (1985).

38. Adapted from Michael E. Clark, *Health Care Fraud Redux?* 15 BUS. CRIMES BULL. No. 11, at p. 7 (July 2008).

ment tool against fraud in the healthcare industry. There are seven distinct types of FCA violations set out in the act.[39] The FCA provides for triple damages and a per claim penalty that recently increased from between $5,500 and $11,000 per false claim to "between $10,781.40 and $21,562.80 per claim, plus three times the amount of damages that the federal government sustains because of the false claim."[40]

The FCA generally authorizes suits to be filed in the name of the government by private whistleblowers (called "relators" or "qui tam plaintiffs") who have *original knowledge* about wrongdoing that involved the submission of false or fraudulent claims for reimbursement from, or payment to, Medicare. Unless the government agrees to intervene and take over the action to recover the fraudulently obtained proceeds,[41] then the whistleblower must otherwise prosecute the ac-

---

39. *See* 31 U.S.C. 3729. Under the FCA, a violation occurs when a person:
   (A) knowingly presents, or causes to be presented, a false or fraudulent claim for payment or approval;
   (B) knowingly makes, uses, or causes to be made or used, a false record or statement material to a false or fraudulent claim;
   (C) conspires to commit a violation of subparagraph (A), (B), (D), (E), (F), or (G);
   (D) has possession, custody, or control of property or money used, or to be used, by the Government and knowingly delivers, or causes to be delivered, less than all of that money or property;
   (E) is authorized to make or deliver a document certifying receipt of property used, or to be used, by the Government and, intending to defraud the Government, makes or delivers the receipt without completely knowing that the information on the receipt is true;
   (F) knowingly buys, or receives as a pledge of an obligation or debt, public property from an officer or employee of the Government ... who lawfully may not sell or pledge property; or
   (G) knowingly makes, uses, or causes to be made or used, a false record or statement material to an obligation to pay or transmit money or property to the Government, or knowingly conceals or knowingly and improperly avoids or decreases an obligation to pay or transmit money or property to the Government.

40. *See* Wendy K. Arends, *False Claims Act Penalties Double as of August 1, 2016*, NAT'L LAW REV. (July 19, 2016), *available at* http://www.natlawreview.com/article/false-claims-act-penalties-double-august-1-2016. Prior to this increase, the penalties were between $5,550 to $11,000 per false claim.

41. The odds a qui tam case will settle increase if DOJ intervenes, which it does in less than 25 percent of filed cases. *See* DOJ, *False Claims Act Cases: Government Intervention in Qui Tam (Whistleblower) Suits* (Oct. 1, 1987—Sept. 30, 2012)

tion on the government's behalf. If successful, the whistleblower can earn a bounty of between 15 and 30 percent of the damages, along with payment of attorneys' fees and costs. Notably, a FCA violation also provides a basis for the OIG to permissively exclude a wrongdoer from further participation in Medicare, a sanction that is so far-reaching that it is almost a death penalty sanction for those in industry.

Courts have allowed qui tam plaintiffs to bootstrap violations of the federal Anti-Kickback Statute and the Stark law into actionable FCA violations even though Congress didn't expressly provide for a private cause of action under either of those laws. Courts have also accepted the so-called "tainted claims" and "false certification" theories of liability, which effectively lower plaintiffs' burdens of proof in prosecuting these suits.[42] Given the enormous risks involved with fighting these cases, most of them settle once the government determines that it will intervene in the case, thereby taking over the responsibility for the litigation.

The same points made earlier about the critical importance of obtaining an independent written valuation opinion as a way to protect the parties involved in a transaction hold true for FCA liability considerations because, as explained, the AKS or Stark law commonly are used as predicate violations for an FCA complaint.

## Tax Exemption Issues

Maintaining tax exemption status is critical for many nonprofit hospitals. When examining proposed joint venture relationships, it is important to be mindful of the dangers of private inurement and other shifting of monies to third parties that could negatively impact a hospital's tax-favored status. Under these circumstances, a valuation report needs to also consider how the IRS defines fair market value. As set out in Revenue Ruling 59–60, fair market value means ". . . the price at which the property would change hands between a willing buyer and a willing seller when the former is not under any compul-

---

available at www.justice.gov/usao/pae/Civil_Division/InternetWhistleblower%20update.pdf. See also www.sidley.com/files/upload/C-FRAUDS_FCA_Statistics%20pdf.pdf.

42. *See generally*, Michael E. Clark, *Whether the False Claims Act is a Proper Legal Tool for the Government to Use for Improving the Quality of Care in Long-Term Care Facilities*, 15 No. 1 HEALTH LAW. 12, 12 (2002).

sion to buy and the latter is not under any compulsion to sell, both parties having reasonable knowledge of relevant facts."[43]

## *Current Regulatory Landscape*

### Current Trends: Qui Tam Growth, Federal Fund Spent on Fraud, etc.

While the growth in the number and recoveries of qui tam suits in the United States isn't exponential, it has been substantial since 1986, when Congress amended the FCA to make filing these actions more attractive to whistleblowers by increasing their potential bounty and including other procedural changes to make it easier to pursue such actions. More recently, through the Fraud Enforcement Recovery Act of 2009 (FERA)[44] and PPACA, Congress made bringing and maintaining these actions even easier by, among other changes, including a statutory definition of the term *knowledge* as it is used under the FCA, and by requiring a defendant to identify and return "known overpayments" within 60 days or else the failure to do so would become an actionable false claim. In the Deficit Reduction Act of 2005,[45] Congress also incentivized states to enact state False Claim Act analogues to the FCA by increasing the share of the recovery that the states could retain, which has resulted in a majority of states now having such a measure on their books.

---

43. *See generally*, IRM Part 4, ch. 72, § 8, *available at* https://www.irs.gov/irm/part4/irm_04-072-008.html.

44. PUB. L. 111–21, S. 386, 123 STAT. 1617 (May 20, 2009). As amended by FERA, the FCA prohibits "knowingly and improperly avoid[ing] ... an obligation to pay" the government *even without a false statement to conceal* the obligation and expansively defines an "obligation" to include a duty to pay the government arising "from the retention of any overpayment." Michael E. Clark & Eric C. Tostrud, *The Physician and Attorney Relationship in a Fraud Audit*, materials prepared for the ABA Physicians Legal Issues Conference 2014. Knowledge under the FCA is now defined broadly as "actual knowledge ... deliberate ignorance of the truth [or] reckless disregard of the truth." 31 U.S.C. § 3729(b).

45. *See generally*, Kirsten V. Mayer, et al., *State False Claims Laws and Compliance with the DRA: What is Required after FERA and PPACA?* materials for the 2010 ABA CIVIL FALSE CLAIMS AND QUI TAM ENFORCEMENT INSTITUTE.

## Recent Case Studies: Fair Market Value Business Valuation Take-Aways and Implications

Two recent FCA cases involving hospitals and physicians illustrate the complexities and risks involved with structuring joint ventures in this industry: *Tuomey*[46] and *Halifax*.[47] These cases were unusual for FCA cases since the hospitals actually litigated them—unfortunately, as it turned out, to their disadvantage.

In the *Tuomey* case, the government alleged that, over a period of years, the hospital had presented false Medicare claims that violated the Stark law—including reimbursement claims for services rendered to patients referred by physicians with whom Tuomey had financial relationships (i.e., compensation relationships).[48] The DOJ contended that the compensation arrangements between Tuomey and physicians with whom it structured a relationship *improperly varied with and took into account* the physicians' actual or anticipated *referrals* to Tuomey.[49]

Significantly, Tuomey *had obtained a fair market value report* about the compensation paid to physicians under part-time employment agreements.[50] The DOJ argued that Tuomey could not have reasonably relied on the report since it reflected that the hospital would pay gastroenterologists over 100 percent of the net collections—which clearly exceeded FMV.[51] Not so said the defense. It argued that the contracts at issue met an applicable Stark law exception, but even had it not, the hospital relied on the advice of counsel and shouldn't be held liable.[52] Tuomey lost and suffered enormous adverse consequences.

In the *Halifax* case, the plaintiff was a former director of physician services at Halifax Hospital Medical Center who alleged that it submitted false claims to Medicare and Medicaid because its compensation arrangement with six oncologists violated the Stark Law.[53]

46. United States ex rel. Drakeford v. Tuomey (4th Cir., 2015)

47. United States v. Halifax Hosp. Med. Ctr., No. 6:09-cv-1002-Orl-31TBS, 2013 WL 6017329, at *10-11 (M.D. Fla. Nov. 13, 2013).

48. Adapted from Clark & Tostrud, *The Physician and Attorney Relationship in a Fraud Audit.*

49. *Id.*

50. Chris M. Morrison, "Evolution of a $237M FCA Health Care Verdict," Law 360 (Nov. 26, 2013.

51. *Id.*

52. Adapted from Clark & Tostrud, *The Physician and Attorney Relationship in a Fraud Audit.*

53. *Id*

As noted in the court's opinion on the competing Motions for Summary Judgment,

> The Defendants argue that the compensation arrangement with the Medical Oncologists fit within the Stark Law exception for bona fide employment relationships and therefore referrals by the Medical Oncologists were not prohibited by the Stark Law. The Defendants also argue that the Government has failed to produce any evidence that the Medical Oncologists actually made referrals of DHS during the pertinent time frame.
>
> It is undisputed that the Medical Oncologists had a financial relationship with Halifax Hospital. Because of this, the burden shifts to Halifax Hospital to show that the compensation arrangement with the Medical Oncologists fit within one of the Stark Law's exceptions. *Rogan*, 459 F. Supp. 2d at 715 (N.D. Ill. 2006). Halifax contends that the Medical Oncologists' compensation arrangement satisfied the exception for bona fide employment relationships . . . .[54]

The judge ruled that Halifax had given prohibited bonuses to these physicians, which exposed it to an enormous liability (approximated at nearly $1 billion), which it ordered to be determined by a jury.[55] In his order, the judge noted the significance of an attorney-client communication that underscored a key Stark law problem with the applicability of the relied-upon exception—i.e., the *physicians' compensation varied with the volume or value of the referrals*.[56] Halifax Hospital Medical Center and Halifax Staffing Inc. later agreed to pay $85 mil-

---

54. United States ex. rel. Baklid-Kunz v. Halifax Hosp. Med. Ctr., No. 6:09-cv-1002-Orl-31TBS, Order, at 14-15 (Nov. 13, 2013)

55. *See* Joe Carlson, *$1 billion Stark case against Fla. hospital headed to trial*, MODERN HEALTHCARE (Nov. 25, 2013).

56. *See* Order in United States ex. rel. Baklid-Kunz v. Halifax Hosp. Med. Ctr., at 16, n.8 ("As described in a February 2009 memo from attorneys retained by Halifax Hospital to assess whether the Incentive Bonus complied with the Stark Law, 'the bonus money available in the incentive pool (15 percent of the operating margin of the medical oncology program) itself would vary with the volume and value of each Oncologist's referrals to the District's hospital and other cancer care facilities.'").

lion to resolve the allegations that they violated the FCA by submitting claims to the Medicare program that violated the Stark law.[57]

## Danger Zones

### Internal vs. External Valuation

As noted, when dealing with highly suspicious regulators, it's essential to have an adequate paper trail that reflects how the analysis was properly prepared by an independent and qualified professional in order to demonstrate, in a verifiable manner, the steps that were used in rendering the opinion. As previously stated, relying upon a contractual provision that reflects something to the effect that the parties agreed that the following constitutes an FMV exchange or an FMV compensation arrangement will, in all likelihood, be given short shrift by government officials. When considering the ruinous costs of having to defend such an action against allegations of improper inducements, it's clear that the relatively low costs involved when retaining and utilizing the services of a qualified valuation expert are well worth it. If that wasn't enough, such services *can* be deducted as a necessary and proper business expense on the front end. But, under applicable federal income tax laws and regulations, if fines and penalties are later incurred in a criminal prosecution, or as a civil penalty imposed by federal, state, or local law, they cannot be deducted. *See* 26 C.F.R. §1.162-21 ("fines and penalties").

### Other Bases for FMV: Benchmarks, Rate Cards—From the Attorney Viewpoint/Why Relying on Generic Surveys May Not Be Good Enough

As noted, regulators are highly suspicious about contractual provisions that simply recite that the parties agreed to an FMV exchange or else agree that a certain arrangement was negotiated at FMV. Published surveys are available that reflect average salaries and income by physicians in different types of practices and in different geographic

---

57. DOJ Press Release, "Florida Hospital System Agrees to Pay the Government $85 Million to Settle Allegations of Improper Financial Relationships with Referring Physicians" (March 11, 2014), *available at* https://www.justice.gov/opa/pr/florida-hospital-system-agrees-pay-government-85-million-settle-allegations-improper.

locations. These publications provide valuable services, but they don't necessarily include other factors that will give regulators the same degree of comfort that a professionally-conducted, independent valuation confers.[58] In short, while these publications provide more independent information about what constitutes FMV than a mere contractual recitation, and can be used to help support a negotiated rate of compensation, they are not as good as one prepared by an independent valuation professional.

## Strategies for Maintaining the Attorney-Client Privilege

In retaining an expert to conduct a valuation, it is also important to consider the nature of the attorney-client privilege and the care that is required to protect against its unintended waiver. As a general rule, unless an attorney is involved in retaining the valuation professional to conduct the service for his or her client, there will be no privilege available to assert. Therefore, it is a best practice for a healthcare provider to have an attorney actively involved in this process so that there can be an attorney-client privilege available to assert.

Of course, such a privilege is not self-executing; rather, it must be scrupulously guarded if inadvertent waiver is to be avoided. Professor Wigmore enumerated eight elements that are required for the privilege to be recognized: (1) legal advice was sought, (2) from a legal advisor, (3) and the communications related to that purpose, (4) were made in confidence, (5) by the client, (6) and at his instance were permanently protected, (7) from disclosure, (8) except for waiver.[59] Simply put, the attorney-client privilege protects *confidential communications* between a client and attorney *made for the purpose of requesting or receiving legal advice.*

---

58. *See* Albert D. Hutzler & Joseph N. Wolfe, *Fundamentals of Health Care Valuation for Health Lawyers and Compliance Officers,* Fraud and Compliance Forum, AHLA (Oct. 6-7, 2014), at 14 (noting that among the problems with survey data are that surveys are voluntary, not random, samples; they are limited by regional and local data; there can be cherry-picking from surveys or tables within surveys; and the underlying data can be misleading, such as physician productivity data).

59. 8 J. WIGMORE EVIDENCE, § 2292 (McNaughton rev. 1961).

Not every communication from or to a lawyer is protected, since the privilege generally prevents disclosure of *legal advice, not the underlying facts.*[60] Indeed, a lesson from the recent *Halifax* case, in which *substantial* False Claims Act liability was imposed on the hospital system despite its arguments that it had relied on the advice of attorneys in structuring the challenged business relationships with associated physicians, is that in order to be privileged, the "primary purpose" of a client's communication with a lawyer must be to request or provide legal advice.[61]

Because many lawyers and law firms routinely disclaim any responsibility for the payment of an expert's fees, this disclaimer should be spelled out in the engagement of the valuation expert. In that situation, the engagement should reflect that the valuation expert will be reporting to the attorney on its work, but will seek payment solely from the attorney's client. The engagement agreement with the attorney should also recite that the valuation professional's work is intended to help the attorney advise the client. Moreover, because this privilege is *personal to the client* who retained the attorney's services to provide legal advice, both the client and the valuation professional must be cautioned to only share the information on a need-to-know basis, since sharing it with others outside the attorney-client relationship likely will waive the privilege.

---

60. Using this framework, courts require that advice given by a lawyer must be "legal" in nature (i.e., it cannot merely be business-related) in order to be protected under the attorney-client privilege. If, however, the lawyer acts as "mere scrivener" (e.g., the lawyer fills out real estate forms or tax returns), such acts are *not* protected because the lawyer isn't rendering legal advice. *See, e.g.,* Canady v. United States, 354 F.2d 849, 857 (8th Cir. 1966) (tax returns); Pollock v. United States, 202 F.2d 281, 286 (5th Cir.), *cert. denied,* 345 U.S. 993 (1953) (real estate forms). Moreover, if the nature of the work being provided by the attorney necessarily contemplates making it public, such as in filing bankruptcy schedules for a client, then that work also won't be protected since it wasn't intended to remain confidential.

61. United States v. Halifax Hosp. Med. Ctr., No. 6:09-cv-1002-Orl-31TBS, 2013 WL 6017329, at *10-11 (M.D. Fla. Nov. 13, 2013). *See also* Clark & Tostrud, *supra,* note 44.

# Fair Market Value Basics and Commercially Reasonable

**2**

Jen Johnson, CFA

---

*Determining if the Commercially Reasonable standard has been met should be completed prior to starting an FMV analysis.*

---

Fair market value (FMV) and commercially reasonable (CR) are both standards typically required for arrangements between healthcare facilities and referral sources. These standards ensure transactions and compensation arrangements are entered into based on sound business reasons (CR) and at a fair price (FMV), *absent the consideration of referrals to the healthcare facility*. The aspect that referrals may not be considered in the valuation or decision process is unique to healthcare.

It is critical that healthcare executives are able to explain the reasons for initiating an arrangement with a referral source. It is also important to step back once the terms are outlined and ensure it makes business sense without considering referrals. Many factors must be considered when determining if an arrangement is CR, including ensuring the transaction or agreement is entered into based on legitimate reasoning to serve a specific purpose, and at a reasonable price or compensation level.

Because this book is primarily focused on valuation, this chapter starts with an FMV overview. However, it is important to note that any transaction or arrangement should be deemed CR prior to proceeding with the work that goes in to an FMV assessment. CR should be established before determining a transaction price or compensation. Please see the Appendix for a *Checklist for Reviewing an FMV Opinion*.

## FMV: Standard of Value

The implications of defining FMV correctly are crucial to healthcare transactions. Regulatory constraints imposed by the Internal Revenue Service (IRS) on tax-exempt organizations, by Centers for Medicare & Medicaid Services (CMS) under the Stark law, and by the Office of Inspector General (OIG) under the anti-kickback statute require FMV as a standard. Published definitions of FMV are similar amongst the business valuation industry and healthcare's regulatory environment. However, healthcare regulations provide additional guidance as it relates to methodologies and data.

### The Business Valuation Definition

Business valuation experts most frequently reference the definition of FMV set forth in Revenue Ruling 59-60, which is as follows:

> The price at which the property would change hands between a willing buyer and a willing seller when the former is not under any compulsion to buy and the latter is not under any compulsion to sell, both parties having reasonable knowledge of relevant facts.[1]

Additionally, an *International Glossary of Business Valuation Terms* was jointly developed by representatives of the American Institute of CPAs (AICPA), the American Society of Appraisers (ASA), the Canadian Institute of Chartered Business Valuators (CICBV), the Institute of Business Appraisers (IBA), and the National Association of Certified Valuation Analysts (NACVA). According to the glossary, the definition of the term FMV is as follows:

---

1. IRS Revenue Ruling 59-60, 1951-1 C.B. 237 IRC Sec. 2031.

The price, expressed in terms of cash equivalents, at which a property would change hands between a hypothetical willing and able buyer and a hypothetical willing and able seller, acting at arm's-length in an open and unrestricted market, when neither is under compulsion to buy nor to sell, and when both have reasonable knowledge of the relevant facts.[2]

This definition comports to that found in IRS Revenue Ruling 59-60.

## Regulatory Definitions and Guidelines

It is important to note that the determination of FMV under healthcare regulations may not always be consistent with generally accepted appraisal standards. CMS maintains that certain departures from standard appraisal practice may be required:

Moreover, the definition of "fair market value" in the statute and regulation is qualified in ways that do not necessarily comport with the usage of the term in standard valuation techniques and methodologies (69 *Federal Register* (March 26, 2004), page 16107).

The methodology must exclude valuations where the parties to the transactions are at arm's-length but in a position to refer to one another (69 *Federal Register* (March 26, 2004), page 16107).

Depending on the circumstances, the "volume or value" restriction will preclude reliance on comparables that involve entities and healthcare providers in a position to refer or generate business (66 *Federal Register* (Jan. 4, 2001), page 945.)

Notable definitions related to FMV as stated in Stark include:

- This provision defines fair market value as the value in arm's-length transactions, consistent with the General Market Value (GMV), with other specific terms for rentals or leases. (66 *Federal Register* (Jan. 4, 2001), page 945).

---

2. NACVA Professional Standards, http://web.nacva.com/TL-Website/PDF/NACVA_Professional_Standards.pdf.

- GMV is compensation that would be included in a service agreement as the result of bona fide bargaining between well-informed parties (66 *Federal Register* (Jan. 4, 2001), page 945).
- The compensation must be set in advance, consistent with fair market value, and not determined in a manner that takes into account the volume or value of referrals or other business generated by the referring physician (69 *Federal Register* (March 26, 2004), page 16,066).

The main points to understand as it relates to FMV is that CMS views reliance on certain types of market data in determining FMV as problematic. For instance, Stark states the FMV may not consider the value or volume of referrals and that one should not rely on data produced by referral relationships.

## Commercially Reasonable Standard

When healthcare executives contemplate entering into a transaction or agreement with a referral source, they must be mindful of federal regulations mandating that these arrangements need to be commercially reasonable (CR). Determining if an arrangement is commercially reasonable requires an understanding of a healthcare facility's operational needs, clinical requirements, and financial alternatives. In addition, expertise in the field of healthcare valuation and healthcare law is necessary. This is due to the fact that the arrangement's compensation must be set at FMV and the agreement must be structured so that it is consistent with regulatory guidance. Furthermore, referrals may not be considered when assessing if this standard is met.

### Regulatory Guidelines

CR is a critical standard that must be adhered to for both service agreements and transactions. The following outlines guidance by various regulatory authorities to assist executives in understanding this standard. Both the Department of Health and Human Resources and Stark law have provided guidance for understanding the CR standard which can be very briefly be summarized as (1), (2):

An arrangement must make business sense, without considering referrals.

Case law is a solid reference point for healthcare executives responsible for making sure an arrangement is CR. *U.S. v. SCCI Hospital Houston* is a 2004 qui tam case in which the U.S. questioned the commercial reasonableness of an arrangement between SCCI Hospital Houston and three medical directors. Specifically, the U.S. argued the compensation paid to the three medical directors by SCCI was not commercially reasonable. The government's expert witness provided certain insight including that in order for an arrangement to be commercially reasonable it must (4):

1. Be essential to the hospital's operations and of sound business purpose
2. Consider factors related to patient needs
3. Identify and address the need for medical direction in coordination with hospital management

In summation, the expert witness concluded there should have been an ongoing assessment of the necessity of medical director duties being provided. Based on this case, one can deduce what the courts would consider in assessing the CR standard. In addition, it is important to understand that several parties are needed to determine whether or not an arrangement is CR but the initial steps should be assessed by those most familiar with the hospital's operational, clinical and financial needs.

## Establish a CR Checklist

Although it takes a joint effort by healthcare executives, legal counsel, and valuation consultants to ultimately determine if an arrangement is CR, establishing a best practices checklist to educate those negotiating a business arrangement will assist leadership in addressing this standard. In addition, referring to a checklist will show regulatory authorities the due diligence leadership has implemented in an effort to adhere to this standard.

Three main categories are provided to consider, along with a broad list of sample questions, as there are numerous questions that should be considered, depending on the nuances of each arrangement. It is important to note that not every question is relevant for every arrangement, while other arrangements may warrant additional questions.

Furthermore, all questions should be answered with the understanding that the *decision process was made absent considering referrals.*

*Operational Assessment—Sample Questions*
- Does the subject arrangement (transaction or agreement) further the strategic goals of the hospital?
- Are the proposed services to be provided post-transaction or post-agreement already provided by the hospital?
- Are the stipulated physician hours reasonable to attain in addition to the other duties and services provided by the physician?

*Clinical Requirements—Sample Questions*
- Will the subject arrangement (transaction or agreement) further patient care, patient satisfaction, and overall public benefit?
- Are physicians of a particular specialty required (for services or in the context of an acquisition) based on the community need?
- Are the number of hours stated in a physician service agreement required to serve the patient population or the health system's mission?

*Financial Considerations—Sample Questions*
- Have the economics of the arrangement been compared to other viable options in the local market and been selected as the best choice?
- Are physicians expected earnings consistent with the services or risk they are undertaking?
- Is the proposed transaction price or compensation consistent with FMV?

## What Is Commercially Unreasonable?

Some referral arrangements, whether a transaction or contractual agreement, may be initiated by personnel not familiar with healthcare compliance and legal nuances. As a result, it is not uncommon for these individuals to misunderstand what is acceptable to consider when evaluating if an arrangement makes good business sense, absent referrals. In order to ensure an arrangement can be supported by defensible reasoning, healthcare executives should make sure any party negotiating with physicians understand and anticipate the questions a court would examine in determining if an arrangement is CR.

Due to the operational, clinical, and financial knowledge required to understand if a potential arrangement is necessary and serves a legitimate business purpose, it is important that those most familiar with the needs of the facility are involved in the decision. Some scenarios where an arrangement could be identified as commercially *unreasonable* early on in assessing a potential arrangement include:

1. The number of administrative hours, or administrative positions, in a proposed arrangement exceeds what is required based on facility needs.
2. Offering payments for quality when there is no mechanism to track improvement or superior performance in quality outcomes.
3. Purchasing a physician-owned entity when there is no strategy or community need for that specialty or service in the market.
4. Leasing equipment to a physician at below market rental rates, or leasing equipment from a physician at above market rental rates.
5. Purchasing any service or equipment which is not necessary for efficient operations of the hospital or to serve the patient population.
6. Proposing compensation to physicians for management services when the hospital has staff providing the same, or very similar, services.
7. Providing on-call payments for a specialty that does not require emergent response times.
8. Proposing compensation consistent with physician salaries to a physician who is providing services that do not require the expertise of a physician.

## CR Final Steps

Once an arrangement is deemed CR from leadlership's perspective, legal counsel and valuation firms are often instrumental in ensuring certain aspects of an arrangement are CR. Legal counsel's responsibilities include making sure the arrangements are structured appropriately from a regulatory perspective, as well as ensuring that the services in the agreement do not overlap with existing agreements. In addition, counsel can assist by making sure the agreement's stated compensation is consistent with any FMV opinions that have been issued related to the arrangement, and not outside the range provided by a valuation on file.

Valuation firms are helpful in determining if the transaction price or compensation stated in the arrangement is consistent with FMV, which is a requirement for CR. In addition, experienced healthcare valuation firms may be able to provide insight as to what has been observed in the market at comparable facilities. However, be cautious of a valuation firm representing that they can provide a CR opinion, as this often comes in the form of a brief paragraph describing that management has represented the terms are CR. This may be suitable for compliance purposes as long as healthcare executives understand there are important factors that must be verified by leadership prior to getting this opinion.

Healthcare executives should make sure any party negotiating with physicians understands the CR standard and ideally have documentation related to the decision making process. Once leadership has determined a subject arrangement is CR, it is important to monitor the arrangement to ensure it continues to make business sense. Enforcing the protocols in place to make sure the physicians are providing the services per the agreement, or that the operations make sense for the hospitals mission is key. Lastly, conducting assessments to prove the health system continues to legitimately require the arrangement will be a key to compliance.

*Sources*

1. Commercial reasonableness is defined by the Department of Health and Human Resources as *"a sensible and prudent business agreement, from the perspective of the particular parties involved, even in the absence of any potential referrals."*
2. The Stark Phase II 69 Fed. Reg. 16,093 (March 26, 2004). *"[a]n arrangement will be considered "commercially reasonable" in the absence of referrals if the arrangement would make*

*commercial sense if entered into by a reasonable entity of similar type and size and a reasonable physician (or family member or group practice) of similar scope and specialty, even if there were no potential DHS referrals."*

3. *Fair Market Value in Health Care Transactions* Haynes and Boone LLP, Lewis Lefko, July 2007.

# Engaging a Valuation Analyst 3

*Colin M. McDermott, CFA, CPA/ABV
and Bridget Triepke, CPA*

---

*The credibility and soundness of the valuation report is critical for compliance purposes.*

---

Business valuation is a highly fragmented industry with low barriers to entry; therefore, many valuation analysts providing their "expertise" are not qualified to perform healthcare business or professional service agreement valuation assignments. Due to the unique aspects of the healthcare industry, it is recommended that a valuation analyst be both an expert in healthcare and in valuation. When evaluating a valuation analyst for an engagement, the following should be addressed during the selection process:

- Does the valuation analyst have appropriate credentials (e.g., CFA, CPA, ASA, CVA, etc.)?
- Does the valuation analyst have significant experience in healthcare in a valuation capacity?

- Can the valuation analyst provide references or a list of prior valuation assignments specific to healthcare and specific to the "sub-industry" (e.g., ambulatory surgery center, acute care hospital, laboratory business, etc.) of the subject arrangement?

Once it is determined that the valuation analyst has the applicable experience and skill set, evaluation of his or her reputation, process, and firm is critical. Often a healthcare valuation report will be utilized to support an arrangement that may ultimately be reviewed by regulatory authorities (see chapter 1 for an overview of key regulatory considerations); therefore, it is necessary that the valuation analyst perform the appropriate steps to develop a comprehensive and supportable analysis. Additionally, it is important that the valuation analyst is associated with an organization with the history to ensure the individual (or the firm) will be available in the future to respond to any questions or comments about the analysis.

Below is a sample list of questions to address with a *valuation analyst* to ensure his or her analysis will be comprehensive:

- What steps will the valuation analyst take to deliver an expert report that will withstand regulatory scrutiny? The following should be included in the valuation analyst's response:
  - o Analysis of both historical and prospective financial performance while understanding the entity operates in a unique and specialized industry with its own "terms of art" (e.g., gross charges, deductions, payor mix, productivity measures, etc.).
  - o An understanding of the highly regulated operating environment, the implications of this environment on the operations of the business, and the resulting valuation work product.
  - o An interpretation of the competitive environment and the impact on the subject business.
  - o Identification of key value drivers and the resulting impact on the economics of the business or agreement.
  - o Development of a depth of understanding of comparable precedent transactions and the applicable valuation metrics.
  - o Application of appropriate valuation methodologies to the subject business (e.g., Income Approach, Market Approach, Cost Approach).

- Is the valuation analyst willing to conduct on-site meetings and perform a physical inspection of the facility (when needed)? Valuable insight that could influence the valuation can be gained from a site visit, such as patient flow and experience, attractiveness and convenience of location, proximity to competition, etc.
- Will the deliverable include a valuation conclusion and report that is comprehensive, can be relied upon by the end users, and is consistent with the proposed transaction structure?
- Will the valuation report be prepared in a manner that is consistent with prevailing appraisal standards (USPAP, NACVA, ASA, etc.)
- Will the valuation analyst (or his or her firm) be available at a future date to address any questions or defend the opinion?
- Will the valuation analyst rely upon any third-party specialists, such as real estate or equipment valuation analysts? If so, will he or she be available to address any questions at a future date? Do the third-party specialists have healthcare experience?

In addition to questioning the valuation analysts directly regarding their experience and process, it is also recommended that their professional references be interviewed. Conversations directly with individuals who have experience with the valuation analyst can provide feedback to ensure the individual has the background for the specific engagement.

The following is a sample list of questions to review with the provided *references*:

- Did the valuation analyst convey adequate expertise in the industry both during the process and in the deliverable?
- Did the valuation analyst approach the project as an independent third party?
- Was the appraisal completed in a timely fashion?
- Were the professional fees consistent with the provided fee quote and the quality of the work product delivered?
- Was the valuation analyst both available and dependable for client conference calls, face-to-face meetings, and deliverable deadlines?

- Were the deliverables (valuation schedules, report, and presentation) comprehensive, and would they stand up to potential regulatory scrutiny?
- Was the valuation analyst willing to participate in discussions or investigations with regulators or other reviewing parties after the submission of the deliverable?

Once a valuation analyst is selected, the individual will propose and be retained through an engagement letter. The retaining party should be defined through this document, and most often the retaining party will be the end-user of the report. There are instances where the valuation analyst should be retained through outside legal counsel so as to maintain attorney-client privilege. To minimize misunderstanding during the valuation process, the purpose of the engagement should be thoroughly defined in the document. Additionally, the following components should be addressed through the engagement letter:[1]

- subject to be valued;
- interest to be valued;
- valuation date;
- purpose and use of the valuation;
- standard of value (e.g., fair market value);
- premise of value (e.g., going concern, liquidation);
- intended users;
- valuation approaches or methods;
- assumptions, limiting conditions, and scope limitations; and
- restrictions on the use of the report.

Given the unique issues surrounding healthcare transactions, utilizing a thorough selection process to identify a valuation analyst, along with appropriately defining the engagement, will ensure that the valuation analysts and their work product will meet or exceed expectations.

---

1. Professional Standards, National Association of Certified Valuators and Analysts (NACVA), Aug. 1, 2015.

# *Part Two:*
## *Business Valuations*

# Overview and Business Valuation Basics

# 4

*Aaron Murski, CVA, Colin M. McDermott, CFA, CPA/ABV, and Bridget Triepke, CPA*

The following section and chapters will discuss business valuation as it applies to healthcare enterprises. While variation occurs in the application of valuation approaches and methodologies for various businesses, much of the framework and considerations applicable to conducting a credible healthcare business valuation are standard regardless of business type. Many types of businesses exist within the continuum of healthcare services. Presented in Figure 4-1 on the next page are the most common businesses in the healthcare services industry that are frequently bought and sold, and therefore the subject of a business valuation.

In the following chapters, the key valuation considerations will be discussed for a majority of these businesses. But first, valuation definitions and approaches, which apply to all business types regardless of the specific sub-industry within healthcare services, will be discussed. This overview includes an explanation of the three standard approaches to value (Cost, Income, and Market). These three approaches should be addressed in most every business valuation analysis. Therefore, every chapter is formatted so that value drivers and nuances, by approach,

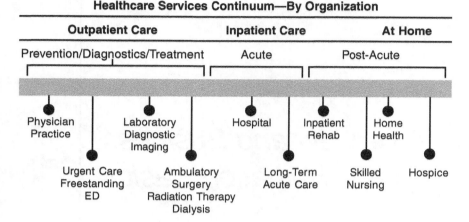

Figure 4-1

are addressed with particular attention to the entity type. This format allows the reader to be able to easily reference general valuation guidelines when reviewing any industry report.

## Components of a Standard Business Enterprise Valuation

A valuation analyst determines a value indication for the subject business at the total invested capital (TIC) or business enterprise value (BEV) level. The value of TIC and BEV is defined as follows:

$$TIC = Equity + Interest\ Bearing\ Debt$$
$$BEV = Equity + Interest\ Bearing\ Debt - Cash$$
$$OR$$
$$BEV = Equity + Net\ Debt$$

Ultimately, both TIC and BEV represent the value of the entire business available to all stakeholders (both debt and equity), and the difference between the two value indications is the treatment of cash.

Standard TIC and BEV fair market value (FMV) indications include all operating assets of the subject business, including a normalized level of working capital, fixed assets, and intangible assets. Working capital includes cash (if using TIC rather than BEV), accounts receivable, and other current assets less non-interest bearing debt that permits a business to conduct day-to-day operations and maintain liquidity. Even though the Cost Approach is the only approach that separately values the working capital, personal property, real estate, and intangible assets of a business, the Income and Market Approaches inherently include these assets as these approaches rely upon the cash flows generated by all of the assets that are needed to operate the business.

Non-operating assets, such as excess land and investments, are typically not captured within a standard BEV, as cash flows related to these assets (if any) are often not reflected in the financials. If non-operating assets are being acquired, the valuation analyst will typically separately assess the FMV of these assets and add it to the concluded BEV.

## *Premise of Value*

*Defining the standard and premise of value is a critical first step to understanding a valuation analysis.*

As defined in the *International Glossary of Business Valuation Terms*, the premise of value is an assumption regarding the most likely set of circumstances surrounding the transaction, which would be applicable to the subject valuation. Establishing the premise of value is a critical step in the valuation process. Generally, the premise of value may either be a "going-concern" premise, or a "liquidation" premise. A going-concern assumption essentially posits that a business will continue to operate and remain in business. Alternatively, a liquidation premise posits that a business will cease operating, selling its assets and settling its debts. The liquidation premise may also carry additional parameters, such as orderly liquidation or forced liquidation. For a viable, cash flow generating enterprise, a going-concern premise is typically utilized. There are additional premises that may be applicable in certain circumstances, such as "value as an assemblage of assets," when assets are not used in connection with producing income.[1]

---

1. SHANNON PRATT & ALINA NICULITA, VALUING A BUSINESS, 5th ed. (McGraw-Hill, 2008), pp. 47, 276.

## Level of Value: Control versus Minority

The valuation analyst must take into consideration the level of value (control versus minority) and make adjustments where appropriate when conducting the FMV analysis. In practice, the amount of control rights or level of minority characteristics associated with a particular equity interest varies and, as such, these concepts exist on a continuum. The level or lack of control associated with a subject interest to be valued can influence the valuation approach used, as well as the valuation assumptions utilized in the approach (e.g., the forecasted cash flows in an Income Approach). In theory, a true minority interest has little to no influence over expansion decisions, cost structure, distributions, or liquidity events; therefore, minority values are typically less than control values, even for the same business with the same projected cash flows. The degree of control or lack thereof may not be a clear-cut issue, as the degree of control can vary depending on the percentage ownership, terms in the operating agreement defining super majority and the powers of minority investors, and state laws governing rights of various percentage ownership interests.

## Valuation Approaches

In conducting an FMV analysis to determine the BEV of the subject business, consideration should be given to the three accepted valuation approaches: the Income, Market, and Cost Approaches. The approach or approaches that the analyst ultimately relies upon are subject to judgment and can be influenced by, but not limited to, the following:

- *Level of value* (control vs. minority): When valuing a security interest directly, valuations of minority interests in closely held companies may rely on the Income Approach as opposed to the Market Approach, as there is generally limited publicly available data regarding minority transactions involving closely held companies.
- *Profitability*: Distressed businesses or businesses with marginal cash flows relative to the value of the tangible and intangible assets are typically valued with the Cost Approach.
- *Availability of market data*: Certain healthcare industries have limited transaction data and few to no pure-play publicly traded

companies. In addition, facts and circumstances of a specific business, such as an out-of-network ASC, may make it too dissimilar to the market comparables.

- *Business stage*: Often, de novos and businesses in the initial years of operations are valued using an Income Approach, as it may be difficult to apply the Market Approach when earnings are not stable and significant growth is expected. Businesses that are not viewed as a going-concern should be valued using the Cost Approach.

## Income Approach[2]

The Income Approach estimates the value of a business based upon the economic benefits that the business is expected to generate in the future. While there are many variations, economic benefits are often measured using cash flow. The Income Approach can utilize a single period capitalization of cash flow or a multi-period discounted cash flow analysis. The single period capitalization method is typically only utilized for mature, stable businesses; consequently, valuation analysts more frequently utilize the multi-period method. While variations exist, the remaining chapters that discuss the Income Approach as applied to business valuation will assume the use of a multi-period discounted cash flow method. An important assumption of any method of the Income Approach is that the business or asset being valued remains a going-concern.

The discounted cash flow method to derive enterprise value comprises three steps:

1. Estimation of the future debt-free net cash flows for a discrete projection period. There is no length requirement. Cash flows should be forecasted until the business has reached a stabilized state.
2. Estimation of the residual or terminal value of cash flows after the discrete projection period.
3. Discounting of the cash flows to present value at a rate of return that takes into consideration the projected cash flow risk and the time value of money.

---

2. SHANNON PRATT & ALINA NICULITA, VALUING A BUSINESS, 5th ed. (McGraw-Hill, 2008), pp. 47, 276.

Since the discounted cash flow method to derive enterprise value[3] estimates the value of a business based on the cash flows available to all stakeholders of the business (both debt and equity), interest expense is eliminated to calculate debt-free net cash flow. Debt-free net cash flow is typically defined as follows:

Earnings Before Interest and Taxes (EBIT)
Less:      Provision for Taxes
Equals:    Debt-Free Net Income
Plus:      Depreciation and Amortization
Less:      Capital Expenditures
Less:      Incremental Working Capital
Equals:    Debt-Free Net Cash Flow

Note that the calculation of debt-free net cash flow calls for the elimination of interest expense and the application of taxes. Both of these calculations are made so that the ultimate cash flow stream utilized matches the appropriate discount rate. The selected discount rate is computed by calculating an industry Weighted Average Cost of Capital (WACC). The WACC incorporates the claims of both debt holders and equity holders in proportion to their relative capital contribution. This approach is consistent with the debt-free cash flows utilized in the business enterprise analysis, which represents the cash flows available to all capital holders (both debt and equity). In addition, the WACC is calculated based upon market data from publicly traded companies that pay taxes. As a result, after tax cash flows are utilized in the discounted cash flow method.

When calculating the discount rate or WACC, the assessment of the specific company risk premium is critical. The specific company risk quantifies the risk associated with the specific operations of the company, or the "unsystematic" risk of the company, which includes the risk associated with achieving the projected cash flows. If volume and/or reimbursement growth appears to be aggressive, or if there is significant speculation and uncertainty in the forecast, a higher than average discount rate should be considered. Please see the industry sections for a list of considerations that are specific to each industry.

3. When utilizing the discounted cash flow method, an equity value, as opposed to an enterprise value, could be derived by inputting the costs of debt financing to calculate the cash flow available to equity holders.

## Market Approach[4]

The Market Approach is an approach that estimates value by using one or more methods that compare the subject business to similar businesses that have been purchased or sold. The underlying premise of the Market Approach to valuation is the economic principle of substitution—a prudent buyer will pay no more for a business or asset than it would cost to acquire a substitute with the same utility. The Market Approach relies on observable market data to estimate indications of value.

*Obtaining transaction data with sufficient information so that it can be adjusted and applied in a business valuation is often challenging.*

The Market Approach comprises two distinct methods:

- *Guideline Public Company Method (GPCM)*: GPCM is a method within the Market Approach whereby market multiples are derived from market prices of stocks of companies that are engaged in the same or similar lines of business and actively traded on a free and open market. Market multiples are developed by dividing the value of a publicly traded company's BEV, TIC, or equity value by a financial measure, such as revenue or EBITDA—these multiples provide an indication of how much a knowledgeable investor in the marketplace is willing to pay for a company. The selected market multiples are then applied to the financial measure of the subject to provide a value indication.

  When utilizing the GPCM, the analyst should take into consideration that external microeconomic and macroeconomic events cause fluctuations in the price of public stocks that can distort multiples. Furthermore, valuation analysts are divided as to whether the guideline public company multiples reflect a control or minority level of value, which creates uncertainty around usage of the GPCM.

---

4. SHANNON PRATT, THE MARKET APPROACH TO VALUING BUSINESSES, 2nd ed. (Wiley, 2005).

- *Merger and Acquisition Method (M&A Method)*: The method within the Market Approach whereby pricing multiples are derived from transactions where the target/seller is engaged in the same or similar lines of business and then applied to the subject business or business interest. This method reviews published data regarding actual transactions in either publicly traded or closely held companies. Sources of transaction multiples include market commentary; public and private transaction data published by third-party sources, such as Irving Levin Associates and Capital IQ; U.S. Securities and Exchange Commission filings; and privileged information from a valuation analyst's internal transaction database.

Valuation analysts typically avoid related party transactions and transactions where the seller is financially distressed, as these circumstances could yield skewed multiples. Transaction multiples typically represent control multiples; however, there are instances in which published information can be found regarding a transaction for a minority interest.

When selecting multiples, the analysts should consider the comparability of the subject business to the market comparables. Items to consider include, but are not limited to, size, growth prospects, service mix diversification, geographic diversification, depth of management, capital structure, and access to capital. In addition, barriers to entry and the subject level of value (control versus minority) should be considered.

The financial metric or multiple utilized is dependent upon the type of business being valued. See the industry sections for commentary regarding common multiples that are utilized for the specific industry.

The selected financial metric of the subject business should reflect a normalized level of earnings that is expected to be sustainable. Any nonrecurring revenue or expense should be excluded from the selected metric. Normalizing adjustments should be made for any material changes in revenue or cost structure that are either expected soon or are not yet fully reflected in the financial metric due to timing (i.e., a change occurred during the last two months of the fiscal year or trailing 12-month period being utilized).

## Cost Approach

The Cost Approach, also known as the asset or build-up approach, is a method that attempts to value a business by identifying and valuing each tangible and intangible asset. The valuation premise used in this method may be one of the following[5]:

- value in continued use as part of a going-concern;
- value in place as part of a mass assemblage of assets; or
- value in exchange as part of an orderly disposition or forced liquidation.

The Cost Approach can be considered to provide a "floor" or lowest minimum value related to a business. This method may be an appropriate method when the Market Approach and Income Approach produce a value lower than the Cost Approach. In determining the applicability of the Cost Approach, the analyst must also consider the earnings generated by the business as indicated in its historical and projected financial statements.

The Cost Approach typically includes tangible assets, and may include identifiable intangible assets. In the context of a business valuation, tangible assets include net working capital and personal property and equipment. Intangible assets may include such things as the business's trade name or, in applicable locales, licensure such as a certificate of need.

Although the tangible and intangible assets are not typically valued separately under the Income and Market Approaches, these approaches still consider the cash flows generated by all assets of the business. In providing an FMV indication of the business enterprise, the Income and Market Approaches include all normalized tangible and intangible assets needed to operate the business.

To apply the Cost Approach, each identified asset is valued according to an appropriate methodology for the asset in question.

- *Working capital components*: To value working capital components, the valuation analyst may rely on available accounting data (i.e., balance sheet values) or, in cases where the subject

---

5. Shannon Pratt & Alina Niculita, Valuing a Business, 5th ed. (McGraw-Hill, 2008), p. 47.

business maintains cash-based financial statements, may rely on metrics to "build up" working capital components (e.g., the business's revenue and an estimate for accounts receivable days outstanding).

- *Personal property and equipment*: Chapter 27 details specific aspects of valuing capital assets. In cases where the Cost Approach will not likely be relied upon (e.g., profitable, cash-flow generating business), many clients or other end-users of the valuation choose to exclude a detailed analysis of a business's personal property in the valuation engagement scope, due to cost or other reasons. In such cases, the valuation analyst will also use available accounting or other data to value the personal property and equipment. Please refer to chapter 27 for more detail concerning the valuation of capital assets.
- *Intangible assets*: Identified intangible assets may be appropriate to include in the application of the Cost Approach to value. These assets may include trade name, medical records in a physician practice, certificate of need, or trained workforce. Whether any of these assets are appropriate for inclusion in any particular valuation engagement will be up to the judgment of the valuation analyst.

The remaining chapters within the Business Valuation section follow the same general outline as discussed above, and highlight particular issues within each of the approaches as they pertain to the various healthcare verticals.

*Sources*

Gary Trugman, *Understanding Business Valuation: A Practical Guide to Valuing Small- to Medium-Sized Business*, 3d ed. (AICPA, 2008)

Shannon Pratt & Alina Niculita, *Valuing a Business*, 5th ed. (McGraw-Hill, 2008).

Shannon Pratt, *The Market Approach to Valuing Businesses*, 2d ed. (Wiley, 2005).

# Physician Practices 5

*Clinton Flume, CVA, and Nikolaus Melder*

---

*In the determination of FMV, it is critical to understand the relationship between provider compensation and productivity.*

---

A physician practice (Practice) is a medical practice comprised of two or more physicians organized to provide patient care services (regardless of its legal form or ownership).[1] Practices are commonly valued in connection with the outright purchase of a practice by a hospital or health system, in order to align with a physician group through direct employment, or a professional services agreement (PSA). Buyers of Practices typically acquire a control position because a minority position limits the buyer's ability to dictate distributions, set employment terms and compensation, influence operations, or leverage buyer attributes post-transaction, not to mention that legal and regulatory restrictions may prohibit outside ownership in a Practice (e.g., corporate practice of medicine doctrine).

---

1. Centers for Medicare & Medicaid Services, www.cms.gov.

In addition to outright acquisitions, hospitals and health systems may find value in the acquisition of a Practice's in-office ancillary services, such as laboratory, therapy, and diagnostic imaging. For many health systems and hospitals, acquisition and alignment of physician practices is a core strategy of achieving health reforms' triple aim of improving the quality and access to affordable medical care.

While the following discussion of Practices make be applicable to a solo practitioner or group of practices, it is not applicable to independent physician associations (IPAs). These types of businesses can carry different dynamics that are beyond the scope of this commentary.

In conducting a fair market value (FMV) analysis, the valuation analyst should consider the Income, Market, and Cost Approaches to value, as outlined in chapter 4.

## *Income Approach*

The Income Approach estimates the value of a Practice by projecting the future cash flow attributable to the subject operations then discounting those earnings back to the present value utilizing an appropriate discount rate that takes into consideration the risk of the operations of the subject business, the forecast utilized, and the industry, among other things. The following outlines the key assumptions to consider when developing a cash flow model for a Practice.

### Volume

Volume for a provider (defined as a physician or mid-level provider) at a Practice can be discussed by using encounter volume or work relative value units (wRVUs). Encounter volume refers to evaluation and management (E&M) current procedural terminology (CPT) codes, which include multiple categories, such as office visits, hospital visits, consultations, and nursing facility visits. Encounter volume is intended to reflect the face-to-face interaction between a provider and a patient. This professional contact excludes ancillary services (e.g., laboratory or diagnostic imaging). wRVUs measure the work effort associated with CPT codes, and reflect professional productivity for a provider. wRVUs do not include technical components of ancillary services. In comparison to encounters, wRVUs are associated with CPT codes, whereas encounters only reflect the E&M CPT codes. Unlike wRVUs, encounters allow a valuation analyst to identify how many patients, on average, a provider examines per day. However, wRVUs provide the most accurate measure of productivity by capturing all professional services and not just services isolated to E&M CPT codes.

Analyzing encounter volume is necessary because it allows a valuation analyst to understand capacity constraints and to benchmark a physician's productivity, revenue, and compensation. Although not all inclusive, a valuation analyst should consider the following when developing or evaluating a forecast for provider volume:

- age of the physicians and any expected retirement dates;
- planned addition of new physician or mid-level provider;
- capacity constraints based on current and future work schedules;
- addition of competing practices in the market;
- an understanding of historical volume trends and fluctuations;
- risk of departure for employed, non-owner physicians (non-compete laws vary from state to state); and
- any one-time personal events that could result in an increase or decrease in volume for a provider (i.e., illness, extended vacation, and coverage for another provider).

The valuation analyst should evaluate local market factors in the form of competition and demographics. Competitors may include a local hospital(s)' employed physicians, new providers entering the market, or changes in the practice habits of the current doctors. If the Practice staffs employed providers who are non-owners, the employed providers may consider alternative employment opportunities, perhaps a local hospital. Hospitals may employ or enter into a contractual relationship with these providers that may impact the future volume (and reimbursement rates) at the Practice. Another determinate of volume growth is the local demographic environment. Developing an understanding of the local community (e.g., age, unemployment rates, average income), along with its population growth rate, will provide insight to the valuation analyst.

Capacity and technological constraints associated with a Practice may impact the volume. A Practice only has a defined number of operating hours and working days. If a Practice is projected to keep the number of doctors stable and increase volume, the valuation analyst should question management personnel on their availability and maximum capacity. Furthermore, with the development and implementation of technological requirements, the valuation analyst should consider down-time associated with application and use of technology (e.g., electronic medical records).

## Reimbursement

In addition to volume, the valuation analyst should address the "price" or reimbursement level to determine the Practice's projected revenue. A Practice's payor mix, procedure mix, and the patient population will define its reimbursment. Typical payors for Practice services include governmental payors (e.g., Medicare, Medicaid, Tricare), commercial or managed-care payors (e.g., Anthem, United Healthcare, Humana, Cigna, Aetna), or the individual (i.e., self-pay). Payor mix provides the necessary information to evaluate future reimbursement levels. The most applicable data for this task is a payor mix report detailed by encounter volume, gross charges, or collections. The valuation analyst can research projected reimbursement for Medicare through a review of the current fee schedule.[2] Commercial and managed care payors can base their rates on Medicare fee schedule rates, but the valuation analyst should discuss managed-care contracting and future expectations with Practice management. Although it is important to understand management's perspective on reimbursement, due to the small scale of operations, Practices typically do not have negotiation leverage with managed-care or commercial payors to impact price. Furthermore, it is important to note that under health reform, including MACRA, physician practice reimbursement models are being discussed and implemented in various markets, including bundled payments, and various value-based models, which will transition practices from the traditional fee-for-service reimbursement, and will put their reimbursement more at risk. A detailed discussion of these reimbursement models is beyond the scope of this chapter.

## Other Considerations

In addition to professional services, some Practices provide in-office ancillary services (e.g., laboratory, therapy, or diagnostic imaging).

---

2. *Id.*

The valuation analyst must thoroughly understand the ancillary services volume and reimbursement and apply similar methodology and scrutiny to the projection of volume and reimbursement for these services. Additionally, the valuation analyst must understand how much of the provider's compensation is derived from ancillary services versus professional services.

## Operating Expenses

Employee salaries and benefits, facility costs, and provider compensation comprise the majority of the operating expenses at a Practice. If a Practice offers ancillary services, then medical supplies, equipment leases, and maintenance expenses can also be a significant component of operating costs.

Employee (non-provider) compensation is typically analyzed in two ways: average salary per full-time equivalent (FTE) employee and number of FTEs per provider. The types of employees at a Practice include nursing staff, medical assistants, and administrative staff. Employee FTEs typically adjust with the number of visits. If a Practice is projected to experience an increase in the number of physicians and mid-levels, the number of FTEs will likely grow to accommodate the additional workload. The opposite applies for departures from a Practice.

Facility costs include rent paid to a third party for the professional space in which the Practice resides. The valuation analyst should take care to review the facility lease when analyzing historical and projected financial operations and determine if the lease is held by a related party or an independent third party. In situations where the Practice leases from a related party, the rent paid may need to be reviewed by a real estate appraiser to determine if it is consistent with FMV. In cases where the Practice owns the property and does not make a charge to the operations, then a real estate appraiser should establish an FMV value or rental rate of the property. This determination will be based on whether or not the buyer is acquiring the land and building. If the Practice excludes the property from a transaction, then the Practice's operations must be burdened with the FMV rental rate. If the property is included in a deal, the appraised amount of the facility would be additive to the valuation of the Practice's business operations once it has been burdened with the appropriate facility rental expense. As always, a valuation analyst must seek advice from a qualified real estate appraiser.

Provider compensation typically represents the single largest component of operating expenses for a Practice. The valuation analyst must understand the actual terms of post-transaction compensation for each provider and burden the Practice with the proposed compensation terms. Proposed compensation can be in multiple forms, including a percentage of pre-compensation earnings (pre-comp split), a percentage of professional collections, per wRVU, salary plus bonus metrics, or a percentage of professional and technical revenue. Valuation analysts must use their best judgment and carefully document rational behind selected compensation assumptions. Also, it is helpful to compare projected provider compensation relative to national benchmarks based on the provider's volume, revenue, and pre-compensation earnings. Significant deviations between provider productivity and compensation can change the risk profile of a Practice.

## Capital Expenditures

Capital expenditures can be used by a Practice to purchase new equipment, make leasehold improvements and upgrades to its facility, maintain the current assets, or fund new projects, such as a new ancillary service. The age of its facility and equipment, the effectiveness and condition of its electronic medical records and technology, the ancillary services provided, the expected growth of the Practice, and the number of providers establishes the amount of capital expenditures a Practice needs. Actual capital expenditure requirements may vary materially depending upon the Practice's existing asset base. However, the ultimate view of capital expenditures should be predicated on the replacement of assets over time to ensure the Practice maintains the same services to deliver the same historical patient quality and achieve its projected growth. The absence of projected investment in the assets of the business will create additional risk.

## Discount Rate Considerations

The forecast utilized by the valuation analyst will include some degree of "forecast" risk. A projection with more optimistic volume assumptions may be riskier than one that assumes the "status quo." The valuation analyst should demonstrate an adequate understanding of the key risks and incorporate a discount rate adjustment for these factors (typically through the specific company risk factor discussed in chapter 4).

Discussion around factors that make a Practice forecast riskier include the departure risk of current providers either due to retirement or alternative employment opportunities; competition within the immediate service area, including alternative sources of care, such as walk-in clinics and urgent care clinics; and community proliferation of provider employment. The latter is especially detrimental to the specialty provider as they rely heavily on referrals from primary care physicians.

## Market Approach

The Market Approach estimates value by comparing the value of similar Practices traded in a free and open market. The underlying premise of the Market Approach to valuation is the economic principle of substitution—a prudent buyer will pay no more for the business or asset than it would cost to acquire a substitute with the same utility. Please refer to chapter 4 for a more detailed discussion on the application of the Market Approach.

### Relevant Multiples

The Market Approach uses relative value measures or "multiples," which are factors by which some fundamental financial variable is multiplied to derive a value indication for the Practice. Types of multiples seen in the healthcare transaction space include revenue and EBITDA multiples. While a valuation analyst should examine the Market Approach in the application of the method, these multiples are rarely used for a Practice for the following reasons:

- *Lack of comparable data*—Practice transactions are primarily conducted by hospital and health systems, both for-profit and not-for-profit. These transaction prices are not often disclosed. Therefore, there are limited data sets available for a valuation analyst to source.
- *Provider compensation* (physician and mid-level provider)— After direct operating expenses (non-provider staff, facility, supplies, contract services, etc.), provider compensation typi-

cally comprises any and all available earnings in a Practice. Therefore, the remainder of the available earnings may render using the Market Approach earnings multiples impractical. As a result, applying an earnings multiple may not result in a meaningful indication of value.

## Sources of Market Data

Sources for market transaction data can be obtained from guideline public companies that have acquired practices (e.g., Davita/HCP; Envision Healthcare; et al.) and from third-party sources, such as Irving Levin. Additionally, survey data from information management companies, such as Medical Group Management Association (MGMA) and Sullivan Cotter and Associates, Inc. (Sullivan Cotter) can serve as a benchmark analytic tool for a valuation analyst. These survey companies aggregate market information from Practice administrators and physicians to understand the underlying financial and operational statistics that drive the professional practice subindustry. A valuation analyst can use these surveys to compare a Practice's operating statistics, provider compensation, and relative productivity to national operating benchmarks. Wide deviations from these studies help a valuation analyst further explore questions within the operations or allow the analysts to understand potential risk better. While these sources do not provide relative transaction measurement multiples, they do provide valuable insight into typical benchmarks of a Practice.

# Cost Approach

The Cost Approach, also known as the asset or build-up approach, is a method that attempts to value a business by identifying and assessing each tangible and intangible asset. This method is primarily used for Practices not generating sufficient cash flows to make its operations more valuable than the underlying value of its assets. The Cost Approach provides a "floor," or lowest minimum value, related to an interest in a Practice and may be appropriate when the Market and Income Approaches produce lower values.

When a valuation analyst deems it appropriate to use a Cost Approach, the components of value included in this methodology typically include tangible assets, and may include identifiable intangible assets. In the context of a business valuation, tangible assets may consist of net working capital and personal property and equipment, leasehold improvements, and real estate. Intangible assets may include a Practice's phone number, medical records, trade name, certificates of need (CONs), physician non-competes, non-physician-trained and assembled workforce, and physician-trained and assembled workforce.

The valuation of the tangible assets of a Practice are fairly straightforward. The most appropriate method to ensure market values are assigned is to conduct a full inventory of the asset base and mark the assets to market. In terms of the identified intangible assets, these carry more subjectivity within the valuation community. Under the Cost Approach, it is important that the valuation analyst consider: (1) whether the identified intangible asset(s) are legally protectable and separately marketable; (2) which premise of value[3] is being applied; and (3) if the premise of value being applied for the selected asset(s) is consistent with the results of the other approaches to value. The inability to address each of these important considerations could result in insufficient support for an identified intangible asset value conclusion under the Cost Approach.

The following identified intangible assets generally are legally protectable and separately marketable if purchased:

1. **Phone number**—A phone number value is the estimated amount it would cost to establish a new number and inform patients of a change in the Practice operations, such as ownership or affiliation.

2. **Medical records**—A medical records value identifies the cost to recreate a medical record in the absence of assuming the charts from the seller. Also, it is worth noting that often times medical records are not purchased but instead a custodial relationship between the Practice and the buyer is entered into.

3. **Trade name**—A trade name seeks to assign value based on the premise that a third-party buyer would pay to avoid the marketing effort and expense involved with creating and promoting a new trade name within the Practice's immediate service area. A trade name value will seek to incorporate the

---

3. See chapter 4 for a discussion of the premise of value in business valuation engagements.

awareness of the Practice's location, physician, and reputation, along with the Practice's relationships with patients and payors and the Practice's historical marketing expenditures.

4. **Certificate of need (CON)**—A CON considers the value the Practice holds with the required licensure to perform certain in-office ancillary services. The most common CON would reside with diagnostic imaging and radiation therapy services.

5. **Non–compete**—A non-compete value is attributable to the estimated dollar impact a seller could inflict to a buyer, should the seller decide to compete for similar services in the market, absent a non-compete. It is important to ensure that the value of a non-compete is not predicated on the volume or value of referrals. Also, in addition to consideration of the premise of value being applied, non-competes are only valid to the extent that local and state laws support the enforcement of the agreement.

Other identified intangible assets in which the valuation community has more divergent viewpoints include non-physician-trained workforce and physician-trained workforce. Please note that the need to address the important considerations listed above remains for these assets.

1. **Non-physician-trained workforce**—The value of the Practice's trained and assembled non-physician workforce takes into consideration the cost associated with rehiring and retraining a non-physician work staff (administrative and clinical). This process is burdensome and results in an inefficient workplace as well as reduced productivity. The value is derived based on the estimated time to hire and retain the existing non-physician staff and the salary and benefit costs related to the workforce.

2. **Physician-trained workforce**—The value of physician-trained workforce likely sparks the most debate of any identified intangible assets under a Practice Cost Approach. A valuation analyst must understand the specific facts and circumstances when this asset is considered. The valuation community has debated extensively whether there is supportable evidence that

a willing buyer of physician-trained workforce could actually sell this asset back to the seller in the event of a divesture. This fact leads many appraisers to question the validity of inclusion of this asset without potential repercussions that the value paid is tied to future referrals.

In addition, it is important to note that if a Practice valuation is supported by an Income- and or Market-based analysis, some valuation analysts may apply a cost-to-recreate methodology, similar to the non-physician-trained workforce, while others may use a residual approach, to attribute a component of the Practice's value over and above the identified tangible and intangible assets (as referred to as goodwill) to physician-trained workforce. Under this scenario, value is in essence allocated to physician-trained workforce and is a component of the value supported by the earnings of the Practice.

Please note that, even though the tangible and intangible assets are not separately valued under the Income and Market Approaches, these approaches consider the cash flows generated by all assets of the business and provide an FMV indication of the business enterprise, which includes all normalized tangible and intangible assets needed to operate the business. Please refer to chapter 4 for further discussion of the Cost Approach in the context of a business valuation.

# Urgent Care Centers and Freestanding Emergency Departments

# 6

*Taryn Nasr and Corey Palasota, CFA*

*Significant risk factors associated with UCCs and FSEDs include the high levels of competition associated with relatively low barriers to entry and community acceptance related to the higher co-pays.*

Urgent care centers (UCCs) and freestanding emergency departments (FSEDs) are facilities that serve patients with varying levels of acuity on a retail basis (i.e., immediate access to care in a convenient location). A UCC is typically open 40 to 60 hours a week and treats common, low-acuity illnesses, such as flu symptoms, cuts and sprains, minor burns, eye issues, bladder issues, and earaches. In contrast, an FSED is open 24/7 and treats patients with higher-acuity symptoms, such as heart attacks, respiratory distress, and severe limb or head injuries. Typically, UCCs or FSEDs are entry points into the healthcare system as patients may be further directed into a hospital or referred to a primary care or specialist physician. UCCs and FSEDs are typically valued for the sale of the entity to a hospital buyer (control level-transactions), contribution to a joint venture (mostly control-level transactions), or individual physician investment (mostly minority-level transactions).

In conducting a fair market value (FMV) analysis, the valuation analyst should consider the Income, Market, and Cost Approaches to value, as outlined in chapter 4.

## *Income Approach*

The Income Approach estimates the value of a UCC or FSED by discounting the projected future free cash flows attributable to the subject operations to a present value. The discount rate takes into consideration the risk of the operations of the subject business, the forecast utilized, and the industry, among other factors. The following outlines the key assumptions that should be considered when developing a cash flow model for a UCC or FSED business.

### Volume

The topline financial performance of a UCC or FSED is dependent upon the number of patient visits. The valuation analyst must evaluate in detail the patient volume performed at the UCC or FSED and develop an understanding of the volume trends along with other local market factors (e.g., competition and demographics) that may impact forecasted volumes.

Historical patient visit volume must be considered by the valuation analyst. Typically, UCC and FSED management will provide average daily patient visit volume that can be used as a proxy to compare the relative activity of the subject UCC or FSED to benchmarks. This information helps the valuation analyst to evaluate historical financial performance and will serve as the base for projecting future utilization. Although not all-inclusive, the following should be considerations of the valuation analyst when developing or evaluating a forecast:

- location, visibility, and accessibility of the UCC or FSED to patients;
- stage of the UCC or FSED in its business cycle; and
- seasonality and persistence of historical patient visit volume levels.

Local market factors in the form of competition and demographics should be evaluated by the valuation analyst. Competition may include a competitor UCC or FSED, a local hospital(s), or even a local physician practice. The barriers to entry for UCCs and FSEDs are relatively low and new competition can significantly impact volume. In addition, location and demographics play a central role in the operations of a UCC or FSED. The more successful UCCs and FSEDs are typically located in high-traffic intersections or in retail strip centers near large neighborhoods and schools. Developing an understanding of the local community (e.g., age, unemployment rates, average income), along with its population growth rate, will provide meaningful insight to the valuation analyst. For example, a UCC located near a high school is more likely to see patients with athletic injuries or flu symptoms, whereas an FSED located near a retirement community may see patients with heart attacks, strokes, or hip fractures.

Capacity and technological constraints are typically not a large factor in UCCs and FSEDs. UCCs have the ability to expand hours of operation if needed and can accommodate patient visit volumes that are significantly higher than average during winter months. Likewise, a typical FSED is open at all times and has the ability to bring in additional staff in order to handle fluctuations in daily visit volume. To the extent a UCC or FSED is overcrowded, patient wait times tend to increase. Consequently, patients may look towards other alternatives. A valuation analyst should consider the need for additional space or staffing if the UCC or FSED experiences a constant overflow of patients.

## Reimbursement

The second component of revenue that should be addressed by the valuation analyst is "price," or reimbursement. Reimbursement is driven by the payor mix of the subject UCC or FSED. Typical payors for UCC and FSED services include commercial or managed care payors (e.g., Anthem, Humana, Cigna, Aetna) or the individual (i.e., self-pay). Government payors (e.g., Medicare, Medicaid, Tricare) are typically low to nonexistent due to the target demographics of UCCs and FSEDs. Payor mix provides the necessary information to evaluate future reimbursement levels that should be considered by the valuation analyst. Typically, the management of the subject UCC or FSED can provide the valuation analyst with payor mix detail reported by patient visit volume, gross charges, or collections. The valuation analyst can apply this information to develop expectations regarding reimbursement growth.

A UCC is typically reimbursed on an in-network standard rate per visit basis or through in-network negotiated menu prices that utilize Medicare's Current Procedural Terminology (CPT) codes. All payments for a UCC are global in nature, which means one payment covers the professional and technical components. Under the rate per visit structure, a UCC will receive one payment without consideration of the patient's diagnosis or ancillary needs (e.g., x-ray, injection, or patch). Under menu pricing, the UCC may bill the payor separately for each service (e.g., patient evaluation, injection, x-ray, etc.). Importantly, reimbursement for services performed by nurse practitioners or physician assistants is typically lower than services performed by physicians.

Reimbursement for FSEDs is somewhat more complex and can vary based on the structure and location of the FSED. If an FSED is affiliated with a health system, the FSED will typically be "in-network" with commercial insurance payors and can bill Medicare patients. Historically, FSEDs were unable to bill government payors if not classified as a department of a hospital. A valuation analyst should understand the current national and state regulations regarding the ability to bill government payors as FSEDs, as this ability may change depending on national and state regulation changes.

Some FSEDs will bill on a global basis, which means one payment is used to cover both the professional and technical components. However, other FSEDs will bill for the technical fee only and the attending physician will bill a professional fee separately.

Reimbursement can be affected by changes in the subject UCC or FSED's patient mix. Higher-acuity patients will typically have higher reimbursement rates while lower-acuity patients will typically have lower reimbursement rates. Technical fees at FSEDs are determined based on patient triage levels of severity (i.e., Levels 1-5). To the extent a UCC or FSED is seeing a disproportionate amount of low acuity patients, future reimbursement may be at risk. A valuation analyst should inquire into the nature and acuity level of the visits.

## Other Considerations

With rising co-pays and deductibles, patients are becoming increasingly aware of their healthcare choices. Patients attracted to UCCs and FSEDs want convenience and immediate care, but may be displeased by the high co-pays and fees at these entities. FSED visits typically incur high out-of-pocket expenses that become the responsibility of the patient. In addition, patient co-pays at UCCs are typically higher than physician office visits. The patient reaction to pricing can impact future volume levels, reimbursement, and bad debt expense (i.e., nonpayment of bill). A valuation analyst should address the issue of community acceptance regarding the UCC and FSED pricing as compared to other alternatives.

## Operating Expenses

Employee salaries, provider compensation, facility costs, and general and administrative expense comprise the majority of the operating expenses at a UCC or FSED. Please note, most expenses for UCCs and FSEDs are fixed in nature; therefore, the contribution margin for incremental patient visit volume above a certain threshold is typically high.

Employee compensation is typically analyzed in two ways: average salary per full-time equivalent (FTE) employee and number of hours per case. The types of employees at a UCC or FSED include nursing staff, technical staff, and administrative staff. Nursing and technical FTE levels will typically adjust with volume. If a UCC or FSED has an influx in volume, the UCC or FSED will increase the number of clinical FTEs in order to accommodate the additional workload. In addition, UCCs may employ physician assistants and nurse practitioners to increase capacity, particularly in areas with a shortage of primary care physicians.

Provider costs reflect the salaries of the physicians to cover the cost of the professional services provided. UCCs and FSEDs typically employ physicians at a base hourly rate or salary. The most common physician specialties employed by UCCs include family medicine, emergency medicine, internal medicine, and pediatrics. UCC physicians can be full-time or part-time. If the UCC relies primarily on nurse practitioners, the provider costs will typically be lower than a UCC that relies primarily on physician providers. Physicians at FSEDs are trained in emergency medicine. The FSED physicians must be at the facility at all times; therefore, the provider costs at an FSED is significantly higher as a percentage of net revenue. The valuation analyst should take care to review the professional services agreement for the physicians when analyzing historical and projected financial operations.

Facility costs are comprised mostly of the rent paid to a third party for the physical space in which the subject UCC or FSED resides. The valuation analyst should take care to review the facility lease when analyzing historical and projected financial operations. In situations where the real estate is owned by investors in the UCC or FSED operations, a real estate appraiser may be requested to verify that the facility rent paid is consistent with FMV. Likewise, a real estate appraisal may be required when the UCC or FSED owns the real estate. In these instances, the real estate is valued and a fair market rental rate is determined. The subject UCC or FSED is burdened with the fair market rental rate for the valuation of the UCC or FSED operations, as most transactions for UCCs or FSEDs do not include the purchase of the real estate. If the real estate is to be purchased, the appraised amount of the real estate would be additive to the valuation of the operations of the subject UCC or FSED once it has been burdened with the appropriate facility rental expense.

General and administrative expenses will usually include any contracted billing and management fees. These fees are typically based on a percentage of revenue; therefore, the expenses will increase and decrease with the revenue of the UCC or FSED. If the subject UCC or FSED contracts for billing and/or management services from a related party, a separate FMV analysis may be required to determine the reasonableness of the fees charged for those services. In addition, general and administrative expenses will usually include the cost of advertising and marketing, which is important for a UCC or FSED to build community awareness of the facility.

## Capital Expenditures

Capital expenditures can be used by a UCC or FSED to purchase new equipment, maintain the current assets, or fund new projects, such as expanding the number of patient rooms. The amount of capital expenditures needed is based on the age of the fixed assets and the expected growth of the UCC or FSED. Actual capital expenditure requirements may vary materially depending upon the subject UCC's or FSED's existing asset base, as over time the asset base will need to be replaced/maintained in order to maintain operations. Hence, another method for estimating capital expenditures is to review the acquisition cost of the existing asset base and the estimated life of the assets.

## Discount Rate Considerations

The forecast utilized by the valuation analyst will include a certain level of "forecast" risk. A forecast with more optimistic volume assumptions may be riskier than one that assumes the "status quo." The valuation analyst should demonstrate an adequate understanding of the key risks and incorporate a discount rate adjustment for these factors (typically through the specific company risk factor discussed in chapter 4).

Other risk factors that the valuation analyst should examine include the following:

- *Sustainability of volume*—Stable UCCs and FSEDs that have shown a historical ability to maintain patient visit volume levels would be considered less risky when compared to newer operations or operations have seen a decline in volume trends.
- *Community acceptance*—UCCs and FSEDs that reside in areas with patients that are more likely to accept higher co-pays would be considered less risky than areas with patients who are price conscience.
- *Reimbursement pressure*—UCCs and FSEDs typically have limited ability to negotiate reimbursement contracts, which can be considered risky for future revenue projections.
- *Market factors*—UCCs or FSEDs in an area with high population growth and low competition would be considered less risky.

## *Market Approach*

The Market Approach estimates value by comparing the value of similar UCCs and FSEDs traded in a free and open market. The underlying premise of the Market Approach to valuation is the economic principle of substitution—a prudent buyer will pay no more for a business or asset than it would cost to acquire a substitute with the same utility. Please refer to chapter 4 for a more detailed discussion on the application of the Market Approach.

## Relevant Multiples

The Market Approach uses relative value measures or "multiples," which are factors by which some fundamental financial variable is multiplied to derive a value indication for the UCC or FSED. The most common multiple utilized to value a UCC or FSED is the EBITDA multiple.

Normalized EBITDA multiples are utilized instead of revenue multiples as they capture the ultimate profitability of the UCCs and FSEDs, and are more closely related to the distributions to owners than are revenue multiples. Since profitability can vary significantly based on a UCC or FSED patient mix and cost structure, the valuation analyst should consider the profitability of the subject versus the identified comparables when selecting revenue multiples instead of EBITDA multiples. In addition, the valuation analyst should consider the stage of the UCC or FSED in its business cycle. If the UCC or FSED is relatively new and lacks stable operations, it would be hard to apply a market multiple to the appropriate financial variable.

## Sources of Market Data

There are currently no public companies that specialize in the ownership and operation of UCCs; however, nearly all public hospital operators have UCCs and frequently comment on the marketplace. There is currently one public company that specializes in the ownership and operation of FSEDs: Adeptus, Inc. (ADPT). Adeptus owns and operates a network of independent freestanding emergency rooms in the United States.

Sources of transaction multiples include market commentary from the public FSED operator noted above; discussions with management of UCC or FSED operators regarding recent transactions; public and private transaction data published by third-party sources, such as Irving Levin Associates and Capital IQ; U.S. Securities and Exchange Commission filings; and nonpublic information from a valuation analyst's internal transaction database that is based upon his or her industry experience. Transaction multiples typically represent control multiples;

however, there are instances in which published information can be found regarding a transaction for a minority interest.

## Factors to Consider When Selecting Multiples

### Comparability of the Subject to the Comparables

It is important to note that there are fundamental differences between small to midsize privately held companies and a publicly traded company. These differences include size, depth of management, capital structure, access to capital, product diversification, geographic diversification, and risk. In addition, external microeconomic and macroeconomic events cause fluctuations in public stock prices that can distort multiples. Therefore, hospital or public company multiples may not necessarily reflect comparable market multiples for any single, privately held UCC or FSED.

Size and growth prospects should also be considered when reviewing transaction multiples, as implied valuation multiples for large multi-site UCC or FSED operators are typically significantly higher than multiples paid for a single location.

### Barriers to Entry

There are minimal to no barriers to entry for UCCs. However, there are barriers to entry for the FSED marketplace, specifically state and federal government licensure and regulation. Each state has its own distinct governance for FSEDs, and some states do not recognize FSEDs. It is important for the valuation analyst to understand specific state restrictions for FSEDs.

### Level of Value

The valuation analyst should always consider if the subject interest being valued represents a minority or controlling interest when selecting market multiples. It should be noted that there is nonconformity in the profession as to how guideline public company multiples should be applied to reflect a control or minority level of value. In any case, when utilizing transaction multiples, the analyst should always ensure that the level of value acquired in the guideline transactions matches the level of value of the subject interest.

### *Other Considerations*

When utilizing transaction multiples, the analyst should identify any transactions that might yield skewed multiples as a result of related party buyers and sellers and a forced or distressed sale.

UCCs and FSEDs with strong concentration of low-acuity cases may have significant potential reimbursement risk in the future. As a result, the multiples utilized in the Market Approach should be adjusted accordingly, or the projected earnings of the UCC or FSED should be adjusted to account for the risk before applying typical market multiples.

## *Cost Approach*

The Cost Approach, also known as the asset or build-up approach, is a method that attempts to value a business by identifying and valuing each tangible and intangible asset. This approach is primarily used for UCCs and FSEDs not generating sufficient cash flows to make their operations more valuable than the underlying value of the assets. The Cost Approach provides a "floor," or lowest minimum value, related to an interest in a UCC or FSED and may be appropriate when the Market and Income Approaches produce lower values.

The Cost Approach typically includes tangible assets, and may include identifiable intangible assets. In the context of a business valuation, tangible assets include net working capital and personal property and equipment. Intangible assets may include items such as the UCC or FSED trade name. Please refer to chapter 4 for further discussion of the Cost Approach in the context of a business valuation.

Please note that all assets identified in the Cost Approach are included within the total enterprise values determined in the Income and Market Approaches.

# Diagnostic Imaging Centers 7

*Taryn Nasr and Chance Sherer, CVA*

---

*Imaging Centers are typically capital
intensive entities and can be limited by
capacity and technological constraints.
The maintenance and replenishment of the
imaging equipment asset base should be
addressed in the valuation.*

---

A diagnostic imaging center (Imaging Center) is a facility
with the equipment to produce various types of radiologic
and electromagnetic images. Imaging Centers include hospital outpatient departments that perform inpatient and
outpatient imaging services, as well as independent diagnostic testing facilities. Imaging Centers are typically valued for the sale of the Imaging Center to a management
company and/or hospital buyer (control-level transactions)
or for contribution to a joint venture (mostly control-level
transactions). In some instances, an Imaging Center will
be valued for individual physician investment (minority-
level transactions).

**71**

In conducting a fair market value (FMV) analysis, the valuation analyst should consider the Income, Market, and Cost Approaches to value, as outlined in chapter 4.

## Income Approach

The Income Approach estimates the value of an Imaging Center by projecting the future cash flow attributable to the subject operations then discounting those earnings back to the present value utilizing an appropriate discount rate that takes into consideration the risk of the operations of the subject business, the forecast utilized, and the industry, among other things. The following outlines the key assumptions that should be considered when developing a cash flow model for an Imaging Center business.

### Volume

The topline financial performance of the Imaging Center is dependent upon scan volume performed at the center. A scan is a noninvasive procedure that is used to generate representations of internal anatomy and functions. A valuation analyst must evaluate in detail the scan volume performed at the Imaging Center and develop an understanding of the referral dynamic from specialists along with other local market factors (e.g., competition and demographics) that may impact forecasted volumes.

Imaging Centers primarily rely upon referrals from specialists and the referral structure must be considered by the valuation analyst. Although not all inclusive, the following should be considerations of the valuation analyst when developing or evaluating a forecast:

- working relationships between the Imaging Center and specialists that will refer scans;
- pre-authorization and authorization procedures and requirements between the Imaging Center and payors;
- implementation of any revenue benefit management programs by commercial payors; and
- any one-time personal events that could result in an increase or decrease in scan volume for radiologist reads (i.e., illness, extended vacation, and/or coverage for another radiologist).

Local market factors in the form of competition and demographics should be evaluated by the valuation analyst. Competition may include a competing Imaging Center, local hospital(s), or even changes to practicing habits of the referring physicians. Another determinate of volume growth is the local demographic environment. Developing an understanding of the local community (e.g., age, unemployment rates, average income), along with its population growth rate, will provide insight to the valuation analyst.

Capacity and technological constraints associated with the Imaging Center may impact the financial forecast. Each modality has limitations on the number of scans that be performed. Older equipment may take longer to perform scans when compared to equipment that was recently purchased. If an Imaging Center is projected to add equipment and/or modalities to increase scan volume, the valuation analyst should question management on the availability of space and time necessary to handle any expected increases in scan volume.

## Reimbursement

The second component of revenue that should be addressed by the valuation analyst is "price" or reimbursement. Reimbursement is driven by the payor mix of the subject Imaging Center. Typical payors for Imaging Center services include governmental payors (e.g., Medicare, Medicaid, Tricare), commercial or managed care payors (e.g., Anthem, Humana, Cigna, Aetna), or the individual (i.e., self-pay). Payor mix provides the necessary information to evaluate future reimbursement levels that should be considered by the valuation analyst. Typically, the subject Imaging Center's management can provide the valuation analyst with payor mix detail reported by scan volume, gross charges, or collections. The valuation analyst can research projected reimbursement for Medicare through a review of the current fee schedule.[1] Many of the commercial and managed care payors base their fee schedules on Medicare fee schedule rates, but the valuation analyst should discuss managed care contracting and future expectations with management. The valuation analyst can apply this information to develop expectations regarding reimbursement growth.

Reimbursement can be affected by changes in the subject Imaging Center's scan mix. The different diagnostic imaging service lines

---

1. Centers for Medicare & Medicaid Services. www.cms.gov.

are referred to as modalities and are typically divided into two categories: advanced imaging and routine imaging. Advanced imaging modalities include magnetic resonance imaging (MRI), computed topography (CT), and positron emission tomography (PET). Routine imaging modalities include general radiology and fluoroscopy (X-ray), ultrasound/echography, mammography, nuclear medicine, and bone densitometry. Advanced imaging scans will typically have higher reimbursement rates than routine imaging scans.

## Other Considerations

An Imaging Center can be reimbursed on a global basis or technical basis. Global reimbursement means that the Imaging Center receives payment for the technical and professional components of the service provided. The technical component includes the use of equipment, facilities, nonprofessional staff, and supplies. The professional component covers the cost of the physician's professional services only. If an Imaging Center bills on a global basis, it will receive full reimbursement and will pay the radiologists their professional component. If an Imaging Center bills on a technical basis, it will be reimbursed for the technical component only and the radiologists will bill their professional component separately. A valuation analyst must understand the billing structure of the Imaging Center in comparing reimbursement with benchmarks.

## Operating Expenses

Employee salaries, professional radiology fees, facility costs, and general and administrative expense comprise the majority of the operating expenses at an Imaging Center.

Employee compensation is typically analyzed in two ways: average salary per full-time equivalent (FTE) employee and number of hours per scan. The types of employees at an Imaging Center include technical staff and administrative staff. Technical FTE levels will typically adjust with volume. If an Imaging Center is projected to have an influx in volume, the number of clinical FTEs will need to grow to accommodate the additional workload. By contrast, if an Imaging Center is expected to lose significant volume, it would be reasonable to assume that management would lower the number of staff hours at the Imaging Center.

Professional fees paid to the radiologist are associated with the diagnostic image interpretations, or read fees. This expense would be present in instances where the Imaging Center bills for services on a global basis. The fee may be structured as a percentage of global net revenues, a fixed annual payment, or a fixed fee per scan type. In the context of a transaction, this expense would typically be checked to ensure the fees paid are also consistent with FMV. It may be necessary to conduct a separate FMV analysis on the payment made to radiologists for professional services.

Facility costs are comprised mostly of the rent paid to a third party for the physical space in which the subject Imaging Center resides. The valuation analyst should take care to review the facility lease when analyzing historical and projected financial operations. In situations where the real estate is owned by investors in the Imaging Center technical operations, a real estate appraiser may be requested to verify that the facility rent paid is consistent with FMV. Also, a real estate appraisal may be required when the Imaging Center owns the real estate. In these instances, the real estate is valued and a fair market rental rate is determined. The subject Imaging Center is burdened with the fair market rental rate for the valuation of the Imaging Center operations, as most transactions for Imaging Centers do not include the purchase of the real estate. If the real estate is to be purchased, the appraised amount of the real estate would be additive to the valuation of the operations of the subject Imaging Center once it has been burdened with the appropriate facility rental expense.

There are other facility-related aspects to consider when valuing an Imaging Center, such as the required electromagnetic shielding for an MRI room. Considering the cost of the leasehold improvements associated with the specific room build-out, it is important that FMV rent or value of any real estate associated with an Imaging Center reflect these intricacies related to the facility.

General and administrative expenses will usually include any contracted billing and management fees. These fees are typically based on a percentage of revenue; therefore, the expenses will increase and decrease with the revenue of the Imaging Center. If the subject Imaging Center contracts for billing and/or management services from a related party, a separate FMV analysis may be required to determine the reasonableness of the fees charged for those services. Other general and administrative expenses to review include the advertising and marketing staff needed to build physician referral relationships and equipment expenses. Imaging Centers can either own or lease the equipment used to perform scans. If the Imaging Center owns the equipment, it will typically have maintenance contracts in place that will need to be considered in the valuation. If the Imaging Center leases the equipment, it will have an equipment lease expense on its income statement. The equipment lease expense may or may not include a related maintenance contract. In any case, given the materiality of the maintenance expenses associated with the imaging equipment, close attention should be paid to this expense item.

## Capital Expenditures

Capital expenditures can be used by an Imaging Center to purchase new equipment, maintain the current assets, or fund new projects, such as systems upgrades. The amount of capital expenditures needed is based on the age of the fixed assets, the modalities performed, and the expected growth of the Imaging Center. Imaging Centers are typically capital-intensive facilities comparable to other healthcare entities. Given the capital intensive nature of Imaging Centers and the constant technological advances in diagnostic equipment, the valuation analyst must also attempt to understand if any of the in place equipment is technologically obsolete from a hypothetical market participant perspective. If the equipment is outdated then significant capital expenditure may be required to maintain scan volume. Actual capital expenditure requirements may vary materially depending upon the subject Imaging Center's existing asset base.

## Discount Rate Considerations

The forecast utilized by the valuation analyst will include a certain level of "forecast" risk. A forecast with more optimistic volume assumptions may be riskier than one that assumes the "status quo." The valuation analyst should demonstrate an adequate understanding of the key risks and incorporate a discount rate adjustment for these factors (typically through the specific company risk factor discussed in chapter 4).

Other risk factors that the valuation analyst should consider include the following:

- *Age of equipment*—An Imaging Center with relatively new equipment would be considered less risky than an Imaging Center with older equipment that may need to be replaced.
- *Diversified scan mix*—A multi-modality Imaging Center would typically be considered less risky than a single-modality Imaging Center.
- *Market factors*—Imaging centers in an area with high population growth and low competition would be considered less risky.

# Market Approach

The Market Approach estimates value by comparing the value of similar Imaging Centers traded in a free and open market. The underlying premise of the Market Approach to valuation is the economic principle of substitution—a prudent buyer will pay no more for a business or asset than it would cost to acquire a substitute with the same utility. Please refer to chapter 4 for a more detailed discussion on the application of the Market Approach.

## Relevant Multiples

The Market Approach uses relative value measures or "multiples," which are factors by which some fundamental financial variable is multiplied to derive a value indication for the Imaging Center. The common multiples utilized to value an Imaging Center are:

- EBITDA multiples
- revenue multiples

Normalized EBITDA multiples are utilized more frequently than revenue multiples as they capture the ultimate profitability of Imaging Centers and are more closely related to the free cash flow available to owners than revenue multiples. Since profitability can vary significantly based on an Imaging Center's scan mix and cost structure, the valuation analyst should consider the profitability of the subject versus the identified comparables when selecting revenue multiples.

## Sources of Market Data

There are currently two public companies that specialize in the ownership and operation of Imaging Centers: RadNet, Inc. (RadNet) and
Alliance Healthcare Services, Inc. (AIQ). RadNet and AIQ are the largest national providers of freestanding, fixed-site, outpatient diagnostic
services in the United States. It should be noted that there is a question
in the profession as to how guideline public company multiples should
be applied to reflect a control or minority level of value.

Sources of transaction multiples include market commentary from
the public Imaging Center operator noted above; discussions with
management of imaging center operators regarding recent transactions; public and private transaction data published by third-party
sources, such as Irving Levin Associates and Capital IQ; U.S. Securities and Exchange Commission filings; and nonpublic information from
a valuation analyst's internal transaction database that is based upon
their industry experience. Transaction multiples typically represent
control multiples; however, there are instances in which published information can be found regarding a transaction for a minority interest.

## Factors to Consider When Selecting Multiples

### Comparability of the Subject to the Comparables

It is important to note that there are fundamental differences between
small to midsize privately held companies and publicly traded companies. These differences include size, depth of management, capital
structure, access to capital, scan mix diversification, geographic diversification, prospective growth rates, liquidity, and risk. In addition,
external microeconomic and macroeconomic events cause fluctuations in the price of public stock prices that can distort multiples. Therefore, RadNet multiples do not necessarily reflect comparable market
multiples for any single, privately held Imaging Centers.

Size and growth prospects should also be considered when reviewing transaction multiples as implied valuation multiples for hospital-based Imaging Center operators are typically significantly higher
than multiples paid for independent Imaging Centers.

### Barriers to Entry

When valuing Imaging Centers that reside in states with certificate of need (CON) requirements, the analyst should examine the state's CON requirements and history of granting Imaging Center CONs. A CON is a permit that requires state government approval for the establishment or modification of healthcare institutions, facilities, or services at designated locations. CONs are typically granted on a modality basis and typically only related to advance imaging. The Imaging Centers that have CONs in states with CON requirements may warrant a higher multiple as the CON acts as a barrier to entry for potential market competitors. In states with CON requirements that have a history of denying the applications for new CONs, the multiple utilized in the Market Approach may be higher. Conversely, if the state has a history of granting most applicants with a CON, the Market Approach may not need to be adjusted as the CON does not provide material protection from future competition.

### Level of Value

The valuation analyst should consider if the subject interest being valued represents a minority or controlling interest when selecting market multiples. When utilizing transaction multiples, the analyst should always ensure that the level of value acquired in the guideline transactions matches the level of value of the subject interest.

Individual investments in an Imaging Center are often for minority interests. A true minority interest has little to no influence over expansion decisions, cost structure, distributions, or liquidity events; therefore, minority multiples for Imaging Centers are typically less than control multiples.

### Other Considerations

When utilizing transaction multiples, the analyst should identify any transactions that might yield skewed multiples as a result of related party buyers and sellers and a forced or distressed sale.

## Cost Approach

The Cost Approach, also known as the asset or build-up approach, is a method that attempts to value a business by identifying and valuing each tangible and intangible asset. This approach is primarily used for Imaging Centers not generating sufficient cash flows to make its operations more valuable than the underlying value of the assets. The Cost Approach provides a "floor," or lowest minimum value, related to an interest in an Imaging Center and may be appropriate when the Market and Income Approaches produce lower values.

The Cost Approach typically includes tangible assets, and may include identifiable intangible assets. In the context of a business valuation, tangible assets include net working capital and personal property and equipment. Intangible assets may include items such as the Imaging Center's trade name or, in applicable locales, licensure, such as a certificate of need. Please refer to chapter 4 for further discussion of the Cost Approach in the context of a business valuation.

Please note that, even though the tangible and intangible assets are not separately valued under the Income and Market Approaches, these approaches consider the cash flows generated by all assets of the business and provide an FMV indication of the business enterprise, which includes all normalized tangible and intangible assets needed to operate the business.

# Laboratory Services 8

*Aaron Murski, CVA*

Laboratory services may encompass any business that provides diagnostic testing and evaluation of medical specimens. Broadly, laboratory businesses may provide clinical laboratory or anatomic pathology services. Clinical laboratory testing is generally performed on whole blood, serum, plasma, and other body fluids (e.g., urine). Common clinical laboratory testing includes blood chemistries, urinalysis, or blood cell counts. Clinical laboratory testing may be performed at a hospital, physician office, or independent laboratory. Clinical laboratory testing is generally considered to be "routine." Anatomic pathology services, including cytology, are performed on human tissue or cells. Anatomic pathology services involve the diagnosis of cancer and other diseases and medical conditions through the examination of the tissue and cells collected from patients. Anatomical pathology services are connected to medical groups consisting of either pathologists or medical specialties that lend themselves to anatomic specimen collection (e.g., gastroenterology, dermatology).

In addition to routine, anatomic pathology, and cytology testing, other testing segments, including esoteric testing and drugs of abuse (toxicology) testing, supplement the laboratory services industry. Esoteric tests are more advanced clinical laboratory tests that are not "routine." Esoteric tests include procedures in the areas of molecular-based diagnostics, protein chemistry, cellular immunology, and advanced microbiology. As esoteric tests become more common, they shift into the category of routine testing. This chapter focuses on the clinical laboratory and anatomic pathology space that comprises the majority of the laboratory industry. Although an important and growing sub-segment of the industry, molecular and genomic laboratories will not be the focus of this chapter.

Examples of typical buyers in the market include large publicly traded laboratory services companies, such as LabCorp or Quest Diagnostics; hospitals and health systems in markets local to the laboratory businesses; and/or private equity investors. Typical stand-alone lab services transactions consist primarily of control-level transactions, either of an independent lab, or a hospital operated lab that is being divested. For a medical group that has a significant lab operation, a minority-level "transaction" may occur when a physician "buys-in," or becomes an owner of the medical group. However, this scenario would not necessarily result in a stand-alone lab transaction, and thus would not be comparable to other transactions due to the unique facts and considerations of the particular medical group involved. As such, this chapter will focus on control-level valuation issues.

In conducting a fair market value (FMV) analysis, the valuation analyst should consider the Income, Market, and Cost Approaches to value, as outlined in chapter 4.

## Income Approach

The Income Approach estimates the value of the laboratory business by projecting the future cash flow attributable to the subject operations, then discounting those earnings back to the present value by utilizing an appropriate discount rate. The discount rate should take into consideration the risk of the operations of the subject business, the forecast utilized, and the industry, among other factors. The following sections outline the key assumptions that should be considered when developing a cash flow model for the business.

## Volume

The test volume performed at any laboratory services business is driven primarily by the underlying network of physicians, including both primary care and specialists who order or request the tests. The range of tests performed by the business and test volume capacity will largely be determined by the type and capabilities of the laboratory equipment, and analyzers deployed by the business. In most mature markets, the laboratory services industry is a crowded space and is highly competitive. In order to maintain their customer base, many laboratory businesses must compete in terms of service price, capability, quality, turnaround times, number and type of tests performed, reputation in the community, information technology (connectivity to physician offices), and patient access to the laboratory business (geographic coverage of laboratory draw stations).

A valuation must take into consideration the historical and projected test volumes of the business. Although not all-inclusive, the following should be considerations of the valuation analyst when developing or evaluating a forecast:

- sources of test volumes—(Do any relationships exist between customers and institutions? What geographic coverage is maintained by the business? Are test volumes concentrated across a small customer base or a large customer base?);
- hours of operation;
- age, type, and capacity of equipment utilized, and equipment repair and maintenance (downtime) needs relative to projected test volume;
- changes in test offerings of the business;
- existing competitive landscape in the local market(s); and
- barriers to entry for new entrants in the market (e.g., licensure or certificate of need (CON) issues).

Local market factors in the form of physician alignment should be evaluated by the valuation analyst. Hospitals continue to acquire physician practices and absorb laboratory test volume much to the dismay of clinical independent laboratories. While demographics are still somewhat relevant, the customer base of a laboratory services business consists of underlying physicians, and institutions where those physicians are employed. Competition may come from national operators such as LabCorp or Quest Diagnostics, hospitals and health systems in markets where the laboratory business operates, or other independent labs, including large medical groups that perform laboratory tests in-house.

Capacity constraints are mostly technological in nature, as chemistry analyzers and other laboratory equipment have some threshold limits to total throughput, notwithstanding the fact that some lab equipment may be operated around the clock. For pathology lab tests, the physician capacity should be considered as well.

## Reimbursement

The second component of revenue that should be addressed by the valuation analyst is "price" or reimbursement. The laboratory business's payor mix and relationship with payors can meaningfully impact the financial performance of the business. Medicare reimburses based on a set fee schedule, and the majority of commercial payors follow suit, either using the Medicare fee schedule or a percentage over or under the Medicare fee schedule. Therefore, understanding any projected increases or decreases in Medicare reimbursement, by current procedure terminology (CPT) code, is critical to forecasting revenues included in the valuation. To the extent the laboratory is associated with a medical group (i.e., path lab), the reimbursement outlook may be different for professional versus technical reimbursement. The valuation analyst can apply this information to develop expectations regarding reimbursement growth. Changes in the laboratory's test offerings may also impact reimbursement. In some markets, payors may only be contracted with one or a few laboratory businesses, which should also be considered.

## Other Considerations

In addition, projected reimbursement should take into account the risks associated with any out-of-network payments from commercial and managed-care payors. A more recent development within certain laboratory services, such as toxicology laboratories, is the reliance on an out-of-network strategy. Since laboratory businesses compete on service, and generally establish a relationship with a referring provider whereby the laboratory business accepts all requisitioned tests, tests associated with patients who do not have out-of-network benefits go unreimbursed. The sustainability of this model has yet to be demonstrated over a long-time horizon, and the risks associated with the sustainability should be considered to the extent that out-of-network reimbursement is expected to be impacted in a particular market. In addition, the changing nature of health insurance plan coverage may create or erode opportunities to bill on an out-of-network basis in the future.

## Operating Expenses

Most lab services businesses exhibit a high degree of operating leverage. As such, maintaining a concise fixed-cost infrastructure can allow for projected margin expansion to the extent volume growth can be supported. Employee salaries and benefits, test transportation costs, and testing supply costs comprise the majority of the operating expenses for a lab services business. In many settings, lab staffing functions as a quasi-fixed cost, as incremental test volumes will not necessarily impact staffing needs for a fully staffed shift (to a point). For an efficient lab, increasing test volume throughput will primarily result in higher transportation costs, higher test supply costs, and higher billing fees.

Employee costs can be influenced by local labor markets. In certain markets, lab directors and other critical licensed personnel required to efficiently operate the business may be in more or less supply. In any case, salary and benefit costs per full-time equivalent (FTE) employee, and wage increases, are primary variables used to forecast salaries and wages. In addition, to the extent that the forecasted volume for the business implies that additional shifts are needed, factors like employee FTE needs, and therefore salary and wage costs, may behave as a step-function.

Transportation and test supply costs (e.g., reagents) are typically stated on a "per test" basis. Laboratory services that cover a broader geography or operate in lower-volume markets will typically outsource transportation services. On the other hand, laboratory services with larger, scaled operations, or businesses that have narrow geographic coverage and economical volume throughput, may keep transportation services in-house.

To the extent that professional physician fees are generated by the business, physician compensation expenses may become a material forecast assumption. Careful consideration should be given to the level of compensation relative to the capacity of the physician workforce.

Facility costs are generally fixed expenses, and should include any draw stations or other space that the laboratory business utilizes in order to collect specimens or house its operations.

If the business relies on outsourced billing services, the fee structure is often contracted as a percent of net revenue, or, alternatively, on a per-test basis, subject to certain floors and caps.

## Capital Expenditures

Capital expenditure forecasts for a lab services business should consider the age, condition, and likely replacement timing of the equipment and other assets utilized, while analyzing the current condition and forecasted level of equipment utilization. The primary equipment utilized by a lab services business consists of analyzers. Automated analyzers can be operated on an around-the-clock basis. Aside from directly purchasing equipment, a laboratory business may also obtain lab equipment through a lease option, offered by many vendors. Under a typical lease, the laboratory business uses the lab equipment in exchange for purchasing all reagents from the vendor.

## Discount Rate Considerations

*Due in part to the continued growth in lab volumes and relationships between labs and referring physicians and the OIG's position that the potential exists for fraud and abuse in the industry, any direct or indirect financial relationships between a laboratory and referring physicians should be disclosed in order to evaluate the risk profile of the subject lab business.*

The forecast utilized by the valuation analyst will include a certain level of "forecast" risk. A forecast with more optimistic volume assumptions may be riskier than one that assumes the "status quo." The valuation analyst should demonstrate an adequate understanding of the key risks and incorporate a discount rate adjustment for these factors (typically through the specific company risk factor discussed in chapter 4).

The particular business model employed by the laboratory may make the subject lab services business more or less risky, as compared to industry peers. For example, if the lab business's customer base is concentrated among one or two sources, it may present a higher risk profile, as opposed to a lab business with a diversified customer base.

## *Market Approach*

The Market Approach estimates value by comparing the value of similar businesses traded in a free and open market. The underlying premise of the Market Approach to valuation is the economic principle of substitution—a prudent buyer will pay no more for a business or asset than it would cost to acquire a substitute with the same utility. Please refer to chapter 4 for a more detailed discussion on the application of the Market Approach.

### Relevant Multiples

The Market Approach uses relative value measures or "multiples," which are factors by which some fundamental financial variable is multiplied to derive a value indication for the lab business. The common multiples utilized to value a lab business are:

- EBITDA multiples
- revenue multiples

Normalized EBITDA multiples are utilized more frequently than revenue multiples, as they capture the ultimate profitability of the business. Since profitability can vary significantly based on the service mix and cost structure, the valuation analyst should consider the profitability of the subject versus the identified comparables when selecting revenue multiples.

## Sources of Market Data

Consistent with the two main methods of Market Approach application, sources of Market Approach data may be found in public company stock prices, as well as transaction data that may be made available when one company acquires another.

Concerning the guideline public company method, there are currently two public companies that specialize in the ownership and operation of laboratory services businesses: Quest Diagnostics Inc. (NYSE ticker "DGX") and Laboratory Corp. of America Holdings (NYSE ticker "LH"). According to information developed by Quest, Quest and LabCorp maintain an 8 percent and 6.2 percent market share, respectively, in the $72 billion lab industry as of 2014, while independent labs maintain a 19.7 percent market share. While many transactions occur in the lab space, it should be noted that there is a question in the profession as to how guideline public company multiples should be applied to reflect a control or minority level of value.

Sources of transaction multiples include market commentary from the public lab operators noted above; discussions with management of operators regarding recent transactions; public and private transaction data published by third-party sources, such as Irving Levin Associates and Capital IQ; U.S. Securities and Exchange Commission filings; and nonpublic information from a valuation analyst's internal transaction database that is based upon his or her industry experience. Transaction multiples typically represent control multiples; however, there are instances in which published information can be found regarding a transaction for a minority interest.

## Factors to Consider When Selecting Multiples

### *Comparability of the Subject to the Comparables*

Regarding the applicability of the guideline public company approach, there are fundamental differences between small to midsize privately held companies and the two publicly traded companies. These differences include size, depth of management, capital structure, access to capital to fund growth, product diversification, geographic diversification, and risk. In addition, external microeconomic and macroeconomic events cause fluctuations in the price of public stock prices that can distort multiples. While the two public company stock prices may be a data point, the DGX and LH trading multiples do not necessarily reflect comparable market multiples for any single, privately held lab business. If applicable, the valuation analyst should adjust the guideline company multiples as appropriate, for differences in factors such as growth, profitability, etc.

Size and growth prospects should also be considered when reviewing transaction multiples, as implied valuation multiples for large-scaled lab businesses are typically significantly higher than multiples paid for smaller, single market or limited geography lab businesses.

## Barriers to Entry

When valuing lab businesses that reside in states with certificate of need (CON) or other licensure requirements, the analyst should examine the federal or state's applicable requirements and history of granting approval for any permits or licenses. In states with CON requirements that have a history of denying the applications for new CONs, the multiple utilized in the Market Approach may be higher. Conversely, if the state has a history of approving most applicants with a CON, the Market Approach may not need to be adjusted, as the CON does not provide material protection from future competition.

Particular commercial payors maintain the practice of contracting exclusive arrangements with certain laboratory businesses, which reduces the available market share for new entrants.

### Level of Value

The valuation analyst should always consider if the subject interest being valued represents a minority or controlling interest when selecting market multiples. When utilizing transaction multiples, the analyst should always ensure that the level of value acquired in the guideline transactions matches the level of value of the subject interest.

### Other Considerations

As previously mentioned, a lab business with an out-of-network reimbursement strategy may have significant potential reimbursement risk or business model risk in the future. As a result, the multiples utilized in the Market Approach should be adjusted accordingly, or, alternatively, the projected earnings of the lab business should be adjusted to account for the risk before applying typical market multiples.

## *Cost Approach*

The Cost Approach, also known as the asset or build-up approach, is a method that attempts to value a business by identifying and valuing each tangible and intangible asset. This approach is primarily used for lab businesses not generating sufficient cash flows to make operations more valuable than the underlying value of the assets. The Cost Approach provides a "floor," or lowest minimum value, related to an interest in a lab business and may be appropriate when the Market and Income Approaches produce lower values.

The Cost Approach typically includes tangible assets, and may include identifiable intangible assets. In the context of a business valuation, tangible assets include net working capital and personal property and equipment. Intangible assets may include things such as the business's trade name, or in applicable locales, licensure such as a certificate of need. Please refer to chapter 4 for further discussion of the Cost Approach in the context of a business valuation.

Although tangible and intangible assets are not separately valued under the Income and Market Approaches, these approaches still consider the cash flows generated by all assets of the business. In providing an FMV indication of the business enterprise, the Income and Market Approaches include all normalized tangible and intangible assets needed to operate the business.

# Ambulatory Surgery Centers  9

*Taryn Nasr and Chance Sherer, CVA*

---

*A key factor in the valuation of an ASC is understanding the physician utilizer attributes, such as ownership percentage, age, specialty, and any expected changes in practice patterns.*

---

An ambulatory surgery center (ASC) is a distinct entity that operates exclusively for the purpose of providing low-acuity surgical procedures that do not require a hospitalization, typically require less than a 24-hour stay, and do not pose a significant safety risk to the patient. ASCs are typically valued for individual physician investment (minority-level transactions), the sale of the ASC to a management company and/or hospital buyer (control-level transactions), and contribution to a joint venture (mostly control-level transactions).

In conducting a fair market value (FMV) analysis, the valuation analyst should consider the Income, Market, and Cost Approaches to value, as outlined in chapter 4.

# Income Approach

The Income Approach estimates the value of an ASC by projecting the future cash flow attributable to the subject operations then discounting those earnings back to the present value utilizing an appropriate discount rate that takes into consideration the risk of the operations of the subject business, the forecast utilized, and the industry, among other things. The following outlines the key assumptions that should be considered when developing a cash flow model for an ASC business.

## Volume

The topline financial performance of the ASC is dependent upon case volume performed at the center. A case is representative of a surgical procedure or group of surgical procedures and is a proxy for a unique patient encounter. A valuation analyst must evaluate in detail the case volume performed at the ASC and develop an understanding of the physician dynamic along with other local market factors (e.g., competition and demographics) that may impact forecasted volumes.

Physician utilization must be considered by the valuation analyst. Typically, ASC management will have case volume data readily available which provides historical detail by physician. This information is invaluable as it provides the necessary information to evaluate historical financial performance and will serve as the basis for projecting future physician utilization. Although not all inclusive, the following should be considerations of the valuation analyst when developing or evaluating a forecast:

- relationship of case volume performed by physician investors versus the case volume performed by non-investors;
- age of the physicians and any expected retirement dates;
- expected addition of new physicians;
- change in a physician's professional practice that could impact the case volume of the ASC (i.e., addition or loss of physicians to the practice of owner physicians); and
- any one-time personal events that could result in an increase or decrease in case volume for a physician (i.e., illness, extended vacation, and/or coverage for another physician).

Local market factors in the form of competition and demographics should be evaluated by the valuation analyst. Competition may include a competitor ASC, local hospital(s), or even changes to the practicing habits of physician utilizers. If the subject ASC facility does not have updated equipment or is not currently providing the investors with an adequate return on their investment, the physician utilizers may consider alternative investment opportunities with a competing ASC. Additionally, the local hospital can be a significant competitor to an ASC. Hospitals may employ or enter into a contractual relationship with the physician utilizers that may impact the future case volume at the ASC. Also, many hospitals have a strategy of employing key primary care physicians. Primary care physicians can be a significant referral source to physician surgical specialists and a driver of case volume. Another determinate of volume growth is the local demographic environment. Developing an understanding of the local community (e.g., age, unemployment rates, average income), along with its population growth rate, will provide insight to the valuation analyst.

Capacity and technological constraints associated with the ASC may impact the financial forecast. An ASC only has a specific number of operating rooms (ORs) and procedure rooms (PRs) outfitted with dedicated equipment to provide certain surgical procedures. If an ASC is projected to add physicians and/or specialties to increase case volume, the valuation analyst should question management on the availability of block time and equipment necessary to perform any expected increases in case volume.

## Reimbursement

The second component of revenue that should be addressed by the valuation analyst is "price" or reimbursement. Reimbursement is driven by the payor mix of the subject ASC. Typical payors for ASC services include governmental payors (e.g., Medicare, Medicaid, Tricare), commercial or managed care payors (e.g., Anthem, Humana, Cigna, Aetna), or the individual (i.e., self-pay). Payor mix provides the necessary information to evaluate future reimbursement levels that should be considered by the valuation analyst. Typically, the subject ASC's management can provide the valuation analyst with payor mix detail reported by case volume, gross charges, or collections. The valuation analyst can research projected reimbursement for Medicare through a review of the current fee schedule.[1] Many of the commercial and managed-care payors base their fee schedules on Medicare fee schedule rates, but the valuation analyst should discuss managed-care contracting and future expectations with management. The valuation analyst can apply this information to develop expectations regarding reimbursement growth.

Reimbursement can be affected by changes in the subject ASC's case mix. This can occur through a shift in cases to a different specialty (e.g., from GI to ortho), along with a change in underlying cases by specialty. Certain specialties (e.g., orthopedics, plastic surgery) typically have a higher reimbursement rate than other specialties (e.g., gastroenterology, pain management). The valuation analyst should consider the subject ASC's case mix when analyzing reimbursement trends.

## Other Considerations

Some ASCs employ a unique payor strategy and remain "out-of-network." An out-of-network strategy is characterized by relatively low case volumes but high average reimbursement per case. Many commercial and managed-care payors have taken steps to eliminate or reduce the level of out-of-network payments. In many markets, commercial and managed-care payors have instituted measures in response to the increased costs of out-of-network payments. Examples of these include the following:

- increased patient responsibility for payment for procedures performed in out-of-network facilities;
- payment to patients rather than to facilities, requiring ASCs to seek payment for out-of-network services from the patient; and
- the requirement that physicians conduct procedures in contracted facilities to receive professional fees.

Though the efforts of the commercial and managed-care payors to curb out-of-network payments have either not been attempted or not been entirely successful, the industry appears to agree that high out-

---

1. Centers for Medicare & Medicaid Services, www.cms.gov.

of-network payments are not likely sustainable over the long term. In some cases, the conversion from out-of-network to in-network rates could be immediate; in others, it could take several years. The valuation analyst should address the risk associated with any out-of-network reimbursement.

## Operating Expenses

Employee salaries, medical supplies, facility costs, and general and administrative expense comprise the majority of the operating expenses at an ASC.

Employee compensation is typically analyzed in two ways: average salary per full-time equivalent (FTE) employee and number of hours per case. The types of employees at an ASC include nursing staff, technical staff, and administrative staff. Nursing and technical FTE levels will typically adjust with volume. If an ASC is projected to have an influx in volume, the number of clinical FTEs will need to grow to accommodate the additional workload. By contrast, if an ASC is expected to lose significant volume, it would be reasonable to assume that management would lower the number of staff hours at the ASC.

Medical supplies and implants are projected on a cost-per-case basis for each specialty. Certain specialties, such as orthopedics and plastic surgery, will incur higher medical supply costs based on the type of supplies needed to perform each procedure. Other specialties, such as gastroenterology and pain management, will incur lower medical supply costs due to the minimal amount of supplies used in each case. Therefore, a single-specialty endoscopy center may have a lower average medical supply cost per case when compared to a multi-specialty surgery center that specializes in orthopedics.

Facility costs are comprised mostly of the rent paid to a third party for the physical space in which the subject ASC resides. The analyst should take care to review the facility lease when analyzing historical and projected financial operations. In situations where the real estate is owned by investors in the ASC technical operations, a real estate appraiser may be requested to verify that the facility rent paid is consistent with FMV. Also, a real estate appraisal may be required when the ASC owns the real estate. In these instances, the real estate is valued and a fair market rental rate is determined. The subject ASC is burdened with the fair market rental rate for the valuation of the ASC operations, as most transactions for ASCs do not include the purchase of the real estate. If the real estate is to be purchased, the appraised amount of the real estate would be additive to the valuation of the operations of the subject ASC once it has been burdened with the appropriate facility rental expense.

General and administrative expenses will usually include any contracted billing and management fees. These fees are typically based on a percentage of revenue; therefore, the expenses will increase and decrease with the revenue of the ASC. If the subject ASC contracts for billing and/or management services from a related party, a separate FMV analysis may be required to determine the reasonableness of the fees charged for those services.

## Capital Expenditures

Capital expenditures can be used by an ASC to purchase new equipment, maintain the current assets, or fund new projects, such as expanding the number of ORs/PRs. The amount of capital expenditures needed is based on the age of the fixed assets, the specialties performed, and the expected growth of the ASC. Actual capital expenditure requirements may vary materially depending upon the subject ASC's existing asset base, as over time the asset base will need to be replaced/maintained in order to maintain operations. Hence, another method for estimating capital expenditures is to review the acquisition cost of the existing asset base and the estimated life of the assets.

## Discount Rate Considerations

The forecast utilized by the valuation analyst will include a certain level of "forecast" risk. A forecast with more optimistic volume assumptions may be riskier than one that assumes the "status quo." The valuation analyst should demonstrate an adequate understanding of the key risks and incorporate a discount rate adjustment for these factors (typically through the specific company risk factor discussed in chapter 4).

Other risk factors that the valuation analyst should consider include the following:

- *Physician ownership*—Physicians that have ownership in the ASC are less risky than physicians who do not have ownership in the ASC.

- *Diversified case mix*—A multi-specialty ASC would typically be considered less risky than a single-specialty ASC.
- *Market factors*—ASCs in an area with high population growth and low competition would be considered less risky.

# Market Approach

The Market Approach estimates value by comparing the value of similar ASCs traded in a free and open market. The underlying premise of the Market Approach to valuation is the economic principle of substitution—a prudent buyer will pay no more for a business or asset than it would cost to acquire a substitute with the same utility. Please refer to chapter 4 for a more detailed discussion on the application of the Market Approach.

## Relevant Multiples

The Market Approach uses relative value measures or "multiples," which are factors by which some fundamental financial variable is multiplied to derive a value indication for the ASC. The common multiples utilized to value an ASC are:

- EBITDA multiples
- revenue multiples

Normalized EBITDA multiples are utilized more frequently than revenue multiples as they capture the ultimate profitability of ASCs and are more closely related to the free cash flow available to owners than revenue multiples. Since profitability can vary significantly based on an ASC's case mix and cost structure, the valuation analyst should consider the profitability of the subject versus the identified comparables when selecting revenue multiples.

## Sources of Market Data

There are currently two public companies that specialize in the ownership and operation of ASCs: AmSurg Corp. (AMSG) and Surgical Care Affiliates, Inc. (SCAI). Both of these companies own and operate hundreds of multi-specialty surgery centers across the United States. It should be noted that there is a question in the profession as to how guideline public company multiples should be applied to reflect a control or minority level of value.

Sources of transaction multiples include market commentary from the public ASC operators noted above; discussions with management of surgery centers regarding recent transactions; public and private transaction data published by third-party sources, such as Irving Levin Associates and Capital IQ; U.S. Securities and Exchange Commission filings; and nonpublic information from a valuation analyst's internal transaction database that is based upon industry experience. Transaction multiples typically represent control multiples; however, there are instances in which published information can be found regarding a transaction for a minority interest.

## Factors to Consider When Selecting Multiples

### Comparability of the Subject to the Comparables

It is important to note that there are fundamental differences between small to midsize privately held companies and publicly traded companies. These differences include size, depth of management, capital structure, access to capital, case mix diversification, geographic diversification, prospective growth rates, liquidity, and risk. In addition, external microeconomic and macroeconomic events cause fluctuations in the price of public stock prices that can distort multiples. Therefore, AMSG and SCAI multiples do not necessarily reflect comparable market multiples for any single, privately held ASCs.

Size and growth prospects should also be considered when reviewing transaction multiples as implied valuation multiples for large multi-site ASC operators are typically significantly higher than multiples paid for a single location.

### Barriers to Entry

When valuing ASCs that reside in states with certificate of need (CON) requirements, the analyst should examine the state's CON requirements and history of granting ASC CONs. A CON is a permit that requires state government approval for the establishment or modification of healthcare institutions, facilities, or services at designated locations. The ASCs that have CONs in states with CON requirements may warrant a higher multiple as the CON acts as a barrier to entry for potential market competitors. In states with CON requirements that have a history of denying the applications for new CONs, the multiple utilized in the Market Approach may be higher. Conversely, if the state has a history of granting most applicants with a CON, the Market Approach may not need to be adjusted as the CON does not provide material protection from future competition.

### Level of Value

The valuation analyst should consider if the subject interest being valued represents a minority or controlling interest when selecting market multiples. When utilizing transaction multiples, the analyst should always ensure that the level of value acquired in the guideline transactions matches the level of value of the subject interest.

Individual physician investments in an ASC are often for minority interests. A true minority interest has little to no influence over expansion decisions, recruitment of new physicians, cost structure, distributions, or liquidity events; therefore, minority multiples for ASCs are typically less than control multiples.

### Other Considerations

When utilizing transaction multiples, the analyst should identify any transactions that might yield skewed multiples as a result of related party buyers and sellers and a forced or distressed sale.

As previously mentioned, ASCs with out-of-network reimbursement strategies may have significant potential reimbursement risk in the future. As a result, the multiples utilized in the Market Approach should be adjusted accordingly or the projected earnings of the ASC should be adjusted to account for the risk before applying typical market multiples.

## Cost Approach

The Cost Approach, also known as the asset or build-up approach, is a method that attempts to value a business by identifying and valuing each tangible and intangible asset. This approach is primarily used for ASCs not generating sufficient cash flows to make its operations more valuable than the underlying value of the assets. The Cost Approach provides a "floor," or lowest minimum value, related to an interest in an ASC and may be appropriate when the Market and Income Approaches produce lower values.

The Cost Approach typically includes tangible assets, and may include identifiable intangible assets. In the context of a business valuation, tangible assets include net working capital and personal property and equipment. Intangible assets may include things such as the ASC's trade name or, in applicable locales, licensure such as a certificate of need. Please refer to chapter 4 for further discussion of the Cost Approach in the context of a business valuation.

Please note that even though the tangible and intangible assets are not separately valued under the Income and Market Approaches, these approaches consider the cash flows generated by all assets of the business and provide an FMV indication of the business enterprise, which includes all normalized tangible and intangible assets needed to operate the business.

# Radiation Therapy 10

*Chance Sherer, CVA, and Zach Sadau*

---

*Radiation therapy is a capital-intensive business; therefore, future capital expenditures required to maintain current assets and fund new equipment must be addressed in the FMV analysis.*

---

A radiation therapy center (RT Center) is a distinct entity that operates exclusively for the purpose of treating cancer (including prostate, breast, lung, and colorectal cancer) and involves exposing the patient to an external or internal source of radiation. Radiation therapy treatment involves a wide range of services for cancer patients that can be broken into two primary phases during the course of treatment: planning and simulation, and treatment delivery through the use of: external beam radiation therapy (ERBT), intensity modulated radiation therapy (IMRT), stereotactic body radiation therapy (SBRT), stereotactic radiosurgery (SRS), and/or brachytherapy. RT Centers are typically valued for the sale of the RT Center to a management company and/or hospital buyer (predominantly control-level transactions) and/or contribution to a joint venture (again, predominantly control-level transactions).

In conducting a fair market value (FMV) analysis, the valuation analyst should consider the Income, Market, and Cost Approaches to value, as outlined in chapter 4.

## *Income Approach*

The Income Approach estimates the value of an RT Center by projecting the future cash flow attributable to the subject operations then discounting those earnings back to the present value utilizing an appropriate discount rate that takes into consideration the risk of the operations of the subject business, the forecast utilized, and the industry, among other things. The following outlines the key assumptions that should be considered when developing a cash flow model for an RT business.

### Volume

The financial performance of an RT Center is primarily dependent upon the volume of patients treated at the RT Center, also referred to as courses of treatment. While a number of revenue-generating services are provided to a patient during a course of treatment, the actual treatments, or fractions, are the primary volume metric to consider. The treatment options that fall under radiation therapy include brachytherapy and various forms of ERBT, IMRT, Cyberknife, and Gamma Knife. Image-guided radiation therapy (IGRT) is used with the various forms of EBRT and IMRT. By far the two most common types of treatments are EBRT and IMRT.

Physician referrals and treatment mix must be considered in the valuation. Medical and surgical oncology practices, along with certain other specialty groups (such as urologists), are key referral sources for RT Centers. The relationship between the RT Center and referring physicians is crucial. In addition, it is important to understand which types of treatments are performed. If the RT Center has a higher EBRT to IMRT treatment mix then it usually has a lower profit margin because EBRT is reimbursed less than IMRT. The RT Center will have treatment data readily available that will serve as the basis for projecting future treatment volume. Although not all inclusive, the following should be considerations of the valuation when developing or evaluating a forecast:

- change in a referring physician's professional practice that could impact the volume of the RT Center (i.e., addition or loss of physicians at the practice);
- investment in new medical equipment (i.e., linear accelerator) to bring additional volume to the RT Center;
- capacity constraints based on the number of linear accelerators; and
- any one-time events that could result in an increase or decrease in treatment volume (i.e., linear accelerator placed out of operation due to maintenance or replacement).

Local market factors in the form of competition and demographics should be evaluated by the valuation analyst. Direct competition may include other RT Centers and local hospital(s). Additionally, the local hospital can be a significant competitor to an RT Center due to its affiliation with local physicians. Hospitals may employ or enter into a contractual relationship with the oncologists that may impact the future treatment volume at the RT Center. Another determinant of volume growth is the local demographic environment. Developing an understanding of the local community (e.g., age, unemployment rates, and average income), along with its population growth rate, will provide insight to the valuation analyst.

Capacity and technological constraints associated with the RT Center may impact the financial forecast. An RT Center only has a specific number of radiotherapy vaults, which are treatment rooms that include a linear accelerator and necessary equipment to provide certain treatments. The valuation analyst should ensure there are no capacity constraints with the level of projected volume as there are only so many treatments and types of treatments that can be performed per day. If an RT Center is projected to increase treatment volume, the valuation analyst should question management on the availability of time and equipment necessary to perform any expected increases in treatment volume.

## Reimbursement

The second component of revenue that should be addressed by the valuation analyst is "price" or reimbursement. Reimbursement is driven by the payor mix of the subject RT Center. Typical payors for radiation therapy services include governmental payors (e.g., Medicare, Medicaid, Tricare), commercial or managed-care payors (e.g., Anthem, Humana, Cigna, Aetna), or the individual (i.e., self-pay). Payor mix provides the necessary information to evaluate future reimbursement levels that should be considered by the valuation analyst. Typically, the subject RT Center's management can provide the valuation analyst with payor mix detail reported by treatment volume, gross charges, or collections. The valuation analyst can research projected reimbursement for Medicare through a review of the current fee schedule. Understanding the current and projected Medicare reimbursement is critical to the valuation as radiation therapy has been subject to significant cuts in reimbursement, primarily for IMRT, over the past decade. The majority of commercial and managed-care payors base their fee schedules on Medicare fee schedule rates, but the valuation analyst should discuss managed-care contracting and future expectations with management. The valuation analyst can apply this information to develop expectations regarding reimbursement growth.

Reimbursement can be affected by changes in the subject RT Center's treatment mix. This can occur through a shift in treatments to a different modality (i.e., from EBRT to IMRT) along with changes in the patient's course of treatment.

## Other Considerations

RT Centers can either bill patients directly for charges related to the use of the RT Center (technical component) or bill patients for both the technical component and for the physicians' professional services rendered (professional component). If the RT Center bills for both the technical and professional component, then it is said to bill globally. It is critical to distinguish between global versus technical only, because if the RT Center bills globally then the appropriate professional fees need to be included in the expenses.

## Operating Expenses

Employee salaries, professional radiation oncology fees, facility costs, and general and administrative expense comprise the majority of the operating expenses at an RT Center.

Employee compensation is typically analyzed in two ways: average salary per full-time equivalent (FTE) employee and number of hours per treatment. The types of employees at an RT Center include radiation therapist, physicist, dosimetrist, and administrative staff. Radiation therapist, dosimetrist, and physicist FTE levels will typically adjust with volume. If an RT Center is projected to have an influx in volume, the number of clinical FTEs will need to grow to accommodate the additional workload. By contrast, if an RT Center is expected to lose significant volume, it would be reasonable to assume that management would lower the number of staff at the RT Center. Radiation therapist, physicist, and dosimetrist staff can either be employed or contracted through a third party. It is important to understand the compensation agreement and ensure the compensation of these positions is reflected in the employee costs.

As mentioned previously, an RT Center is reimbursed either globally or technically for services performed. This can be determined by examining the expenses of the subject RT Center to see if there is compensation for professional physician medical services. If this expense is present, then the subject RT Center's revenue represents both technical and professional reimbursement (global). It is essential that the professional compensation expense on the income statement reflects the physician services agreement. These professional fees are typically paid as a percentage of net collections or the professional components relating to the physicians services provided at the RT Center. If the RT Center bills globally, then a separate FMV analysis may be required to determine the reasonableness of the professional fees paid for those services.

Facility costs are comprised mostly of the rent paid to a third party for the physical space in which the subject RT Center resides. The valuation analyst should take care to review the facility lease when analyzing historical and projected financial operations. Furthermore, the valuation analyst needs to understand the unique features of the subject RT Center, such as significant tenant improvements for shielding and build-outs related to the radiotherapy vaults. In situations where the real estate is owned by investors in the RT Center's technical operations, a real estate valuation may be requested to verify that the facility rent paid is consistent with FMV. Also, a real estate appraisal may be required when the RT Center owns the real estate. In these instances, the real estate is valued and a fair market rental rate is determined. The subject RT Center is burdened with the fair market rental rate for the valuation of the RT Center's operations, as most transactions for RT Centers do not include the purchase of the real estate. If the real estate is to be purchased, the appraised amount of the real estate would be additive to the valuation of the operations of the subject RT Center once it has been burdened with the appropriate facility rental expense.

General and administrative expenses will usually include any contracted billing and management fees, as well as equipment maintenance fees. Billing and management fees are typically based on a percentage of revenue; therefore, the expenses will increase and decrease with the revenue of the RT Center. If the subject RT Center contracts for billing and/or management services from a related party, a separate FMV analysis may be required to determine the reasonableness of the fees charged for those services. Because of the high equipment costs, most RT Centers contract with third parties to provide maintenance on the equipment. These fees should be based on the maintenance agreement over the defined period. These payments are either monthly, quarterly, or annually and must be reflected in the subject RT Center's expenses.

## Capital Expenditures

Capital expenditures can be used by an RT Center to purchase new equipment, maintain the current assets, or fund new projects, such as increasing the number of radiotherapy vaults. The amount of capital expenditures needed is based on the age of the fixed assets and the expected growth of the RT Center. Owning and operating an RT Center is a highly capital intensive business. Linear accelerators and CT scanners are the two primary equipment needs that have a combined price tag in the millions. Actual capital expenditure requirements may vary materially dependent upon the subject RT Center's asset base, as over time the asset base will need to be replaced/maintained in order to sustain operations. Hence, another method for estimating capital expenditures is to review the acquisition cost of existing asset base and the estimated life of the assets.

## Discount Rate Considerations

The forecast utilized by the valuation analyst will include a certain level of "forecast" risk. A forecast with more optimistic volume assumptions may be riskier than one that assumes the "status quo." The valuation analyst should demonstrate an adequate understanding of the key risks and incorporate a discount rate adjustment for these factors (typically through the specific company risk factor discussed in chapter 4).

Discussion around factors that the valuation analysis should consider include the following:

- *Equipment*—The age and condition of the equipment will dictate the capacity of the RT Center as new equipment typically has faster treatment times. In addition, older equipment risks being clinically obsolete and may result in referrals migrating to centers with newer equipment.
- *Market factors*—RT Centers in an area with high population growth and low competition would be considered less risky.
- *Nature of the RT Center and competition*—Is the RT Center connected to a urology practice or medical oncology practice, or a freestanding business with a broad customer base?

# *Market Approach*

The Market Approach estimates value by comparing the value of similar RT Centers traded in a free and open market. The underlying premise of the Market Approach to valuation is the economic principle of substitution—a prudent buyer will pay no more for a business or asset than it would cost to acquire a substitute with the same utility. Please refer to chapter 4 for a more detailed discussion on the application of the Market Approach.

## Relevant Multiples

The Market Approach uses relative value measures or "multiples," which are factors by which some fundamental financial variable is multiplied to derive a value indication for the RT Center. The common multiples utilized to value an RT Center are:

- EBITDA multiples
- revenue multiples

Normalized EBITDA multiples are utilized more frequently than revenue multiples as they capture the ultimate profitability of RT Centers and are more closely related to the distributions to owners than revenue multiples. Since profitability can vary significantly based on an RT Center's treatment mix and cost structure, the valuation analyst should consider the profitability of the subject versus the identified comparables when selecting revenue multiples.

## Sources of Market Data

There are currently two public companies that specialize in the ownership and operation of imaging and radiation therapy centers: RadNet, Inc. (RDNT) and Alliance Healthcare Services, Inc. (AIQ). Both of these companies own and operate radiation therapy centers across the United States. It should be noted that there is a question in the profession as to how guideline public company multiples should be applied to reflect a control or minority level of value. Additionally, though RDNT and AIQ operate radiation therapy centers, their primary operations are related to diagnostic imaging that is not directly comparable to radiation therapy.

Sources of transaction multiples include market commentary from the public radiation therapy operators noted above; discussions with management of radiation therapy operators regarding recent transactions; public and private transaction data published by third-party sources, such as Irving Levin Associates and Capital IQ; U.S. Securities and Exchange Commission filings; and nonpublic information from a valuation analyst's internal transaction database that is based upon their industry experience. Transaction multiples typically represent control multiples; however there are instances in which published information can be found regarding a transaction for a minority interest.

## Factors to Consider When Selecting Multiples

### Comparability of the Subject to the Comparables

It is important to note that there are fundamental differences between small to midsize privately held companies and publicly traded companies. These differences include size, depth of management, capital structure, access to capital, case mix diversification, geographic diversification, prospective growth rates, and risk. In addition, external microeconomic and macroeconomic events cause fluctuations in the price of public stock prices that can distort multiples. Due to the reasons stated above and the fact RDNT and AIQ perform imaging services, their multiples do not necessarily reflect comparable market multiples for any single, privately held RT Center.

Size and growth prospects should also be considered when reviewing transaction multiples as implied valuation multiples for large multi-site radiation therapy operators are typically significantly higher than multiples paid for a single location.

### Barriers to Entry

When valuing RT Centers that reside in states with certificate of need (CON) requirements, the analyst should examine the state's CON requirements and history of granting RT Center CONs. A CON is a permit that requires state government approval for the establishment or modification of healthcare institutions, facilities, or services at designated locations. CONs for RT Centers are typically granted on a per vault/linear accelerator basis. The RT Centers that have CONs in states with CON requirements may warrant a higher multiple as the CON acts as a barrier to entry for potential market competitors. In states with CON requirements that have a history of denying the applications for new CONs, the multiple utilized in the Market Approach may be higher. Conversely, if the state has a history of granting most applicants with a CON, the Market Approach may not need to be adjusted as the CON does not provide material protection from future competition.

### Level of Value

The valuation analyst should always consider if the subject interest being valued represents a minority or controlling interest when selecting market multiples. When utilizing transaction multiples, the analyst should always ensure that the level of value acquired in the guideline transactions matches the level of value of the subject interest.

### Other Considerations

When utilizing transaction multiples, the analyst should identify any transactions that might yield skewed multiples as a result of related party buyers and sellers and a forced or distressed sale.

As previously mentioned, reliance on a primary physician oncology group to maintain volume levels as well as an unfavorable treatment mix may pose potential volume risk in the future. As a result, the multiples utilized in the Market Approach should be adjusted accordingly or the projected earnings of the RT Center should be adjusted to account for the risk before applying typical market multiples.

## Cost Approach

The Cost Approach, also known as the asset or build-up approach, is a method that attempts to value a business by identifying and valuing each tangible and intangible asset. This approach is primarily used for RT Centers not generating sufficient cash flows to make its operations more valuable than the underlying value of the assets. The Cost Approach provides a "floor," or lowest minimum value, related to an interest in an RT Center and may be appropriate when the Market and Income Approaches produce lower values. Operating an RT Center is a capital-intensive business, so there is usually a substantial amount of tangible value derived under the Cost Approach.

The Cost Approach typically includes tangible assets, and may include identifiable intangible assets. In the context of a business valuation, tangible assets include net working capital and personal property and equipment. Intangible assets may include things such as the RT Center's trade name or, in applicable locales, licensure such as a certificate of need. Please refer to chapter 4 for further discussion of the Cost Approach in the context of a business valuation.

Please note that even though the tangible and intangible assets are not separately valued under the Income and Market Approaches, these approaches consider the cash flows generated by all assets of the business and provide an FMV indication of the business enterprise, which includes all normalized tangible and intangible assets needed to operate the business.

# Acute Care Hospitals

# 11

*Colin M. McDermott CFA, CPA/ABV,
and Corey Palasota, CFA*

---

*Hospitals often rely on subsidy payments
from states and the federal government. The
valuation analyst should understand the
source and amount of these payments to
evaluate the future risk of these dollars.*

---

Acute care is a treatment level in which a patient receives
care for a brief but severe episode of illness as a result of
disease, trauma, or surgery. An acute care hospital (Hospital) provides short-term services for these patients in an inpatient or an outpatient setting. In the inpatient setting, a
patient can be characterized as requiring medical or surgical attention that may involve multiple overnight stays. In
the outpatient setting, Hospitals provide care through hospital outpatient departments (HOPDs), which may include
a broad array of same-day services.

Transactions for Hospitals are usually highly visible to
the public and command scrutiny from regulators and stakeholders alike. In many circumstances, the transaction will
be reviewed by regulatory bodies including the Federal

Trade Commission and/or the state attorney general office. Hospital valuations are typically performed prior to sale, purchase, or lease on behalf of the buyer or the seller, for review by regulatory authorities, or for banks or other financing organizations associated with a transaction.

In conducting a fair market value (FMV) analysis, the valuation analyst should consider the Income, Market, and Cost Approaches to value, as outlined in chapter 4.

# Income Approach

The Income Approach estimates the value of a Hospital by discounting the projected future free cash flows attributable to the subject operations to a present value. The discount rate takes into consideration the risk of the operations of the subject business, the forecast utilized, and the industry, among other factors. The following outlines the key assumptions that should be considered when developing a cash flow model for a Hospital business.

## Volume

Hospital management typically reports and evaluates inpatient and outpatient volume separately, and the valuation analyst should understand the key metrics reviewed by management.

### Inpatient volume

In general, inpatient volume involves medical and surgical services that require a patient to be admitted into the facility. The following key metrics are often evaluated related to inpatient volume:

- *Admissions*—The number of patients admitted into the Hospital in any given year for inpatient care (i.e., typically requiring monitoring over several nights). These patients may enter the Hospital for a scheduled surgery, through the emergency room, or on a recommendation by a physician for nightly observation. Instead of admissions, some Hospitals report discharges, a similar metric, that captures the number of patients who left the Hospital from inpatient stay during the period.

- *Average length of stay (ALOS)*—The average number of days each patient stays in the Hospital for inpatient care. The ALOS may be lower or higher depending on the acuity and service mix.
- *Patient days*—Calculated as the number of admissions multiplied by ALOS. A variety of Hospital revenue and expense items are evaluated by management on a per patient day basis.
- *Case mix index (CMI)*—A measure of patient acuity (i.e., severity of illness) reflecting the diversity, clinical complexity, and the resources required by the population inside the Hospital. A higher CMI is indicative of a higher acuity patient population.

### Outpatient Volume

Generally, a Hospital's outpatient volume is generated through the emergency department or a variety of physician-driven services, such as outpatient surgery, radiology, clinical laboratories, or catheterization laboratories (collectively, these service offerings represent HOPDs). The following key terms are used to analyze a Hospital's outpatient volume:

- *Outpatient visits*—While each Hospital may utilize a different definition of a "visit," generally outpatient visits involve patients in the emergency department (not admitted as an inpatient), outpatient surgery department, radiology department, or other HOPD. Typically, each unit represents one patient encounter.
- *Service-line volume*—Oftentimes, Hospital management will report specific outpatient visit statistics, such as emergency room visits, outpatient surgeries, or imaging scans. Annual trends in these statistics may help a valuation analyst better understand the underlying dynamics within each HOPD.

Although not all inclusive, the following should be considered by the valuation analyst when developing or evaluating a forecast for a Hospital:

- changes in service lines offered by the Hospital;
- management initiatives and significant events;

- regulatory changes regarding utilization or patient classification (e.g., observation verses inpatient status);
- seasonality of volume;
- payment changes that may influence patient behavior;
- population and local community demographics; and
- consideration of macro trends, such as the movement of services from inpatient to outpatient setting.

In an attempt to reflect the overall activity in a Hospital, industry participants oftentimes refer to adjusted admissions and adjusted patient days. These statistics "combine" inpatient and outpatient volume into a single metric as defined below:

- *Adjusted admissions*—Increases the number of admissions by a multiplier factor that incorporates the relative contribution of outpatient revenue to total revenue (calculated as total gross charges divided by inpatient revenue). This calculation effectively converts the total revenue generated from outpatient visits into an equivalent number of incremental admissions.
- *Adjusted patient days*—Increases the number of patient days by a multiplier factor that incorporates the relative contribution of outpatient revenue to total revenue (calculated as total gross charges divided by inpatient revenue). This calculation effectively converts the total revenue generated from outpatient visits into an equivalent number of incremental patient days.

The valuation analyst should also evaluate the capacity of the subject Hospital. Metrics that offer insight on inpatient capacity include:

- *Average daily census (ADC)*—Calculated as the average number of patients in the Hospital at any given time.
- *Percent occupancy*—The ADC of the Hospital divided by the number of total beds available. If a Hospital is already operating at a high occupancy level, the valuation analyst should question management on the ability to further absorb volume growth without spending additional capital to increase capacity.

Assessing capacity limitations for HOPDs is less straightforward and requires discussions with management to understand which HOPDs are under or over capacity. For example, the valuation analyst might inquire about operating room (OR) utilization and the ability to support additional surgical case volume. There is not a single metric that provides insight into capacity constraints for outpatient services.

Due to the diversity of services offered, a Hospital's competition typically includes a variety of market participants. The inpatient services of a Hospital face competition from other acute care facilities along with surgical specialty hospitals while the HOPDs can face competition from a variety of sources, including physician in-office ancillary services, ambulatory surgery centers for outpatient surgical volume, freestanding emergency departments, freestanding diagnostic imaging operators, or other ancillary service providers.

### Other Volume Considerations

Physician employment and alignment trends in the marketplace can have an impact on Hospital utilization. The valuation analyst must understand local market factors affecting physician employment or alignment and the resulting impact on the Hospital. Management should provide detail regarding the Hospital's recruiting efforts for consideration by the valuation analyst. Additionally, a valuation analyst should inquire into trends with respect to physician ownership of ambulatory surgery centers and specialty hospitals in the marketplace.

## Reimbursement

The second component of revenue that should be addressed by the valuation analyst is "price," or reimbursement. Typical payors for Hospital services include governmental payors (e.g., Medicare, Medicaid, Tricare), commercial or managed-care payors (e.g., Anthem, Humana, Cigna, Aetna), or the individual (i.e., self-pay). In addition to these standard payors, many Hospitals have charity policies to serve patients with no insurance. Self-pay (i.e., patients with no insurance) and bad debt are higher in Hospitals compared to other healthcare entities. Annual trends in reimbursement reflect changes in contracted rates with payors, payor mix shifts within the patient composition, and/or acuity mix shifts based on service levels. A valuation professional should inquire into which factor or set of factors are driving observed changes in reimbursement rates. As a starting point, the subject Hospital's management can provide the valuation analyst with a historical snapshot of payor mix reported by volume, gross charges, or collections.

The Medicare program pays for inpatient and outpatient services under different fee schedules. Payments for inpatient services are generally made pursuant to the inpatient prospective payment system (IPPS). This system is relies on a predetermined reimbursement for each admission based on the patient's diagnosis (oftentimes referred to as a diagnosis-related group (DRG)). Alternatively, CMS groups various outpatient services into ambulatory payment classifications (APCs) on the basis of clinical and cost similarity. All services within an APC have the same payment rate.

The Hospital negotiates rates with its commercial and managed-care payors and may have a contract that covers several years with predetermined escalators or is reevaluated on an annual basis. Conversations with management will provide guidance on future commercial reimbursement changes.

Specific areas to consider when evaluating the reasonableness of reimbursement projections include the following:

- published Medicare reimbursement rates for the next year;
- contract renegotiations with commercial payors and/or current annual rate inflators;
- mix shifts amongst the various payor classes (i.e., shifting population towards Medicare from commercial insurance products); and
- changes in patient acuity due to service-line initiatives.

## Other Considerations

Federal, state, and local governments have various programs that subsidize Hospitals for their service to the indigent population and disproportionate share of Medicare or Medicaid patients. Other government programs are available to incentivize Hospitals to comply with various quality initiatives or to make certain investments. In many instances, the dollars received from these programs are critical to the Hospital. The valuation analyst should understand the program(s) with which the Hospital is a participant and the impact of potential future changes to these programs.

## Operating Expenses

Employee salaries, medical supplies, facility costs, and general and administrative expenses constitute the majority of the operating expenses at a Hospital. Expenses are usually evaluated and forecasted as a percentage of revenue, amount per adjusted admission/patient day, or as increasing with inflation.

Employee salary expense is typically analyzed at a high level for valuation purposes as a Hospital typically is one of the larger employers in the community in which it operates; however, certain instances may dictate the necessity for a deeper analysis. The types of employees at a typical Hospital include nursing staff, technical staff, executive staff, and administrative staff. Additionally, some Hospitals may operate physician clinics and report physician salary expense separately. Average salary per full-time equivalent (FTE) employee and the number of FTEs should be evaluated by the valuation analyst. To properly compare these metrics with other operators, the analyst should consider the Hospital's use of purchased services (e.g., dietary, laundry, environmental services, and security) that may not be included in the benchmark FTE data. Discussions with management are required to understand the average annual merit increase for Hospital employees along with how FTE levels should be adjusted with changes in volume (i.e., often an increase in volume does not result in a one-to-one increase in FTEs as the Hospital should experience some efficiencies).

Medical supplies are usually projected on a cost per unit basis or as a percentage of revenue. In the Hospital setting, medical supplies can encompass a variety of categories, such as surgical supplies and implants, pharmaceuticals, and non-surgical supplies. Typically, medical supply expense represents 15 to 20 percent of net revenue; however, the service lines offered by the Hospital can dictate whether these expenses are higher or lower as a percentage of revenue. A valuation analyst should understand dynamics driving supply costs to appropriately develop the forecast. Areas to discuss with management include contractual changes with group purchasing organizations (GPO) and changes in contracts with major medical device manufacturers.

Generally, Hospitals own the land and building where they operate (i.e., owner-occupied); therefore, no rent is paid. In addition to rent, facility costs may include repairs and maintenance, janitorial services, and utilities expense. If applicable, the valuation analyst should take care to review the facility lease when analyzing historical and projected financial operations.

General and administrative expenses will usually encompass a variety of expenses, including licenses, equipment rental, information technology, insurance, billing expenses, advertising, purchased services, and legal and professional fees. For Hospitals that belong to a multi-facility healthcare system, direct and indirect corporate overhead expenses may be significant. The valuation analyst should inquire into the types of services included within direct and indirect overhead to determine whether any adjustments are necessary.

## Capital Expenditures

Capital expenditures can be used by a Hospital to maintain the current asset base (e.g., building, improvements, equipment, and technology) or fund new projects. General maintenance capital expenditures can be estimated based on the age and remaining useful life of the existing fixed assets. These annual maintenance outlays are necessary to keep the Hospital operating in its steady state. For Hospitals with low earnings, cash flow from operations available for capital expenditures is minimal and regular maintenance items may be deferred. A valuation analyst should determine whether a backlog of these maintenance items exists. Alternatively, growth-related capital expenditures are more nonrecurring in nature and should be discretely forecasted (e.g., the construction of a new tower). It should be noted that growth-related capital outlays should be accompanied by additional revenue in the forecast.

## Discount Rate Considerations

The forecast utilized by the valuation analyst will include a certain level of "forecast" risk. A forecast with more optimistic volume assumptions may be riskier than one that assumes the "status quo." The valuation analyst should demonstrate an adequate understanding of the key risks and incorporate a discount rate adjustment for these factors (typically through the specific company risk factor discussed in chapter 4).

Specific factors to consider regarding Hospitals include the following, among many others:

- impact of healthcare reform specific to its locality;
- trends in market reimbursement and relationships with payors;
- existence of any significant concentration of risk within any particular service line or for any specific key physician or physician group;
- reputation in the local community;
- competitive factors;
- physician alignment; and
- shift from inpatient to outpatient medicine.

# Market Approach

The Market Approach estimates value by comparing the value of similar Hospitals traded in a free and open market. The underlying premise of the Market Approach to valuation is the economic principle of substitution—a prudent buyer will pay no more for a business or asset than it would cost to acquire a substitute with the same utility. Please refer to chapter 4 for a more detailed discussion on the application of the Market Approach.

## Relevant Multiples

The Market Approach uses relative value measures or "multiples," which are factors by which some fundamental financial variable is multiplied to derive a value indication for the Hospital. The common multiples utilized to value a Hospital are:

- EBITDA multiples
- revenue multiples

Revenue multiples are frequently utilized when the subject Hospital has low or negative EBITDA margins. In instances where the subject Hospital has normal profit margins, an EBITDA multiple may become more relevant. There is a direct correlation between Hospital profitability and the implicit revenue multiple paid by the buyer. Whether applying a revenue or EBITDA multiple, the valuation analyst should consider the comparability of the subject Hospital to the characteristics of the observed transactions.

## Sources of Market Data

There are currently five public companies that specialize in the ownership and operation of Hospitals: Community Health Systems, Inc. (CYH), LifePoint Hospitals, Inc. (LPNT), HCA Holdings, Inc. (HCA), Tenet Healthcare Corp. (THC), and Universal Health Services, Inc. (UHS). These companies have diversified operations across the United States and represent a significant sample of the industry.

Sources of transaction multiples include market commentary from the public Hospital operators noted above, Irving Levin publications, Capital IQ, *The American Hospital Directory* (AHD), Electronic Municipal Market Access (EMMA), U.S. Securities and Exchange Commission filings, state attorney general offices, and online research. Additionally, the valuation firm may have developed an internal transaction database with nonpublic and confidential information to use at the aggregate summary level, such that the identity of any particular individual reference is protected. Transaction multiples typically represent control multiples; however, there are instances in which published information can be found regarding a transaction for a minority interest.

## Factors to Consider When Selecting Multiples

### Comparability of the Subject to the Comparables

There are fundamental differences between small and midsize privately held Hospitals and publicly traded companies. These differences include size, depth of management, capital structure, access to capital, case mix diversification, geographic diversification, prospective growth rates, and risk. In addition, external microeconomic and macroeconomic events cause fluctuations in the price of public stock prices that can distort multiples. Therefore, a valuation analyst should understand these differences when deciphering the applicability of the publicly traded multiples to the subject Hospital.

Factors influencing comparability to merger and acquisition comparables include the following:

- facility size and location;
- reliance on subsidy dollars;

- stage in business cycle (i.e., start-up, growth, mature, declining);
- local competitor dynamics;
- physician organization; and
- payor mix.

### Barriers to Entry

When valuing Hospitals that reside in states with certificate of need (CON) requirements, the analyst should examine the state's CON requirements and history of granting Hospital CONs. A CON is a permit that requires state government approval for the establishment or modification of healthcare institutions, facilities, or services at designated locations. The Hospitals that have CONs in states with CON requirements may warrant a higher multiple as the CON acts as a barrier to entry for potential market competitors. In states with CON requirements that have a history of denying the applications for new CONs, the multiple utilized in the Market Approach may be higher. Conversely, if the state has a history of granting most CON applications, the Market Approach may not need to be adjusted as the CON does not provide material protection from future competition.

### Level of Value

The valuation analyst should always consider if the subject interest being valued represents a minority or controlling interest when selecting market multiples. It should be noted that there is nonconformity in the profession as to how guideline public company multiples should be applied to reflect a control or minority level of value. In any case, when utilizing transaction multiples, the analyst should always ensure that the level of value acquired in the guideline transactions matches the level of value of the subject interest.

### Other Considerations

When utilizing transaction multiples, the analyst should identify any transactions that might yield outlier or skewed multiples. Additionally, the analyst should ensure the market transaction data set excludes affiliations between two not-for-profit operators. It should be noted that the purchase price and terms in an affiliation (which involves a not-for-profit member substitution) is typically not determined through an actual competitive auction process, and typically consists of an assumption of debt.

Additionally, price-per-bed multiples, although popular, are not utilized by actual market participants when determining an offer price.

## Cost Approach

The Cost Approach, also known as the asset or build-up approach, is a method that attempts to value a business by identifying and valuing each tangible and intangible asset. This approach is primarily used for Hospitals not generating sufficient cash flows to make their operations more valuable than the underlying value of the assets. The Cost Approach provides a "floor," or lowest minimum value, related to an interest in a Hospital and may be appropriate when the Market and Income Approaches produce lower values.

The Cost Approach typically includes tangible assets, and may include identifiable intangible assets. In the context of a business valuation, tangible assets include net working capital and personal property and equipment. Intangible assets may include items such as the Hospital's trade name or, in applicable locales, licensure such as a CON. Please refer to chapter 4 for further discussion of the Cost Approach in the context of a business valuation.

Please note all assets identified in the Cost Approach are included within the total enterprise values determined in the Income and Market Approaches.

### Other Considerations

Hospitals tend to have additional nuances outside the Income, Market, and Cost Approaches that should be addressed by the valuation analysis:

- *Separately saleable businesses*—Hospitals are diversified healthcare entities and many provide patient care beyond typical "acute" care services, including home health, skilled nursing, psychiatric, and rehabilitation services, or may own real estate assets that can be monetized. In certain instances, it may be appropriate to isolate and separately value these service-line or real estate assets (i.e., the sum of the parts is worth more than the whole).

- *Non-operating assets*—The business valuation of a Hospital typically encompasses all assets used to operate the Hospital. However, Hospitals may also have many non-operating assets, such as excess land and charitable trusts that will be represented on the balance sheet. The value of these non-operating assets may not be captured in the business valuation and may need to be addressed separately.

- *Post-transaction arrangements*—In some instances, certain agreements post transaction should be considered in the valuation, particularly in instances of a joint venture. If one party is contributing a cash-flow stream after agreed-upon management or royalty rates, the projected financials used for valuation should reflect these agreements. Additionally, all parties should mutually agree how future corporate allocations will be charged to the joint venture and should be considered as part of the valuation.

# Inpatient Rehabilitation Facilities

# 12

*Clinton Flume, CVA*

---

*Market-level reimbursement should be at the forefront of the analysis of an IRF. The FMV of any IRF has to consider the reimbursement any willing market participate can achieve, not a specific buyer/seller.*

---

An inpatient rehabilitation facility (IRF) is a post-acute entity that provides treatment and therapy services to patients after stabilization of acute care services. An IRF is required to meet admission standards designated by Medicare. For example, a percentage of the total patient admissions (Medicare and all other) must meet one of 13 diagnoses requiring concentrated rehabilitation therapy, referred to as the 60 percent rule. Also, the patient must be able to tolerate three hours of therapy a day and show progression to meet a plan. Other patient criteria apply. During an IRF stay, treatment is typically administered in the form of physical therapy (mobility and function), speech therapy (speech and communication disorders), or occupational therapy ("everyday living" development). IRFs can be a freestanding entity (Freestanding) or a distinct unit in an acute care hospital (Department). Either designation will require the entity to meet IRF licensure standards to accept Medicare patients.

In 2014 there where approximately 1,180 IRFs, of which for-profit accounted for 338 IRFs or 29 percent. The other IRFs were categorized as not-for-profit or government-based entities. Given the fragmentation of this post-acute segment, both for-profit and management company operators look to gain efficiencies and market share through consolidation. The most common transactions in the market include outright acquisitions and joint-venture models (JV) (both typically control-level transactions). While the former is prevalent, the market is leaning more heavily towards the JV model as the independent operator can leverage health system payor relationships, and the health system can take advantage of the independent operator's access to intellectual property around patient and staff management along with capital.

In conducting a fair market value (FMV) analysis, the valuation analyst should consider the Income, Market, and Cost Approaches to value, as outlined in chapter 4.

## *Income Approach*

The Income Approach estimates the value of an IRF by projecting the future cash flow attributable to the subject operations then discounting those earnings back to the present value utilizing an appropriate discount rate that takes into consideration the risk of the operations of the subject business, the forecast utilized, and the industry, among other things. The following outlines the key assumptions to consider when developing a cash flow model for an IRF business.

### Freestanding vs. Hospital Department

There are many considerations in the Income Approach of an IRF when the standard of value is FMV. However, the revenue and expense structure that any willing buyer can reasonably expect to achieve is the leading factor. Therefore, if the IRF currently operates as a Department, the valuation analyst must consider the facts and circumstances of the IRF as a Freestanding entity.

A Freestanding IRF has a distinct tax identification number and operates autonomously. A Department IRF is typically located within a hospital, bills under the hospital's provider number, and shares in an overhead structure. While both entities are comparably reimbursed under Medicare's IRF prospective payment system (PPS), a valuation analyst must understand the commercial payors in the local market. One of the primary differences between a Freestanding and Department relates to the financial reporting and cost accounting structure of these entities. Under the Freestanding setting, the IRF does not share efficiencies through aggregate management, billing, supply chain services, or leveraged staffing models. The costs incurred by a Freestanding IRF are direct. Under the Department setting, much of the IRF's cost structure is incurred by the host hospital and allocated down to the Department IRF through an "overhead" or direct and indirect charges. In most instances, the overhead charge is a formulaic cost accounting measure to distribute the hospital's total expense structure to all service lines. For example, the entire administrative and non-clinical staff of a hospital can be allocated to a Department IRF based on the number of host-hospital patient days. This allocation could unfavorably increase the staffing profile beyond what is reasonable for a Freestanding IRF. The resulting impact of an improper burden expense profile could result in an inaccurate value of the IRF at a freestanding level. Therefore, in the review of any FMV appraisal of an IRF, it first must be established whether the entity is a Department or Freestanding. If the former, there will be critical valuation analyses and assumptions a valuation analyst will have to consider. These will be addressed in tandem with Freestanding IRFs in the next sections.

## Volume

The financial performance of an IRF is largely dependent upon its admission volume and patient type. An admission is characterized by the formal acceptance by the IRF of a patient who resides full-time at the IRF for a length of stay and provided with room, board, and continuous nursing and therapy services. For both Freestanding and Department IRFs, the majority of admissions are sourced from hospital referrals. Freestanding IRFs also drive patient admissions through relationships with local physicians and long-term care facilities.

Even with a steady admissions trend at an IRF, some capacity limitations must be considered, including number and type of beds (private or semi-private) and gender and comorbidity of the patient. An IRF that has 100 percent private beds could achieve a rather high occupancy percentage if there is a significant demand for the services; however, if an IRF has semi-private beds, occupancy percentages will be constrained based on patient placement. In a review of an IRF, admission growth projections must be closely monitored to ensure that there is adequate size and bed structure to accept patients.

Although not all inclusive, a valuation analyst should consider the following when developing or evaluating a forecast for provider volume:

- 60 percent rule compliance—This rule helps distinguish an IRF from an acute care hospital. IRFs that cannot demonstrate compliance are reimbursed under the inpatient prospective payment system (IPPS), which will impact profitability and increase risk of the forecasted earnings.
- Acuity of the patient (case mix index or CMI) and how long the patient stays at the IRF (average length of stay or ALOS). In general, if an IRF has a high ALOS, the overall admissions will be lower on a relative basis. While a higher CMI and ALOS may drive higher reimbursement, based on the acuity of the patient, variable expenses such as staffing may flex and increase too. IRF operators work efficiently to maximize the balance between CMI and ALOS to ensure a maximum occupancy level while maintaining an efficient cost structure.

## Reimbursement

In addition to volume, the valuation analyst should address the "price" or reimbursement level to determine the IRF's projected revenue. The patient distribution for IRFs tends to favor Medicare. Whether the IRF is a Department or a Freestanding entity, all Medicare patients are reimbursed based on the IRF PPS. There are certain nuances to the payment that take into consideration the acuity of the patient, the length of stay, geographical factors, and qualifying facilities (rural, academic, low income); however, all IRFs start with a base reimbursement level. The fiscal year 2017 base discharge rate can be found on the CMS.gov website.

The other primary payors for IRFs include commercial, managed care, Medicaid, self-pay, and charity care. Under a Freestanding setting, these payors are likely to reflect "market," however, in a Department setting these rates could be higher or lower. For example, as a Department IRF, the entity is likely to bill under a hospital's provider number and subsequently reimbursed based on a negotiated rate between the hospital and payor. Sometimes this reimbursement will not reflect the market. In some payment structures, the payor could have included a payment that is 200 percent of Medicare, while another payor set rates at 90 percent of Medicare. Commercial and managed-care reimbursement depend on negotiated rates between the hospital and payor. Again, it is important to understand how the commercial rates compare to Medicare and determine whether the willing buyer would be able to achieve these rates.

Overall, a review of the reimbursement should focus on the Medicare rate given the type of patients and assessment of the commercial and managed-care rate. Historically, Medicare has seen net price increases of between 0.5 percent and 2 percent and commercial carriers are market dependent.

## Other Considerations

Although not an exhaustive list, other considerations that might impact the forecasted earnings include an IRF medical director's tenure of service and experience, as well as the Department IRF's charity care policy.

Clinically strong medical directors have an active admissions process for eligible IRFs patients. Consistency within the medical director position can have a positive impact on risk and growth rates of an IRF.

A Department IRF's host hospital's policy on charity care could have an adverse impact on the profitability. Certain religious affiliations, for example, dictate that hospitals (including all departments) accept a percentage of charity patients within the community.

## Operating Expenses

The following are key considerations for understanding historical and projected operating costs. Employee salaries, wages and benefits, facility expenses, medical supplies and pharmaceuticals, patient support services, and general and administrative expenses constitute the majority of the operating profile at an IRF.

Employee salaries, wages, and benefits typically include the largest portion of spending at an IRF. The types of employees at an IRF include therapy staff, nursing staff, technical staff, support staff, and administrative staff. Under a Freestanding model, the staffing structure will likely include all the required therapy, clinical, and technical staff required to run the operations. Some Freestanding entities will contract with third parties to provide oversight and operational services. In a Department setting, particular attention must be paid to identify whether all direct and support employees of the IRF are accounted in the cost report. It is not uncommon for a Department IRF to not allocate or under-allocate support staff from the hospital because their positions fall under a different hospital department cost report. A valuation analyst must pay careful attention to these details as the operating expense profile must include the appropriate staffing model for any willing buyer to assume operations.

Facility costs primarily include rent paid for the physical space in which the IRF resides. This cost can also include ground leases, common area expenses, utilities, and facility support services. In a review of a third-party lease, careful attention should be paid to the lessor of the establishment. In any instance whereby the landlord of the facility is a related party to the business operations to be acquired, an FMV real estate appraisal should be considered. Under a Department model, the IRF space is often owned by the hospital. Therefore, the Department IRF will likely incur a depreciation cost allocation from the hospital and not a traditional facility lease expense. The space requirements for an IRF include patient rooms, nursing stations, therapy rooms, common area rooms for patient gatherings, clinical/operational storage, shared space, and administrative space. In this situation, a real estate appraiser must determine the footprint of the Department within the hospital and appropriately account for a market rent to be allocated to the IRF. Ultimately, an FMV rent rate appraisal should ensure that the rental rate charged to the IRF by the related party is FMV and not a preferred rate.

General and administrative expenses will usually include billing and management fees, purchased services, repairs and maintenance, marketing, indirect management, and property taxes. For Freestanding IRFs, billing and management fees can be sourced from third parties and are typically charged as a percentage of revenue. For a Department IRF, the valuation analyst should review all cost allocations to ensure these services are accounted for in the expense profile. If the subject IRF contracts for billing and management services from a related party, a separate FMV analysis may be required to determine the reasonableness of the fees charged. Also, under the circumstance where management and billing agreements are entered into post-transaction by the buyer and seller, the analysis should reflect the agreed-upon terms of these contracts. Purchased services include ancillary services administered to patients, such as laboratory, x-ray, and dialysis to name a few. In a Freestanding setting, purchased services are built into the operating structure; however, in a Department IRF setting, a cost allocation may need to be made from the host hospital. While the total cost of these services may be fully allocated to a Department IRF, a valuation analyst should benchmark and confirm the associated cost for accuracy.

## Capital Expenditures

Capital expenditures are required by an IRF to purchase new equipment, maintain the current assets, maintain the facility, or fund new projects, such as increasing the number of beds or bringing the facility up to code. The amount of capital expenditures needed is based on the age of the fixed assets and the expected growth of the IRF. A rule of thumb for a valuation analyst to use when determining the appropriate level of capital expenditures is $3,500 to $5,000 per bed per year if no significant capital expenditures are projected. Actual capital expenditure requirements may vary materially, dependent upon the subject IRF's asset base when considering the leasehold improvements and information technology needs. Also, if the deal terms for an IRF transaction include the assumption of real estate, and the property has been considered an integrated operating assets in the appraisal, the capital expenditures should account for the ongoing maintenance and replacement of the property.

## Discount Rate Considerations

The forecast utilized by the valuation analyst will include some degree of "forecast" risk. A projection with more optimistic volume assumptions may be riskier than one that assumes the "status quo." The valuation analyst should demonstrate an adequate understanding of the key risks and incorporate a discount rate adjustment for these factors (typically through the specific company risk factor discussed in chapter 4).

Examples of factors with the potential to increase an IRF's risk with respect to the IRF industry include whether the IRF possesses a certificate of need; the local competition of inpatient rehabilitation services, including skilled nursing facilities; analysis of commercial reimbursement compared to a "market" participate; revenue or expense profile not consistent with a Freestanding IRF; and capacity constraints based on bed layout.

## Market Approach

The Market Approach estimates value by comparing the value of similar IRFs traded in a free and open market. The underlying premise of the Market Approach to valuation is the economic principle of substitution—a prudent buyer will pay no more for the business or asset than it would cost to acquire a substitute with the same utility. Please refer to chapter 4 for a more detailed discussion on the application of the Market Approach.

### Relevant Multiples

The Market Approach uses relative value measures or "multiples," which are factors by which some fundamental financial variable is multiplied to derive a value indication for the IRF. The common multiples utilized to value an IRF are:

- bed multiples
- EBITDA multiples
- revenue multiples

Normalized EBITDA multiples may be used more frequently than revenue multiples. While the EBITDA metric is not a proxy for cash flow, EBITDA multiples more closely relate to the distributions to owners than revenue multiples. Since profitability can vary significantly based on an IRF's admission mix and cost structure, the valuation analyst should consider the profitability of the subject IRF versus the identified comparables when selecting revenue multiples.

## Sources of Market Data

Market data available for the analysis of an IRF can be sourced from public and private transaction data published by third-party sources, such as Irving Levin Associates and Capital IQ, or proprietary databases from transaction firms. Also, key operational and financial metrics can be obtained from public companies, such as HealthSouth Corporation, Kindred Healthcare, Inc., and Select Medical Holdings Corporation. While each of these public companies has a focus on inpatient rehabilitation, each also has alternative segments focused in post-acute care, such as home health, long-term acute care, and outpatient physical therapy. Annual reports, annual filings, and quarterly filings are excellent sources of information to extract the latest trends within the industry.

## Factors to Consider When Selecting Multiples

### Comparability of the Subject IRF to the Comparables

It is important to note that there are fundamental differences between small to midsize privately held companies and publicly traded companies. These differences include size, depth of management, capital structure, access to capital, case mix diversification, geographic diversification, prospective growth rates, and risk. In addition, external microeconomic and macroeconomic events cause fluctuations in the price of public stock prices that can distort multiples. Therefore, public company multiples do not necessarily reflect comparable market multiples for any single, privately held IRF.

### Barriers to Entry

When valuing IRFs that reside in states with certificate of need (CON) requirements, the valuation analyst should examine the state's CON requirements and history of granting IRF CONs. A CON is a permit that requires state government approval for the establishment or modification of healthcare institutions, facilities, or services at designated locations. The IRFs that have CONs in states with IRF requirements may warrant a higher multiple as the CON acts as a barrier to entry for potential market competitors. In states with CON requirements that have a history of denying the applications for new CONs, the valuation analyst should use corresponding market transaction multiples. Conversely, if the state has a history of granting most applicants with a CON, the Market Approach may not need to be adjusted as the CON does not provide material protection from future competition.

### Level of Value

The valuation analyst should always consider if the subject interest being valued represents a minority or controlling interest when selecting market multiples. When utilizing transaction multiples, the analyst should always ensure that the level of value acquired in the guideline transactions matches the level of value of the subject interest.

As a guideline, if two IRFs contribute their respective equity to a new joint venture, the premise of value will typically be at the control level. Also, if a buyer purchases 100 percent of the equity of an IRF, the value premise will be at the control level. Considerations for a minority level stake could include a health system's alignment strategy with a third-party provider in the community or potentially a third-party management company purchasing an interest in the IRF.

### Other Considerations

When utilizing transaction multiples, the valuation analyst should identify any transactions that might yield skewed multiples as a result of related party buyers and sellers and a forced or distressed sale.

Also, an analyst should consider transactions wherein IRFs lease the facility versus own the facility. Regarding the latter, market multiples will tend to be skewed due to the absence of a facility lease expense. A valuation analyst with a robust private transaction database will likely have a better understanding for this potential adjustment, because of the lack of transaction terms in public sales.

Based on these factors, the multiples utilized in the Market Approach should be adjusted to account for special considerations or the valuation analysts will run the risk of misapplication of this relative value methodology.

## Cost Approach

The Cost Approach, also known as the asset or build-up approach, is a method that attempts to value a business by identifying and assessing each tangible and intangible asset. This method is primarily used for IRFs not generating sufficient cash flows to make its operations more valuable than the underlying value of the assets. The Cost Approach provides a "floor," or lowest minimum value, related to an interest in an IRF and may be appropriate when the Market and Income Approaches produce lower values.

The Cost Approach typically includes tangible assets, and may include identifiable intangible assets. In the context of a business valuation, tangible assets include net working capital and personal property and equipment. Intangible assets may include things such as the IRF's trade name, or in applicable locales, licensure such as a CON. Please refer to chapter 4 for further discussion of the Cost Approach in the context of a business valuation.

Please note, that even though the tangible and intangible assets are not separately valued under the Income and Market Approaches, these approaches consider the cash flows generated by all assets of the business and provide an FMV indication of the business enterprise, which includes all normalized tangible and intangible assets needed to operate the IRF.

# Dialysis 13

*David LaMonte, CFA, Silas Eldredge,*
*and Bridget Triepke, CPA*

*Dialysis centers rely disproportionately on a small minority of patients covered by commercial payors in order to generate a profit. Therefore, understanding the current and projected commercial patient base is crucial to any dialysis center valuation.*

A dialysis center is a distinct entity that offers life support service for patients that suffer from lost kidney function due to either short-term acute renal failure or long-term chronic kidney disease, also known as end stage renal disease (ESRD). Dialysis treatments are offered by freestanding facilities, hospitals, and at-home hemodialysis machines. Nephrologists typically refer patients to an outpatient dialysis center for treatment of ESRD. The nephrologist's physician practice operations are separate from the operations of the dialysis center. Dialysis centers will typically have medical director agreements with physicians to oversee its clinical operations. Reasons for performing a valuation of a dialysis center may include individual physician investment (minority level transactions) and the sale of the dialysis center to or from a management company, national or regional operator, and/or hospital buyer (control-level transactions).

In conducting a fair market value (FMV) analysis, the valuation analyst should consider the Income, Market, and Cost Approaches to value, as outlined in chapter 4.

## Income Approach

The Income Approach estimates the value of a dialysis center by projecting the future cash flow attributable to the subject operations, then discounting those earnings back to the present value by utilizing the selected discount rate that takes into consideration the risk of the operations of the subject business, the forecast utilized, and the industry, among other factors. The following sections outline the key assumptions that should be considered when developing a cash flow model for a dialysis center.

### Volume

The financial performance of a dialysis center is primarily dependent upon the patient census and the resulting treatment volume performed at the particular center. A typical patient will receive three dialysis treatments per week, or approximately 156 treatments per year. Patient census and the resulting treatment volumes at a dialysis center are primarily driven by the demographics of the surrounding area. Areas with a higher proportion of low-income residents may experience higher rates of kidney-related diseases due to poor nutrition options. Additionally, because Medicare provides dialysis treatment coverage to all patients with ESRD regardless of age, the volume of a dialysis center is not dependent on insurance coverage characteristics of the relevant population to the same extent as other outpatient healthcare businesses.

A valuation must take into consideration the historical and projected patient census and resulting treatment volume at the dialysis center. Although not all inclusive, the following should be considerations of the valuation analyst when developing or evaluating a forecast:

- patient demographics in the center's local marketplace;
- current levels of capacity at the nearby centers;
- Medicare certification status;
- legal staffing requirements impacting ability to accept additional patients;
- technological advances associated with ESRD treatments;
- development of or migration to competing dialysis centers; and
- one-time events that could result in an increase or decrease in the stable attainable patient census for the center (i.e., illness of a medical director, shift in the hours of operation, construction, etc.).

In addition to understanding the demographics in the surrounding area and physician referrals of the subject dialysis center as it relates to patient census and treatment volume, the valuation must also consider any capacity and technological constraints associated with the center. A dialysis center operates with a given number of hemodialysis machines, each of which can only accommodate a single patient for a given period. If a dialysis center is projected to have an increase in patient census, the valuation analyst should question management on the availability of machines and the appropriateness of the current level of staffing. Average treatments per day per machine can be reviewed to assist in assessing any potential capacity constraints. A typical turnover time for each treatment is approximately four hours. Therefore, a single hemodialysis machine at a dialysis center can be reasonably estimated to accommodate two patient treatments in an eight-hour period.

## Reimbursement

Reimbursement levels represent another key revenue determinant of financial performance. Since 1972 the U.S. government has provided Medicare coverage to all ESRD patients regardless of age or financial situation. As a result, typically 90 percent or more of a dialysis center's treatment volume is reimbursed through Medicare Part B. A patient who has commercial insurance when beginning a dialysis treatment program will automatically convert to Medicare after a 33-month period. Because dialysis centers are typically out-of-network with commercial payors, the payments from commercial payors for dialysis treatment typically are significantly above the Medicare payment rate, often in excess of two times Medicare rates. DaVita Healthcare Partners, Inc., the largest dialysis provider in the United States, has communicated to the investor market that, "The payments we receive from commercial payors generate nearly all of our profits."[1] Therefore, understanding any projected increases or decreases in Medicare reimbursement, as well as the expected commercial patient attrition, is critical to the valuation.

## Operating Expenses

Employee salaries, medical supplies, facility costs, and general and administrative expense comprise the majority of the operating expenses at a dialysis center.

The types of employees at a dialysis center include nursing staff, patient care technicians and administrative staff. Employee compensation is typically analyzed in two ways: average salary per full-time equivalent (FTE) employee and number of hours per treatment. Nursing and technical FTE levels will typically adjust with patient census and treatment volume. Patient care technicians initiate, monitor, and terminate the dialysis treatments under the supervision of a nurse. Administrative staff, which typically varies less with volume, includes administrators, social workers, dieticians, clinical coordinators, reception, and billing employees. If a dialysis center is projected to have an influx in volume, the number of nursing and technical FTEs will need to grow to accommodate the additional workload, as well as to meet regulations. By contrast, if a dialysis center is expected to lose significant volume, management would typically lower the number of staff at the dialysis center, provided the levels do not fall below the required minimums.

Medical supplies are projected on a cost-per-treatment basis. Generally, medical supply costs primarily consist of medications such as erythropoietin (EPO) and various other medical supplies required for each treatment. Since these types of supplies are required for each treatment a patient receives, they are usually assumed to increase with overall treatment volume.

---

1. Davita Healthcare Partners, Inc. Form 10-K for the fiscal year ended Dec. 31, 2015.

Facility costs are composed primarily of the rent paid to a third party for the physical space in which the dialysis center resides. The valuation analyst should take care to review the facility lease when analyzing historical and projected financial operations. In situations where the real estate is owned by investors in the dialysis center's operations, a real estate appraiser may be requested to verify that the facility rent paid is consistent with FMV. Also, a real estate appraisal may be required when the dialysis center owns the real estate. In these instances, the real estate is valued and a fair market rental rate is determined. The subject dialysis center is burdened with the fair market rental rate for valuation of the dialysis center's operations, as most transactions for dialysis centers do not include the purchase of the real estate. If the real estate is to be purchased, the appraised amount of the real estate would be added to the valuation of the business operations of the subject dialysis center once it has been burdened with the appropriate facility rental expense.

General and administrative expenses will usually include any contracted billing and management fees. These fees are typically based on a percentage of revenue; therefore, the expenses will increase and decrease with the revenue of the dialysis center. If the subject dialysis center contracts for billing and/or management services from a related party, a separate FMV analysis may be required to determine the reasonableness of the fees charged for those services. Other types of general and administrative costs include laboratory expenses, repairs and maintenance, equipment lease costs, nonmedical supplies, and non-income taxes.

## Capital Expenditures

Capital expenditures can be used by a dialysis center to purchase new equipment, maintain the current assets, or fund new projects, such as an update and/or expansion of the facility. The amount of capital expenditures needed is based on the expected patient census growth and the age of the current fixed asset base. The analyst should be primarily concerned with the age of the hemodialysis machines, which are the major required fixed asset for a dialysis center. Additionally, the analyst should consider the effectiveness and condition of the center's electronic medical records and technology assets. Generally, capital expenditures at a dialysis center are relatively low, as the cost of a hemodialysis machine typically ranges from $10,000 to $20,000. The average expected life of a hemodialysis machine is approximately five years, but can vary depending on utilization. Overall capital expenditures are typically estimated based on the number of hemodialysis machines and other capital assets needed to support the expected patient census.

## Discount Rate Considerations

The forecast utilized by the valuation analyst will include a certain level of "forecast" risk. A forecast with more optimistic volume assumptions may be riskier than one that assumes the "status quo." The valuation analyst should demonstrate an adequate understanding of the key risks and incorporate a discount rate adjustment for these factors (typically through the specific company risk factor discussed in chapter 4). Factors that may influence the forecast risk for a dialysis center include, but are not limited to, any pending Medicare certification, ability to successfully recruit trained nursing staff, ability to grow patient census, and level of competition from other local dialysis providers.

## *Market Approach*

The Market Approach estimates value by comparing the value of similar dialysis centers traded in a free and open market. The underlying premise of the Market Approach to valuation is the economic principle of substitution—a prudent buyer will pay no more for a business or asset than it would cost to acquire a substitute with the same utility. Please refer to chapter 4 for a more detailed discussion on the application of the Market Approach.

## Relevant Multiples

The Market Approach uses relative value measures, or "multiples," which are factors by which some fundamental financial variable is multiplied to derive a value indication for the dialysis center. The common multiples utilized to value a dialysis center are:

- EBITDA multiples
- revenue multiples
- patient census multiples

Normalized EBITDA multiples are utilized more frequently than revenue multiples, as they capture the ultimate profitability of dialysis centers and are more closely related to the distributions to owners than are revenue multiples. Since profitability can vary significantly based on a dialysis center's payor mix (commercial versus Medicare) and cost structure, the valuation analyst should consider the profitability of the subject versus the identified comparables when selecting revenue multiples. Patient census multiples are also frequently considered by operators. Typically, a dialysis center with a higher proportion of commercial insured patients will command a higher patient census multiple, while a dialysis center with a higher proportion of government insured patients will command a lower patient census multiple.

## Sources of Market Data

There are currently three public companies that specialize in the ownership and operation of dialysis centers. DaVita Healthcare Partners, Inc. (DVA) and Fresenius Medical Care AG & Co. KGaA (FME) are the two largest dialysis center operators in the United States. Each company owns and operates thousands of dialysis centers across the United States. Recently, American Renal Associates Holdings, Inc. (ARA) also became a publicly traded dialysis center operator; however, ARA is much smaller than DVA and FME in terms of number of dialysis centers currently operated. It should be noted that there is a question in the profession as to how guideline public company multiples should be applied to reflect a control or minority level of value.

Sources of transaction multiples include market commentary from the public dialysis center operators noted above; discussions with management of dialysis center operators regarding recent transactions; public and private transaction data published by third-party sources, such as Irving Levin Associates and Capital IQ; U.S. Securities and Exchange Commission filings; and nonpublic information from a valuation analyst's internal transaction database that is based upon his or her industry experience. Transaction multiples typically represent control multiples; however, there are instances in which published information can be found regarding a transaction for a minority interest.

# Factors to Consider When Selecting Multiples

## *Comparability of the Subject to the Comparables*

There are fundamental differences between small to midsize privately held companies and publicly traded companies. These differences include size, depth of management, capital structure, access to capital, geographic diversification, prospective growth rates, and risk. In addition, external microeconomic and macroeconomic events cause fluctuations in the price of public stock prices that can distort multiples. Therefore, public company multiples do not necessarily reflect comparable market multiples for a single, privately held dialysis center.

Size and growth prospects should also be considered when reviewing transaction multiples, as implied valuation multiples for large multi-site dialysis center operators are typically significantly higher than multiples paid for a single location.

## *Barriers to Entry*

When valuing dialysis centers that reside in states with certificate of need (CON) requirements, the analyst should examine the state's CON requirements and history of granting dialysis center CONs. A CON is a permit that requires state government approval for the establishment or modification of healthcare institutions, facilities, or services at designated locations. The dialysis centers that have CONs in states with CON requirements may warrant a higher multiple, as the CON acts as a barrier to entry for potential market competitors. In states with CON requirements that have a history of denying the applications for new CONs, the multiple utilized in the Market Approach may be higher. Conversely, if the state has a history of granting most applicants with a CON, the Market Approach may not need to be adjusted, as the CON does not provide material protection from future competition.

## *Level of Value*

The valuation analyst should always consider if the subject interest being valued represents a minority or controlling interest when selecting market multiples. When utilizing transaction multiples, the analyst should always ensure that the level of value acquired in the guideline transactions matches the level of value of the subject interest.

Individual physician investments in a dialysis center are often trans-
acted at minority interests. A minority interest in a smaller, single-
location dialysis center can sometimes influence expansion decisions,
cost structure, future volume growth, and distributions or liquidity
events. Minority interest valuation multiples for ownership in large,
multi-site dialysis businesses are typically less than control multiples,
as a minority investor often has little influence on major decisions.
Operating agreements and other governing legal documents should
be reviewed when assessing the rights and influence of a minority
investor.

### Other Considerations

When utilizing transaction multiples, the analyst should identify any
transactions that might yield skewed multiples as a result of related
party buyers and sellers and a forced or distressed sale.

Dialysis centers with a large proportion of commercial insured
patients may have significant potential reimbursement risk in the future. As a result, the multiples utilized in the Market Approach should
be adjusted accordingly, or the projected earnings of the dialysis center should be adjusted to account for the risk before applying typical
market multiples.

## Cost Approach

The Cost Approach, also known as the asset or build-up approach, is a
method that attempts to value a business by identifying and valuing
each tangible and intangible asset. This approach is primarily used for
a dialysis center not generating sufficient cash flows to make its operations more valuable than the underlying value of the assets. The
Cost Approach provides a "floor," or lowest minimum value, related
to an interest in a dialysis center and may be appropriate when the
Market and Income Approaches produce lower values.

The Cost Approach typically includes tangible assets, and may
include identifiable intangible assets. In the context of a business valuation, tangible assets may include net working capital, personal property and equipment, leasehold improvements, and real estate. Intangible
assets may include things such as the dialysis center's trade name and,

in applicable locales, licensure such as a certificate of need. Please refer to chapter 4 for further discussion of the Cost Approach in the context of a business valuation.

Although tangible and intangible assets are not separately valued under the Income and Market Approaches, these approaches still consider the cash flows generated by all assets of the business. In providing an FMV indication of the business enterprise, the Income and Market Approaches include all normalized tangible and intangible assets needed to operate the business.

# Home Care Services

*Aaron Murski, CVA*

**14**

*Due to the low cost per day of home care relative to other settings (e.g., hospital, skilled nursing), continually improving medical technology, and the imperatives of healthcare reform and the "triple aim," the home care industry may see continued growth and expansion by taking market share from other healthcare verticals.*

The post-acute home care industry is comprised of a wide range of healthcare services and businesses, including home healthcare agencies, hospice providers, durable medical equipment (DME) suppliers, infusion and oxygen services, and private duty businesses. A home care business may specialize in one or more of these areas. Not surprisingly, the predominant demographic across all home care services sectors are seniors. However, wide variation can exist depending on the specific area of focus within the industry. For example, a high-risk obstetrics home health operation would cater to a demographic very different from a hospice provider.

As of 2015, there were over 12,000 Medicare certified-home health agencies, as well as more than 4,000 unique Medicare certified hospice providers. The home health market has been estimated at over $87 billion, including Medicare certified providers as well as non-Medicare certified providers.

The home care industry is highly fragmented, even by healthcare standards. Examples of typical buyers in the market include large publicly traded companies, hospitals and health systems in markets local to the target, and privately held management companies. Typical home care transactions consist primarily of control-level transactions. As such, this chapter will focus on control-level valuation issues.

In conducting a fair market value (FMV) analysis, the valuation analyst should consider the Income, Market, and Cost Approaches to value, as outlined in chapter 4.

## Income Approach

The Income Approach estimates the value of an the home care services business by projecting the future cash flow attributable to the subject operations then discounting those earnings back to the present value utilizing an appropriate discount rate that takes into consideration the risk of the operations of the subject business, the forecast utilized, and the industry, among other things. The following sections outline the key assumptions that should be considered when developing a cash flow model for the business.

### Volume

Depending on the home care services sector, volume may include, but not be limited to, home visits, episodes of care, DME sales or rentals, or days. For example, home health services are paid for by Medicare in units of 60-day episodes, with coding adjustments that can vary depending on the clinical needs of the patient and the functions provided by the home health personnel. Home health services, for example, can include occupational or speech therapy, skilled nursing, or other social services.

The business's volume by type of service should be considered by the valuation analyst. Although not all inclusive, the following should be considerations of the valuation analyst when developing or evaluating a forecast:

- specific services offered and personnel available to provide services;
- marketing and customer acquisition strategy;
- local demographic trends and market share;
- existing competitive landscape in the local market(s); and
- barriers to entry for new entrants in the market (e.g., licensure moratoriums or certificate of need issues).

For home care services dependent on personnel, evaluating employee turnover and employee wages and incentive programs can be helpful in determining the specific business's competitive position in the local market. Aside from local population growth, developing a detailed understanding of the local community (e.g., age, unemployment rates, average income) along with its population growth rate will provide insight to the valuation analyst.

Depending on the services provided by the business, the business may face capacity constraints. For home health services, capacity can be dependent on available personnel, as total staff hours available may be the limiting factor with respect to the number of home care visits possible in a given year.

## Reimbursement

The second component of revenue that should be addressed by the valuation analyst is "price" or reimbursement. Considering the demographics of the majority of home care services patients, understanding and modeling Medicare reimbursement is paramount for the valuation analyst to adequately assess reimbursement changes in any forecast of revenue. Through Medicare proposed rules, MedPac recommendations, and other sources, a valuation analyst can gain an understanding of what the future may hold for Medicare payments and changing reimbursement models for each specific home care services sector. Medicaid is also a large payor in many home care services businesses;

as such, reimbursement should also be modeled and forecast in a manner that reflects the likely trends.

Notably, like many other sectors, Medicare has begun a value-based payment program, as well as a quality reporting initiative for home health. In particular, during 2016, Medicare continued to cut reimbursement for home health services.[1] To the extent the reimbursement forecast has not specifically considered these types of issues, the forecast could be materially incorrect.

Reimbursement can be affected by changes in the subject business's service mix and patient acuity mix as well. For example, this can occur through a shift in visits to provide more services.

## Operating Expenses

The operating expense profile of any home health entity is usually dominated by employee salaries and benefits, as well as mileage reimbursement. Pertaining to DME businesses, a material expense (whether classified as capital or operating) would also include the cost of goods sold or depreciation associated with rental items.

Employee costs can be influenced by local labor markets, in that in certain markets, the nursing or therapy personnel are in greater demand than others. In any case, salary and benefit costs per full-time equivalent (FTE) employee and wage increases are primary variables used to forecast salaries and wages. In addition, to the extent that the forecasted volume for the business implies that additional FTE staff are needed, employee FTE needs, and therefore salary and wage costs, should increase accordingly.

Mileage reimbursement should be forecast to fluctuate with some measure of volume, such as visit volume, as mileage reimbursement costs will be influenced by the number of visits to the patient and patient locations.

For DME businesses, the valuation analyst must pay careful attention to how the business has historically treated sales and rental items from an expense recognition perspective. Rental items may be depreciated and corresponding expenses will be capitalized while sales items are expensed as sold. In any case, a distinct cost of sale and rental items forecast should be tied to the sales and rental revenue forecast,

---

1. For example, for durable medical equipment, Medicare has moved to a bid process that has materially impacted many industry participants.

to be appropriately considered. Also, ownership of the actual DME assets may or may not transfer to the patient, at certain usage levels.

## Capital Expenditures

Capital expenditure forecasts for a home care services business are typically minimal, as these businesses do not rely on significant equipment of facilities in order to provide care. While any capital expenditure forecast should consider the age and condition of the equipment and other assets utilized, the likely dollar amount of the capital needs may be relatively low. One area that is becoming increasingly important and can be costly to implement and use are IT systems, which manage operations and control inventory, costs, and quality. Any necessary investments in IT infrastructure should also be considered.

## Discount Rate Considerations

The forecast utilized by the valuation analyst will include a certain level of "forecast" risk. A forecast with more optimistic volume assumptions may be riskier than one that assumes the "status quo." The valuation analyst should demonstrate an adequate understanding of the key risks and incorporate a discount rate adjustment for these factors (typically through the specific company risk factor discussed in chapter 4).

# *Market Approach*

The Market Approach estimates value by comparing the value of similar businesses traded in a free and open market. The underlying premise of the Market Approach to valuation is the economic principle of substitution—a prudent buyer will pay no more for a business or asset than it would cost to acquire a substitute with the same utility. Please refer to chapter 4 for a more detailed discussion on the application of the Market Approach.

## Relevant Multiples

The Market Approach uses relative value measures, or "multiples," which are factors by which some fundamental financial variable is multiplied to derive a value indication for the home care business. The common multiples utilized to value a home care business are:

- EBITDA multiples
- revenue multiples

Normalized EBITDA multiples are utilized more frequently than revenue multiples, as they capture the ultimate profitability of home care businesses and are more closely related to the distributions to owners than are revenue multiples. Since profitability can vary significantly based on the specific service mix, payor mix, and cost structure, the valuation analyst should consider the profitability of the subject versus the identified comparables when selecting revenue multiples.

## Sources of Market Data

Consistent with the two main methods of Market Approach application, sources of Market Approach data may be found in public company stock prices, as well as transaction data that may be made available when one company acquires another. Concerning the guideline public company method, there are many public companies that specialize in the ownership and operation of home health and related services, such as Amedisys, Inc. (ticker "AMED"); Gentiva Health Services, Inc. (ticker "GTIV"); LHC Group, Inc. (ticker "LHCG"); and Almost Family, Inc. (ticker "AFAM"). It should be noted that there is a question in the profession as to how guideline public company multiples should be applied to reflect a control or minority level of value.

Sources of transaction multiples include market commentary from the public home care operators noted above; discussions with operators regarding recent transactions, public and private transaction data published by third-party sources, such as Irving Levin Associates and Capital IQ; U.S. Securities and Exchange Commission (SEC) filings; and nonpublic information from a valuation analyst's internal transaction database that is based upon his or her industry experience. Transaction multiples typically represent control multiples; however, there are instances in which published information can be found regarding a transaction for a minority interest.

## Factors to Consider When Selecting Multiples

### Comparability of the Subject to the Comparables

Regarding the applicability of the guideline public company approach, there are fundamental differences between small to midsize privately held companies and the publicly traded companies. These differences include size, depth of management, capital structure, access to capital to fund growth, product diversification, geographic diversification, and risk. In addition, external microeconomic and macroeconomic events cause fluctuations in the price of public stock prices that can distort multiples. While the public company stock prices may be a data point, public company trading multiples do not necessarily reflect comparable market multiples for any single, privately held business. If applicable, the valuation analyst should adjust the guideline company multiples as appropriate, for differences in things such as growth, profitability, etc.

Size and growth prospects should also be considered when reviewing transaction multiples, as implied valuation multiples for large, scaled businesses are typically significantly higher than multiples paid for a home care services business that covers a limited geography.

## Barriers to Entry

When valuing home care businesses that reside in states with certificate of need (CON) moratoriums or other licensure requirements, the analyst should examine the state's specific regulatory regime and history of granting approval to operate. To the extent the home care business is protected from new entrants into the market due to a regulatory barrier, a higher multiple may be warranted (depending on the location of the transactions comprising the comparable data set). Conversely, if approval is needed and the specific state has a history of granting approval for most applicants, the Market Approach may not need to be adjusted, as the regulatory approvals needed to operate may not provide material protection from future competition.

## Level of Value

The valuation analyst should always consider if the subject interest being valued represents a minority or controlling interest when selecting market multiples. When utilizing transaction multiples, the analyst should always ensure that the level of value acquired in the guideline transactions matches the level of value of the subject interest.

## Cost Approach

The Cost Approach, also known as the asset or build-up approach, is a method that attempts to value a business by identifying and valuing each tangible and intangible asset. This approach is primarily used for home care businesses not generating sufficient cash flows to make its operations more valuable than the underlying value of the assets. The Cost Approach provides a "floor," or lowest minimum value, related to an interest in a home care business and may be appropriate when the Market and Income Approaches produce lower values.

The Cost Approach typically includes tangible assets, and may include identifiable intangible assets. In the context of a business valuation, tangible assets include net working capital and personal property and equipment. Intangible assets may include things such as the home care business's trade name or, in applicable locales, licensure such as a certificate of need and Medicare licensure. Please refer to chapter 4 for further discussion of the Cost Approach in the context of a business valuation.

Although tangible and intangible assets are not separately valued under the Income and Market Approaches, these approaches still consider the cash flows generated by all assets of the business. In providing an FMV indication of the business enterprise, the Income and Market Approaches include all normalized tangible and intangible assets needed to operate the business.

# Long-Term Acute Care Hospitals

William Teague, CFA

*The FMV analysis must address the impact of significant new regulations, such as the 25% Rule and Site Neutral Payments on future operations.*

Long-term acute care hospitals (LTACHs) treat patients with clinically complex problems that require hospital-level care for relatively extended periods. Currently, to be certified as an LTACH eligible for Medicare payments, a facility must have an average length of stay (ALOS) greater than 25 days for its Medicare patients. Services offered by LTACHs generally include comprehensive rehabilitation, respiratory therapy, head trauma treatment, and pain management. Typically, patients admitted to an LTACH will see a physician daily and be treated by a team of nurses and therapists to gradually strengthen the respective patient. LTACHs can be either freestanding facilities (Freestanding) or located within an acute care hospital (ACH), in which they are called hospitals within hospitals (HWHs). While HWHs are located within an ACH, they operate as a separate entity. According to Medpac's March 2015 report to Congress, approximately 78 percent of LTACHs are for-profit organizations and approximately 51 percent of all LTACH facilities are owned by Kindred Healthcare and Select Medical.

LTACHs are typically valued to calculate relative equity contributions to a potential joint venture (JV) or for outright acquisition (both scenarios usually being performed under an enterprise or controlling level of value). When an LTACH is acquired, operators hope to achieve cost/revenue synergies, expanded market share, and more negotiating leverage with commercial payors. Under the JV model, independent operators can leverage health system relationships and the health system can utilize the independent operator's management expertise and access to capital.

In conducting a fair market value (FMV) analysis, the valuation analyst should consider the Income, Market, and Cost Approaches to value, as outlined in chapter 4.

## Income Approach

The Income Approach estimates the value of an LTACH by projecting the future cash flow attributable to the subject operations then discounting those earnings back to the present value utilizing an appropriate discount rate that takes into consideration the risk of the operations of the subject business, the forecast utilized, and the industry, among other things. The following outlines the key assumptions that should be considered when developing a cash flow model for an LTACH business.

### Volume

Since October 2002, LTACHs have been reimbursed by Medicare under a prospective payment system (PPS) in which patients are classified into distinct diagnosis-related groups (DRGs) based upon specific clinical characteristics and expected resource needs. There are adjustments to the Medicare payments based on high-cost outliers, short-stay outliers, and other factors. As a result, volume metrics for LTACHs have primarily been dependent upon total patient admission/discharge volume, the number of total days patients spent in the facility, and each patient's associated DRG. For both Freestanding and HWH

LTACHs, the majority of admissions are derived from ACH referrals and relationships with local physicians.

Although not all inclusive, the following should be considerations of the valuation analyst when developing or evaluating a forecast.

### Patient Acuity

The acuity of the patient (case mix index or CMI) is an important factor when projecting volume for an LTACH. In general, if a patient has a higher CMI, the patient will require a longer ALOS. The longer a patient stays in the facility, the lower amount of patient turnover. As a result, the LTACH will, on average, have fewer admissions/discharges than an identical facility with a lower CMI.

### Capacity

A valuation analyst must consider capacity constraints, such as the total number of beds, the breakdown of bed type (private or semi-private), patient gender, and ALOS, when developing admission growth assumptions. LTACHs utilizing only private beds could hypothetically achieve a 90 percent or greater occupancy level. Facilities with semi-private beds would not be able to achieve that level of occupancy due to discharge timing and patient placement issues. As a result, admission growth and ALOS projections must be closely monitored to ensure that there is an adequate number of beds and respective bed type.

### LTACH Facility Moratorium

From a competition standpoint, the entrance of new market participants was limited when Congress passed the Medicare, Medicaid, and SCHIP Extension Act of 2007 (MMSEA). MMSEA imposed a three-year moratorium on new LTACHs, LTACH satellite units and new beds in LTACHs subject to certain exceptions. The moratorium was extended by the Affordable Care Act of 2010 for an additional two years, which expired in December of 2012. Recently, the Pathway for SGR Reform Act of 2013 (SGR Reform Act) reinstated the moratorium from April 1, 2014, to September 30, 2017. Therefore, if an LTACH is close to capacity, additional beds may be unobtainable, limiting future volume growth opportunities. In addition, new entrants will not be able to enter the market, reducing the risk the subject LTACH will lose volume due to competition.

## The 25% Rule

The 25% Rule was established by CMS in 2005 to prevent LTACHs from functioning as units of ACHs. Under the rule, CMS would reduce payments to LTACHs that received more than 25 percent of its referrals from a single source. The initial rule applied only to LTACH HWHs and LTACH satellites, however in 2007 CMS extended the 25% Rule to apply to Freestanding LTACHs. Under the SGR Reform Act, CMS has delayed full implementation of the 25% Rule so that most HWHs and satellites will be paid standard LTACH rates as long as the percentage of Medicare admissions from the host ACH does not exceed 50 percent. In addition, the SGR Reform Act delayed the application of the 25% Rule to Freestanding LTACHs.

As a result, when projecting future volume for an LTACH HWH, a valuation analyst must understand the LTACH's historical referral patterns and sources. Forecasted admission volume must be adjusted if greater than 50 percent of the subject LTACH's historical referrals are generated by a single source. Otherwise, a valuation analyst must consider showing a substantial decline in reimbursement. It is possible for the subject LTACH to maintain current volume and reimbursement levels if it is able to achieve a single-source referral percentage below 50 percent through other referral source volume growth and diversification. A valuation analyst would need to document and have a clear understanding of the sources of these projected new referrals. In addition, many times extra cost may be incurred through the hiring of clinical liaisons and marketing personnel to support the projected admission growth and diversification.

Finally, a valuation analyst must take into account the risk that CMS will eventually fully implement the 25% Rule for both HWH and Freestanding LTACHs. A valuation analyst would appropriately account for this risk through the cost of capital or by making further adjustments in the out years of the cash flow projections.

## Local Market Factors

Market factors in the form of competition and demographics should be evaluated by the valuation analyst. Competition may include a competitor LTACH, local hospital(s), or even changes to practice habits of the local physicians. With regulations like the 25% Rule, understanding local referral patterns is critical. In addition, employment of referring physicians by competitor hospitals could negatively impact volume as they refer to an affiliated facility. This could also impact compliance with the 25% Rule. While new competition is limited with the government moratorium, the universe of patients eligible for LTACH stays is also limited so the competitive environment must be scrutinized. Finally, a valuation analyst must carefully consider the local demographic environment. Developing an understanding of the local community (e.g., age, unemployment rates, health, average income), along with its population growth rate, will provide meaningful insight.

## Reimbursement

The second component of revenue that should be addressed by the valuation analyst is "price" or reimbursement.

As previously discussed, LTACHs are currently reimbursed by Medicare under a PPS system pursuant to which patients are classified into distinct DRGs based upon specific clinical characteristics and expected resource needs. There are adjustments to the Medicare payments based on high-cost outliers, short-stay outliers, and other factors. In addition, payments are adjusted based on the acuity of the patient (CMI), the length of stay, geographical factors, and qualifying facilities (rural, academic, low income). According to MedPac, Medicare accounts for approximately two-thirds of total LTACH admissions and half of total LTACH revenue.

Commercial and managed-care reimbursement depends on negotiated rates between the LTACH and payor. It is important to understand how the commercial rates compare to Medicare and determine whether the willing buyer would be able to achieve these rates.

A valuation analyst should carefully review payor mix information provided by the LTACH in order to accurately understand the LTACH business and for the development of future projections.

In addition, the following should be considerations of the valuation analyst when developing or evaluating a reimbursement forecast (see following page):

### The 25% Rule

As previously discussed, the 25% Rule will reduce payments to LTACHs that received more than 25 percent of their referrals from a single source. Under the SGR Reform Act, CMS has delayed full implementation of the 25% Rule so that most HWHs and satellites will be paid standard LTACH rates as long as the percentage of Medicare admissions from the host ACH does not exceed 50 percent. In addition, the SGR Reform Act delayed the application of the 25% Rule to Freestanding LTACHs. As a result, if the volume projections for a HWH LTACH do not satisfy the requirements of the 25% Rule, the reimbursement rates for the LTACH would need to be adjusted accordingly. In addition, a valuation analysis would need to take into account the risk that CMS will eventually fully implement the 25% Rule for both HWH and Freestanding LTACHs through further reimbursement adjustments or through the cost of capital.

### Site Neutral Payments

The SGR Reform Act established site-neutral payments for specified cases in LTACHs beginning in the fiscal year 2016. Under the law, the LTACH PPS rate will only apply LTACH discharges that had an ACH stay immediately preceding the LTACH admission and for which the ACH stay included at least three days in the intensive care unit (ICU) or the discharge is assigned to the DRG based on the receipt of mechanical ventilation services for at least 96 hours. All other discharges, regardless of ICU use, will be paid at the lower of the ACH inpatient prospective payment system (IPPS) rate or the LTACH PPS rate. These site-neutral payments were phased in over a two-year period beginning in fiscal year 2016 and 2017. During this time period, discharges that do not meet the criteria for payment under the LTACH PPS stated above will receive 50 percent of the standard LTACH PPS rate and the 50 percent of the site-neutral payment. Beginning October 1, 2017, LTACHs will be reimbursed under the site-neutral methodology. CMS will also modify the calculation of ALOS for purposes of qualification as an LTACH. Beginning in FY 2016, the LTACH length of stay requirement will only be calculated for discharges that are not subject to the site-neutral payments. Any accurate FMV analysis should include consideration for the effects of this new regulation and adjust reimbursement accordingly, based on the expected type of patient volume (neutral-site vs. PPS).

## *Other Considerations*

One major item to consider when evaluating or developing projections is the effect of the bundle payment methodology on future LTACH industry reimbursement. Bundled payment systems are beginning to take hold in the post-acute care industry and a valuation analyst should note if any of the major participants in the market have begun to move forward with this methodology. This could affect referral patterns and how the LTACH would be paid going forward.

### Operating Expenses

Employee salaries, medical supplies, purchased services, occupancy costs, and general and administrative expense comprise the majority of the operating expenses at an LTACH.

The expense structure included in an FMV analysis should reflect what any willing buyer/seller can reasonably expect to incur. In other words, the appraisal must simulate operations of the LTACH on a Freestanding basis. For example, while a HWH LTACH might operate as a separate entity from the host ACH, certain expenses might be charged or allocated to the HWH through a purchased services agreement with the host ACH. Common functions charged to HWHs by the host ACHs include, but are not limited to, the following: management, billing and collection, laboratory, dietary, laundry and linens, supplies, and pharmaceuticals. Please note, many times the services provided by the host ACH are charged to the HWH LTACH based on the ACH's total cost allocated on a per patient day/admission basis, as a percentage of revenue, or as a fixed monthly payment. Therefore, the payments included in the purchased service arrangements might not represent the actual costs required to operate the LTACH by a hypothetical willing buyer/seller. The resulting impact of an improperly burdened expense profile may in turn result in an inaccurate value indication for the LTACH. A separate FMV analysis may be required to determine the reasonableness of the fees included in the purchased services arrangements.

Employee costs are usually the largest expense incurred by an LTACH. The types of support staff employed typically include nursing, therapy, dietary/nutrition, social worker, tech, clinical liaison, and administrative staff. When analyzing the staffing model at a subject LTACH, a valuation analyst should confirm that the model reflects LTACH operations on a Freestanding basis. Under an HWH model, staff is oftentimes shared with an ACH and allocated to the LTACH. Many times the expense reflected on the financials does not fully reflect all the staff utilized by the LTACH (especially administrative/management personnel) and results in a less than fully burdened expense profile. An analyst should perform a benchmarking analysis and confirm that the employees per occupied bed and hours per patient day are consistent with industry norms when developing a forecast.

Occupancy costs can include facility rent to related or third parties, ground leases, common area expenses, utilities, and facility support services. In a review of a third-party lease, careful attention should be paid to the lessor. In any instance whereby the landlord of the installation is a related party, an FMV analysis should be considered. The space requirements for an LTACH include patient rooms, nursing stations, therapy rooms, common area rooms, clinical/operational storage, and administrative space. For an HWH LTACH, a valuation analyst must determine the footprint of the subject LTACH within the ACH and ensure the occupancy costs fully reflect the costs incurred to operate the LTACH on a Freestanding basis. Ultimately, an FMV appraisal will help ensure that the rental rate charged to the LTACH by the related party is FMV and not a preferred rate.

## Capital Expenditures

Capital expenditures can be used by an LTACH to purchase new equipment, maintain the current fixed assets, or fund new projects such as renovating space. The amount of capital expenditures needed is based on the age and condition of the existing fixed assets and any new equipment requirements. Major equipment generally employed by LTACHs include ventilators, patient-monitoring systems, patient beds, and nursing stations. Actual capital expenditure requirements may vary materially depending upon the subject LTACH's asset base. If a transaction includes the value of the real estate, the capital expenditures should account for the ongoing maintenance and replacement of the subject property.

## Discount Rate Considerations

The forecast utilized by the valuation analyst will include a certain level of "forecast" risk. A forecast with more optimistic volume assumptions may be riskier than one that assumes the "status quo." The valuation analyst should demonstrate an adequate understanding of the key risks and incorporate a discount rate adjustment for these factors (typically through the specific company risk factor discussed in chapter 4).

Current compliance with new regulations regarding volume, referrals, and reimbursement must be considered when developing a discount rate. If current operations do not show compliance, and the LTACH projections are not adjusted accordingly, a high-risk factor should be utilized. In addition, the risk of the government fully implementing the 25% Rule should be accounted for. Finally, bundled payment methodology represents a considerable risk to the industry as LTACHs are a higher cost provider compared to skilled nursing facilities and other post-acute care providers.

# *Market Approach*

The Market Approach estimates value by comparing the value of similar LTACHs traded in a free and open market. The underlying premise of the Market Approach to valuation is the economic principle of substitution—a prudent buyer will pay no more for a business or asset than it would cost to acquire a substitute with the same utility. Please refer to chapter 4 for a more detailed discussion on the application of the Market Approach.

## Relevant Multiples

The Market Approach uses relative value measures or "multiples," which are factors by which some fundamental financial variable is multiplied to derive a value indication for the LTACH. The common multiples utilized to value an LTACH are:

- bed multiples
- EBITDA multiples
- revenue multiples

Normalized EBITDA multiples may be used more frequently than revenue multiples. While the EBITDA metric may or may not be a proxy for cash flow, EBITDA multiples often more closely related to the distributions to owners than revenue multiples. Revenue multiples require more scrutiny as profitability can vary widely based on patient mix, CMI, payor mix, and expense profile.

## Sources of Market Data

Market data available for the analysis of an LTACH can be sourced from individual transaction databases, such as Capital IQ, Irvin Levin, or proprietary databases. Public transaction databases will oftentimes include the synergistic value of the buyer, which would not be consistent with the FMV standard of value. The best source of information would be the proprietary data from respected firms that have experience in the LTACH space. The multiples sourced from these databases will more closely align with the market and likely provide more of a real-time measure of value.

There are currently two public companies that specialize in the ownership and operation of LTACHs: Kindred Healthcare, Inc., and Select Medical Holdings Corporation. As previously discussed, 51 percent of all LTACH facilities are owned by Kindred Healthcare and Select Medical.

## Factors Impacting the Selection of Multiples

### Comparability of the Subject to the Comparables

There are fundamental differences between small to midsize privately held companies and publicly traded companies. These differences include size, depth of management, capital structure, access to capital, geographic diversification, and risk. In addition, external microeconomic and macroeconomic events cause fluctuations in the price of public stock prices that can distort multiples. Therefore, public company multiples do not necessarily reflect comparable market multiples for any single LTACH. It should be noted that there is a question in the profession as to how guideline public company multiples should be applied to reflect a control or minority level of value.

Size and growth prospects should also be considered when reviewing transaction multiples as implied valuation multiples for large multi-site LTACH operators are typically significantly higher than multiples paid for a single location.

### Barriers to Entry

As previously discussed, there is a moratorium currently in place for the development of new LTACHs or addition of new beds. As a result, barriers to entry are extremely high in the marketplace.

### Level of Value

The valuation analyst should always consider if the subject interest being valued represents a minority or controlling interest when selecting market multiples. When utilizing transaction multiples, the analyst should always ensure that the level of value acquired in the guideline transactions matches the level of value of the subject interest. As previously discussed, LTACHs are typically valued to calculate relative equity contributions to a potential joint ventures or for outright acquisition (both scenarios usually being performed under an enterprise or controlling level of value).

### Other Considerations

The valuation analyst should take into consideration certain key factors in the application of the Market Approach. Examples include, but are not limited to, the following:

- LTACHs with commercial reimbursement materially different from market;
- LTACHs with a disproportionate share of Medicaid, self-pay, and charity care;
- LTACHs with high capital-expenditure requirements; and
- LTACHs that lease the facility versus own the real estate. Regarding the latter, market multiples will tend to be lower, because the facility lease expense does not impact EBITDA.

## Cost Approach

The Cost Approach, also known as the asset or build-up approach, is a method that attempts to value a business by identifying and valuing each tangible and intangible asset. This approach is primarily used for

LTACHs not generating sufficient cash flows to make its operations more valuable than the underlying value of the assets. The Cost Approach provides a "floor," or lowest minimum value, related to an interest in an LTACH and may be appropriate when the Market and Income Approaches produce lower values.

The Cost Approach typically includes tangible assets and may include identifiable intangible assets. In the context of a business valuation, tangible assets include net working capital, personal property, and equipment. Intangible assets may include things such as the LTACH's trade name or, in applicable locales, licensure such as a certificate of need. Please refer to chapter 4 for further discussion of the Cost Approach in the context of a business valuation.

Please note that even though the tangible and intangible assets are not separately valued under the Income and Market Approaches, these approaches consider the cash flows generated by all assets of the business and provide an FMV indication of the business enterprise, which includes all normalized tangible and intangible assets needed to operate the business.

# *Part Three:*
## *Compensation Agreement Valuations*

# Overview and Agreement Types 16

*Jen Johnson, CFA*

---

*Understanding the agreement terms and services should be the first step in valuing any type of compensation arrangement.*

---

The healthcare industry has experienced significant growth in the number and types of physician integration strategies, as well as contractual arrangements with physicians and physician-owned entities. Obvious reasons, such as declining reimbursement, expensive information technology, and anticipation of new reimbursement methods based on quality and cost savings, are prompting physicians and hospitals to consider new arrangements to work together. Some of these strategies have existed for years, such as medical directorships and direct employment, while others are relatively new, such as compensating physicians for quality outcomes.

Regardless of the arrangement type, when healthcare executives contemplate entering into an agreement, ensur-

**169**

ing the arrangement is commercially reasonable (CR) and consistent with fair market value (FMV) is highly recommended. Aspects of what should be considered when determining if an arrangement is CR are addressed in chapter 2. As previously noted, the CR standard should be met, and ideally documented, prior to going through the process of ensuring the compensation is set at FMV. Once CR is established, the FMV process and documentation should begin.

## Valuation Approach

Similar to business valuations, when determining if an arrangement is FMV, the valuation should consider the Cost, Market, and Income Approaches. Although these approaches appear different when assessing compensation arrangements, and are sometimes irrelevant, the valuation analysis should be comprehensive and consider these valuation fundamentals when determining FMV. Formal definitions for these approaches are provided in chapter 4 to provide a better understanding of the financial theory perspective. The following provides a high-level explanation related to how these approaches are considered in the context of a compensation arrangement.

The Cost Approach typically assesses the cost to hire and train staff, or the cost to buy the services, and may include a reasonable market-based return. The Market Approach considers similar fees for comparable services, and ideally relies upon non-referral relationships in considering comparable market fees. The Income Approach quantifies the earning stream from the arrangement and is often inappropriate when valuing a compensation arrangement.

There are numerous types of agreements and regulatory considerations surrounding compensation agreements. Therefore, the three standard approaches to value (Cost, Market, and Income) cannot be generally addressed and applied to all types of arrangements as they would in a business valuation but should be addressed in the unique context of each arrangement. Therefore, each compensation agreement chapter addresses standard approaches to value for that type of agreement.

## Agreement Types

As the industry moves from fee-for-service to pay-for-performance (P4P), new arrangements continue to evolve. Today, both traditional and evolving payment models coexist. The most traditional compensation arrangements include payment for clinical services, medical directorships, and call coverage. Recently, there have been more arrangements utilizing physicians in leadership positions, as well as general management. Lastly, at the forefront of today's compensation arrangement environment, P4P models are rapidly evolving. Also known as alternative payment models, these are arrangements that engage physicians to assist in improving quality and lower costs.

When assessing the value of any compensation arrangement, understanding the terms outlined in the contractual agreement is critical. Ultimately, the valuation should outline the agreement terms since the terms provide important information related to the value of the services. Many contractual agreements include various services. As an example, one agreement could include clinical services, a medical directorship, and a payment for quality. In these arrangements, the valuation should value each of the services separately, as each may require a different valuation approach and data.

It is important to understand that different services require different valuation approaches. Therefore, the following chapters are organized by type of service. Each chapter first provides an overview of the type of service and common fee structures seen in the market. Subsequently, in order to help executives understand what drives compensation, each chapter then outlines valuation drivers of compensation. Lastly, relevant approaches to value and key questions when reviewing an FMV analysis are listed.

# Clinical Services 17

*Jonathan Helm, CVA*

*Compensation practices for employed physicians are shifting to match the current reimbursement landscape. Greater portions of a physician's clinical compensation will be determined based on value or positive patient outcomes versus volume of care.*

Physicians perform a broad range of clinical services, including office visits, surgical procedures, and a variety of diagnostic and therapeutic services that all play a critical role in the delivery of healthcare in the United States. These services are furnished in all healthcare settings, including physicians' offices, hospitals, ambulatory surgery centers, skilled nursing facilities, hospices, outpatient dialysis facilities, clinical laboratories, and other post-acute care settings.

Reimbursement for clinical services has traditionally been provided on a fee-for-service basis. However, this structure is evolving and with the passage of the Medicare

**173**

Access and CHIP Reauthorization Act of 2015 (MACRA), participating providers will be paid based on the quality and effectiveness of the care they provide. This means that a (growing) percentage of physician reimbursement will be based on value rather than volume of services.

Clinical services have been traditionally provided by physicians operating in independent group practices. However, there has been an increasing trend away from independent practice toward direct employment and/or exclusive independent contractor arrangements with hospitals and health systems. The *Merritt Hawkins' 2014 Review of Physician and Advanced Practitioner Recruiting Incentives* proclaims the high percentage of physicians seeking employment is being driven by "a growing reluctance among physicians to assume the financial risks and administrative responsibilities of private practice ownership in today's problematic medical practice environment." Additionally, younger physicians are progressively more focused on work-life balance and less concerned with the autonomy of operating an independent practice.[1]

Additionally, according to *The Complexities of Physician Supply and Demand: Projections from 2013 to 2025,* prepared by IHS, Inc., for the Association of American Medical Colleges (AAMC), demand for physician services is projected to grow substantially faster than supply. According to the AAMC study, in 2025 the United States is projected to face a shortage of physicians in the range of 46,100 to 90,400 across all specialties. The growing shortage of physicians has further incentivized hospitals to explore integration opportunities with physicians.

Ultimately, the aforementioned considerations have contributed to the employment of approximately 63 percent of practicing physicians, according to the *2015 Medscape Physician Compensation Report.*

As hospitals and health systems continue to explore integration opportunities with physicians for their clinical services, identifying compensation amounts and ongoing payment structures that are consistent with fair market value (FMV) remains critical.

---

1. Jeffrey Bendix, *Millennials in Medicine*, MEDICAL ECONOMICS (November, 2015), *available at* http://medicaleconomics.modernmedicine.com/medical-economics/news/millennials-medicine?page=0,0.

## *Clinical Services Fee Structures*

Physician compensation models over the past decade have shifted from flat salary structures to predominantly production-based models. Aligning the incentives of physician employees and the hospital/employer was the overarching goal of these models. With reimbursement models now shifting away from fee-for-service toward value-based structures, many compensation models are again evolving to take into consideration clinical quality and patient access to care. According to the Sullivan Cotter & Associates *2015 Physician Compensation and Productivity Survey Report*, approximately 70 percent of primary care respondents and 64 percent of surgical specialist respondents reported compensation structures based on productivity measures that accounted for 57 percent and 51 percent of total compensation, respectively. Approximately 54 percent of primary care respondents and 42 percent of surgical specialists used quality incentives as a determinant of compensation representing 8 percent and 9 percent of total compensation, respectively. Although this chapter describes structures that include quality incentives, a discussion of assessing an FMV related to quality payments to physicians is included in chapter 24.

Regardless of whether the provider is classified as an employee or an independent contractor, the fundamental valuation approaches used to assess clinical compensation remain constant. The difference between the two classifications from a valuation perspective is the accounting for reasonable and applicable expenses. In employment situations, the employer generally covers the costs of all expenses incurred by the provider. In an independent contractor structure, the contracting physician often bears responsibility for some or all of the expenses required to provide the services. The most common expenses include provider benefits and malpractice insurance. However, depending on the specific arrangement, reasonable costs may also include billing/collection fees, non-provider support staff, office rent, and supplies, among numerous other items.

### Flat or Fixed-Salary Structure

This structure provides the physician with regular intervals of compensation that do not vary during the term of the agreement. It typically requires the physician to commit a certain amount of time to the services (i.e., a minimum of 40 hours per week). This structure shifts the financial risk of the arrangement to the employer.

## Variable Structure

This structure provides the physician with compensation that is solely tied to individual performance with no guaranteed compensation. Productivity metrics commonly used in this structure include personally performed work relative value units (RVUs), professional collections, and/or hours worked. This structure shifts much of the financial risk of the arrangement to the physician.

## Combination (Fixed and Variable) Structure

The combination structure provides the physician with a base compensation or salary and also the opportunity to earn an incentive if certain performance goals are achieved. The two most common types of incentives include production-based incentives[2] and quality/outcomes-based incentives. An example of a production incentive would be an annual work RVU baseline target (typically aligned with the base salary[3]). For each work RVU performed above this target, the physician would receive a bonus per work RVU. An example of a quality or outcomes incentive would be a percentage of base compensation that is paid if the physician achieves improvement or superior outcomes in the selected quality metrics. It is not uncommon for physician service agreements to include both types of incentives. This structure places financial risk on both the employer and the physician.

## *Value Drivers Impacting Clinical Services Compensation*

There are a few key value drivers that may assist management with the selection of an appropriate clinical compensation amount. The following are only guidelines, as both economic and noneconomic factors, as well as the facts and circumstances surrounding an arrangement, should be considered:

---

2. Typically based on personally performed work RVUs or professional collections.

3. For example, if the base salary were set at the 25th percentile of market data, the work RVU productivity target would be set at the 25th percentile of work RVU volumes.

1. *Personally performed work RVUs*[4]*:* Currently, work RVUs are the most commonly used productivity metric for non-hospital based specialties.[5] This metric is preferred by many employers as it measures work effort by physicians in a consistent manner across specialties. However, work RVUs are payor-neutral and do not account for reimbursement/ collection levels.

2. *Personally performed professional collections:* Takes into consideration the specific payor mix of the patient population treated, as well as local reimbursement levels. However, in a situation where little control over payor mix exists, professional collections alone may understate the work effort of a physician.

3. *Community need/supply and demand:* Understanding the supply and demand of physicians in a particular market is an important factor in determining compensation. In markets with significant shortages and unsuccessful recruitment efforts, compensation levels necessary to obtain services may be higher than normal.

4. *Hours worked in position:* Depending on the nature of the position, hours worked can be an important factor for determining compensation. This is most often the case with shift-based specialties, such as hospitalists, emergency medicine, and nocturnists.

5. *Historical and forecasted net earnings*: For independent physicians, compensation levels may be driven by practice economics and not by market survey data. As such, a physician's historical and/or projected compensation levels can be important data points in determining reasonable clinical compensation. If the physician is operating his/her practice in a manner that is more efficient than the market (as defined in the market surveys), physician net earnings will demonstrate this fact. However, it is important to exclude nonbusiness and nonrecurring expenses from the earnings stream, as well as any income not related to services provided under the prospective service agreement.

---

4. It is important to note that for the specialty of anesthesiology, American Society of Anesthesiologists (ASA) units are used in place of work RVUs.

5. Per the Sullivan Cotter & Associates *2015 Physician Compensation and Productivity Survey Report* (table 3.2).

6. *Payor mix:* The mix assists with understanding the patient population treated by the physician, as well as explaining variances in physician collections information relative to published data.

7. *Patient panel size:* Reflects the number of patients assigned to a physician to manage on a consistent basis. Due to the increased focus on patient access to clinical care by qualified practitioners, there is an increasing trend to consider patient panel size and management as factors in determining clinical compensation rates.

8. *Other productivity metrics:* Other productivity metrics that are less frequently considered include total RVUs, patient encounters/visits, and professional gross charges; however, there are valuation drawbacks to these metrics.

In addition to the above factors, other services such as medical directorships, on-call coverage, and quality may be included within the clinical compensation arrangement. Specific discussions on each of these components are included in separate chapters.

## Key Considerations in Assessing Clinical Services Compensation FMV Opinions

Although the analysis of clinical services compensation may consider the Market, Cost, and Income Approaches, the Market Approach is most commonly utilized. It considers published survey data and the underlying productivity levels of the physician. As an example, if a physician's work RVUs and professional collections approximate the 75th percentile of market survey data, the Market Approach would select a compensation rate consistent with the 75th percentile. An additional application of the Market Approach may consider the selection of a published compensation rate per work RVU or compensation to professional collections ratio applied to the productivity levels of the physician. Typically, the median reported ratios are selected. Use of an above-median ratio may lead to a misalignment of total compensation and total productivity.

There are a number of available compensation surveys in the market. It is important that valuations rely upon multiple surveys when available based on regulatory guidance. In addition, selecting surveys that provide data associated with both total compensation and productivity data (work RVUs and professional collections) is important for benchmarking.

Under the Cost Approach, the compensation related costs to obtain the services of a physician are considered. Compensation data may be obtained from physician recruiters or from published recruitment surveys. This approach is commonly utilized when a physician is relocating to the local market and no historical productivity or financial information is available.

Under the Income Approach, the net earnings of a physician's practice, after normalization for nonrecurring/nonbusiness expenses and reduction for cost of capital,[6] are considered. With the application of this approach, it is important to ensure that the prospective services match the services associated with the net earnings of the physician. For example, if a physician historically generated compensation from outside consulting services and will continue to generate this income outside of the prospective arrangement, then this compensation should be excluded from the practice's net earnings.

The development of an Income Approach may be challenging in a situation where the physician is already employed by a hospital or health system. Depending on the structure of the group practice, it may be necessary to significantly adjust the employed physician's income statement to account for reasonable expense allocations and the exclusion of hospital-specific expenses/allocations.

The following is a list of questions to help clarify if an FMV analysis considered appropriate factors:

- **Have the clinical compensation services been clearly defined and do they match the services being addressed in the valuation?** It is imperative that the valuation analysis clearly identify the services being provided and ensure that they match the corresponding services agreement. For example, does the valuation assume a full-time surgeon working 40 hours per week, while the services agreement specifically addresses a part-time family practitioner working 20 hours per week?

---

6. The cost of capital reflects the return on investment the owner of the practice should be paid for the outlay of required capital/resources (i.e., net working capital, fixed assets, etc.) to operate the practice.

- **Have appropriate adjustments been made to reflect the physician's contractual arrangement?** Additional compensation for benefits, malpractice insurance, and other costs may need to be included if the subject physician operates as an independent contractor. Similarly, a reduction in fees may be warranted if the physician is retaining professional collections.
- **Have multiple, objective market surveys been considered as part of the analysis?** The valuation should rely on multiple, objective sources of market survey data. If only one survey is utilized, it is important that the valuation provide sufficient reasoning to explain the departure from use of multiple surveys.
- **Does the valuation rely heavily on any market data that could be tainted with referral relationships?** The valuation analysis should not rely heavily on data that could be perceived as tainted from a referral relationship perspective. For example, the compensation rate paid by a competing hospital in the same market should not constitute the sole basis for FMV within the valuation report. Other credible and objective methods/approaches should be considered and relied upon.
- **Does the selected specialty within the survey data match the required specialty under the agreement?** The survey data used in the valuation should match the specialty of services required under the arrangement.
- **Does the underlying productivity information match the survey data to which it has been applied?** It is common for survey data to be misapplied. Some examples of common errors and misapplications are as follows:
  o Productivity data (i.e., work RVUs and professional collections) is not 100 percent personally performed and includes productivity from other physicians or advanced-practice clinicians (APCs). This error would overstate the productivity and resultant compensation for the physician.
  o Work RVUs have not been adjusted for the impact of modifiers. This error would overstate the work RVU counts and the resultant compensation for the physician.
  o Productivity metrics are compared to the incorrect benchmark. Common examples include:

— total RVUs are incorrectly compared to/benchmarked against work RVUs or vice versa.

— total collections are incorrectly compared to/ benchmarked against professional collections or vice versa.

- **Does total clinical compensation reasonably align with total productivity?** Since a majority of clinical compensation is derived from productivity-based services, the total compensation determined should reasonably align with total productivity. For example, if the physician's work RVUs and professional collections are at the 90th percentile, total compensation (for clinical services) should reasonably be in line with the 90th percentile of market data.

- **If net physician earnings are considered (Income Approach), have they been adjusted to account for outside services or nonrecurring/nonbusiness related expenses?** If the clinical services valuation is based fully or in part on physician net earnings (historical or forecasted), those earnings must match the prospective services to be provided. Compensation related to services outside of the arrangement should be excluded from the net earnings indication. Additionally, the net earnings indication should be normalized to account for nonbusiness/non-recurring expenses and an adjustment for cost of capital.[7]

- **For arrangements with additional services beyond clinical, have the stacked set of services and compensation been considered?** If additional services are being stacked on top of the clinical services, it is imperative that the valuation take into consideration all services. Additional services may include on-call coverage, medical directorships, and quality incentives. The valuation should address whether any adjustments to the underlying clinical survey data are warranted and whether the total bundle of services can be reasonably performed by the physician (i.e., are there enough hours in the week to fulfill all service obligations?).

---

7. The cost of capital reflects the return on investment the owner of the practice should be paid for the outlay of required capital/resources (i.e., net working capital, fixed assets, etc.) to operate the practice.

# Medical Directorships and Physician Executives

18

*Jonathan Helm, CVA*

---

*As hospitals and health systems move from volume-based reimbursement models to value-based models, there is a growing need to engage and utilize the expertise of qualified physicians in administrative and leadership roles.*

---

Physicians are moving into a variety of administrative positions in hospitals and hospital-affiliated organizations, such as health maintenance organizations, independent practice associations, management service organizations, and physician service organizations. Although commonly referred to as medical directorships,[1] these arrangements may include a wide range of physician administrative services, such as traditional medical directorships, physician executive services (such as chief medical officers, chief medical

---

1. For purposes of this chapter, the terms "medical director" and "medical directorship" are intended to include all physician administrative positions and arrangements.

informatics officers, etc.), and/or department chairs/chiefs, among others. For the purposes of this chapter, the term physician executive will encompass the majority of physician executive roles, inclusive of medical directors.

There has been significant growth in the number of physicians serving in administrative and leadership roles as evidenced by the American Association for Physician Leadership (AAPL),[2] whose membership has grown to more than 11,000 since its inception.[3] According to the AAPL, factors driving the growth in the positions include:[4]

- The shift from a volume-based to a value-based reimbursement system.
- The public health-oriented focus on the management of populations toward wellness.
- The fundamental redesign of clinical care models in several settings.
- The financial payment models that have begun rewarding healthcare organizations for clinical excellence and coordinated care at reduced cost.
- The emerging shared risk, capitation, and bundled payment strategies.

Physician executives can be a source of independent clinical expertise. Because they can interpret raw clinical data, medical directors can be especially useful to hospitals and health systems. Quality and efficiency metrics often require careful interpretation by medical professionals. Physician executives can turn the data into meaningful information. In addition, physician executives must be familiar with various local, regional, and national regulatory and accreditation requirements pertaining to the organization's clinical, research, and educational programs. Finally, physician executives can provide leadership

---

2. Formerly known as the American College of Physician Executives.

3. Press release (August 2015), *Survey Finds Support for the Affordable Care Act Among Physician Leaders, available at* http://www.physicianleaders.org/news/press-releases/2015/08/03/value-of-physician-leaders-press-release.

4. P. Angood, *The Value of Physician Leadership,* 2014, American Association for Physician Leadership, *available at* http://www3.acpe.org:8082/docs/default-source/pej-archives-2014/the-value-of-physician-leadership.pdf?sfvrsn=8.

to the structure and function of the clinical enterprise. According to the AAPL, matured physician leadership will be essential for healthcare to continue moving toward higher quality, consistent safety, stream-lined efficiency, and becoming value-based.[5]

As hospitals and health systems continue to engage physician executives, identifying compensation amounts and ongoing payment structures that are consistent with fair market value (FMV) remains critical.

## Physician Executive Services Fee Structures

Due to the administrative nature of the services provided in physician executive arrangements, the corresponding compensation models are typically straightforward and related to time spent in the position. These services are often provided through independent contractor arrangements, but can also be provided as part of an employment arrangement. In employment situations, the employer generally covers the costs of provider benefits and malpractice insurance. In an independent contractor structure, the contracting physician often bears responsibility for some or all of these costs. The following describes commonly observed compensation structures:

### Fixed-Fee Structure (Stipend)

This structure provides the physician with regular intervals of compensation that do not vary during the term of the agreement. It typically requires the physician to commit a certain amount of time to the services (i.e., a minimum of 20 hours per month). Although the valuation will typically be based on an hourly rate analysis, assumed minimum hours are applied to derive a stipend. Under this structure, the physician may work additional hours beyond the minimum required and receive no additional compensation.

### Variable Structure (Hourly)

This structure provides the physician with compensation that is tied solely to hours worked in the specific position. It ties compensation specifically to hours worked and it is common for these structures to

---

5. *Id.*

have a maximum number of hours for which the physician will be compensated.

## Value Drivers Impacting Medical Directorship Services Compensation

There are a few key value drivers that may assist management with the selection of an appropriate medical directorship compensation amount. The following are only guidelines, as both economic and noneconomic factors, as well as the facts and circumstances surrounding an arrangement, should be considered:

1. *Qualifications:* Due to the non-clinical nature of physician executive services, there are no productivity benchmarks to which performance can be compared. As such, understanding the qualifications of the physician and documenting these factors within the valuation report become important tasks of the valuation professional. Factors to be considered may include degrees, certifications, awards, recognitions, years of clinical experience, articles published, and presentations made, among others.

2. *Similar previous experience:* In addition to general qualifications, prior experience in a similar role provides value as the physician is generally able to perform the specific duties more rapidly and/or at an advanced level.

3. *Hours worked in position:* The number of hours that the physician will work in the physician executive role are critical in determining the total value of the compensation. The relationship is linear—the greater the number of hours worked, the greater the total annual compensation that can be supported within the valuation. However, it is important that the organization engaging the physician document why the paid hours are reasonably necessary for the organization.

4. *Required specialty*: It is imperative that the valuation professional identify the medical specialty required for the position. If the position requires a specific medical specialty, survey data for that specialty should be considered within the valuation.

As an example, a neurosurgeon who has 20 years of clinical experience and five years of similar previous experience could potentially demand a higher level of compensation than a neurosurgeon who has five years of clinical experience and one year of similar previous experience. Additionally, relying on survey data for the specialty of family medicine may understate compensation if the position requires a neurosurgeon.

## Key Considerations in Assessing Medical Directorship Services Compensation FMV Opinions

The analysis of physician executive compensation will rely primarily on the Market and Cost Approaches. Under the Market Approach, published compensation survey data for similar positions and services is analyzed. There are a few surveys that report compensation data for physician executive roles. The survey sources often provide general descriptions of the reported positions, which can aid the valuation professional in the selection of appropriate data. Many of the surveys report compensation on an hourly rate basis. However, certain surveys only report compensation on an annual basis and these rates must be converted to hourly rates to match the other surveys.

Once comparable market data has been selected, the specific qualifications of the physician are analyzed to derive a conclusion of value. As an example, a highly qualified and experienced physician may warrant the 75th percentile hourly rate. Depending on the structure of the arrangement, it may be necessary to convert the selected hourly rate into a fixed fee based on the number of expected hours in the position.[6]

A limitation of the Market Approach is that the underlying survey data could be tainted since many of the respondents reflect hospital-physician relationships (i.e., hospitals paying physicians).[7] The mar-

---

6. This would simply be done by multiplying the FMV hourly rate by the expected hours of service. For example, if the proposed fee structure was a flat monthly stipend, the valuation professional would multiply its hourly rate conclusion by the number of expected monthly hours of service.

7. The argument being that the respondents may be reporting compensation rates that are not at FMV due to referral relationship between the respondent parties.

ket surveys, which are independently published, still remain the most relevant and comparable source of data for these services. However, it may be prudent to consider additional sources of information when available in deriving an FMV conclusion.

Under the Cost Approach, the compensation-related costs to obtain the services of a physician are analyzed. This cost often reflects the compensation physicians would otherwise earn in the market for their clinical services.

It is important to understand that this data primarily reports compensation for clinical services rather than administrative services. Previous Stark law guidance notes that there is a difference between FMV compensation for clinical services and administrative services.[8] Furthermore, a valuation relying solely on opportunity cost data may be problematic, especially when the data reflects compensation in excess of typical administrative compensation. Additionally, the compensation reported in these surveys is stated on an annual basis and must be converted to an hourly rate. The Cost Approach findings are often used as a supplemental and corroborating method to the Market Approach.

The following is a list of questions to help clarify if an FMV analysis considered appropriate factors:

- **Have the services been clearly defined and do they match the services being addressed in the valuation?** The agreement should clearly identify the services being provided and the analysis should rely on the appropriate survey titles (CMO, medical director, committee member, etc.). In addition, the valuation analysis should utilize the same number of hours as identified in the agreement.

- **Are the medical directorship services and budgeted hours reasonable and necessary?** It is important that the operational and clinical need for the services be established by the engaging organization prior to entering into the arrangement.

- **Have appropriate adjustments been made in light of the physician's employment status?** Additional compensation for benefits and malpractice insurance may need to be included if the subject physician operates as an independent contractor.

---

8.  51012 Fed. Reg. vol. 72, no. 171 (Sept. 5, 2007).

- **Does the position require the skills/training of a physician?** If the position does not require a physician, use of physician compensation survey data would likely be inappropriate. The survey data should match the skills/training required for the position.
- **Does the position require the skills/training of a physician in a particular medical specialty?** If the position does not have a specific specialty requirement, then use of subspecialty survey data would likely be inappropriate. The survey data should match the required specialty for the services.
- **Have multiple, objective market surveys been considered as part of the analysis?** The valuation should rely on multiple, objective sources of market survey data. If only one survey is utilized, it is important that the valuation provide sufficient reasoning to explain the departure from use of multiple surveys.
- **Are the physicians required to document time and services prior to receiving payment for the services?** Requiring physicians to submit time logs in order to receive payment is best practice from a compliance perspective.

# Non-Clinical Administrative (Management and Billing Services)

## 19

*Sean Dowd and Alexandra Higgins*

---

*Having a detailed list of services in a term sheet or agreement is key for the valuation of an administrative services fee. The services provided dictate the appropriate valuation approaches employed and relevance of market comparables.*

---

For a variety of operational and financial reasons, healthcare facilities may elect to contract with another party for the provision of administrative services. These are non-clinical services required for the business function. While these general administrative services can vary widely, two of the most common arrangements involve a party assuming the management functions or billing and collection functions for a healthcare facility.

Other services arrangements may include the provision of development, marketing, consulting, and other administrative functions. Especially in cases where a healthcare facility and administrative services provider are in a position to generate referrals, it is crucial to have FMV documentation for these services. The majority of these non-clinically focused administrative services arrangements are for management or billing and collection services. In order to assess reasonable compensation for these arrangements, it is important to understand typical management and billing and collection services in the market. Once comparability of the services is confirmed, how much reliance can be put on market fee data can be assessed.

The following are generally considered typical management services:

- financial management and annual operating budgets,
- administration of accounting and purchasing functions,
- human resource management,
- information technology management,
- public relations,
- development plans of the facilities or their services,
- maintenance of all necessary licenses and regulatory compliance,
- design, institution, and supervision of the physical and administrative operations of the entity,
- preparation and submission of all cost reports, and
- negotiation and consummation of agreements and third-party contracts.

The following are generally considered typical billing and collection services:

- contract analysis and review (limited support),
- maintaining payor fee schedules,
- providing and maintaining billing information,
- charge entry,
- claims follow-up,
- claims denial analysis and reporting,
- maintaining billing and financial information,
- payment posting,
- providing monthly financial/operational reporting,

- submission of claims, and
- verification of claims per fee schedule.

Generally, three types of entities may be enlisted to provide administrative services to healthcare facilities, which are outlined below. Depending on the ownership of the company providing and receiving administrative services, various aspects should be considered to ensure compensation compliance.

## Health System-Owned Administrative Services Companies

Health systems may assume the provision of management or other administrative services since the health system already provides a host of management services on a larger scale. It is also common in joint ventures with a health system that the health system provides the managed care contracting services, since health systems often have greater negotiating power when it comes to reimbursement rates. This may help to lower office personnel costs and may create management efficiencies, allowing the providers to focus more on patient care. In the case of a health system providing administrative services, it is imperative that the organization does not charge a fee that is below FMV, as it may be seen as an inducement for referrals if charged to a physician-owned facility or other referral source.

## National Administrative Services Companies

National administrative services companies often specialize in developing, owning, and operating a particular type of healthcare facility (such as ambulatory surgery centers or imaging centers). These companies often form joint venture entities with hospitals and/or physicians, in which the administrative services company is both partial owner of the business and provider of the administrative services. Management and other administrative services fees payable to national administrative services companies are typically paid as a percent of net revenue in the market. In the case of a national administrative services company, there may not be a referral relationship. However, many joint ventures want to ensure the administrative services fee is reasonable and independent of the ownership relationship.

## Physician-Owned Administrative Services Companies

It is becoming more common with larger physician groups or a physician with a strong business background to create management or administrative services companies that specialize in management of a particular type of facility. The facility seeking administrative services can benefit from the expertise of the physician or group in that particular sector and may be able to provide efficiencies the entity may not otherwise have. In the case of a physician-owned administrative services company providing administrative services to a health system, it is important that the management company does not receive a fee above FMV.

## Administrative Services Fee Structures

### Percent of Net Revenue

It is common for typical management and billing and collection services to be stated as a percentage of facility net revenue in exchange for subject services. These services are most often performed by managerial or clerical positions and do not reflect physician required (clinical) services. However, if physicians own the entity providing the services, and are being compensated on a percent of revenue for certain services, legal counsel should consider regulatory guidance and compliance issues around this fee structure.

### Fixed Fee

In some cases, administrative services may be paid based on a predetermined monthly or annual fixed fee. While this structure may be observed for administrative services arrangements between non-referring parties, it is typically the preferred method of remuneration when determining administrative services compensation between healthcare facilities and physicians (or physician-owned administrative services companies), as a fixed fee does not vary based on facility referral volume.

## One-Time Fixed Fee

For a distinct set of administrative services to be performed within a set date, such as development services provided to aid in the construction and start-up of a healthcare facility, a one-time fixed fee is most common. This structure is most appropriate given that the administrative services are not ongoing.

# *Valuation Drivers Impacting Administrative Services Compensation*

There are a few key value drivers that may assist management with the selection of an appropriate administrative services fee. The following are only guidelines, as both economic and noneconomic factors, as well as the facts and circumstances surrounding an arrangement, should be considered.

1. **Net revenue of the facility:** Typically, higher net revenue facilities pay lower administrative services fees as a percentage of net revenue, as the administrative services provider covers its costs at a lower threshold than it would servicing a lower revenue facility. Conversely, lower net revenue facilities pay higher administrative services fees as a percentage of net revenue.

2. **Expertise of the administrative services provider:** As with any arrangement, administrative services providers with deep experience in the administration of a particular healthcare facility type warrant a premium over those with less knowledge in the effective management of similar facilities.

3. **Breadth of services:** When additional services are provided outside the scope of typical management or billing and collection services, a premium to typical fees may be warranted. Conversely, if the administrative services provider does not provide all the typical services, or if the healthcare facility retains responsibility over certain aspects of typical services, a discount should be applied to the market-based fee.

4. **Cost structure/efficiency of administrative services provider:** When administrative services providers have higher cost struc-

tures than competitors, further analysis is typically required. In the case that higher cost are vetted and warranted by additional services, more experience, or other relevant factors that benefit the subject healthcare facility, a premium to a typical market fee may be considered.

5. **Supply and demand:** In the case of a low supply of administrative services providers or high facility demand, the fee may warrant a premium. Conversely, in cases of high supply of administrative services providers or low facility demand, a discount to the fee may be warranted.

6. **Physician vs. non-physician services:** Some physician-owned administrative services companies provide clinical management or administrative services (versus typical management services). In this case, it would be more appropriate to consider physician executive, or administrative, compensation versus market-based management or administrative fees for non-physician management services. In this instance, the administrative services fee might be calculated as an annual stipend by multiplying the hourly rate (at FMV) for physician work by annual hours for clinical management/oversight. It is important to note that some physician-owned administrative services companies may provide both typical and clinical management services.

## Key Considerations in Assessing Administrative Services Compensation FMV Opinions

The analysis of administrative services fees should consider a Cost Approach and a Market Approach. The Market Approach considers similar fees for comparable services, and should primarily rely upon non-referral relationship data points in considering market-based fees. The Cost Approach is typically considered in conjunction with the Market Approach to ensure the cost of providing the services, along with a market-based return, is earned. Ideally these two approaches provide consistent indications of value.

If the services are highly comparable to those in the market and there are numerous market-based fees, the Market Approach may hold more validity and can be simpler to understand and explain. If the services are unique and there are limited or no comparable fees for the set of service, a Cost Approach may be more supportable to rely upon.

The following is a list of questions to help clarify if an FMV analysis considered appropriate factors:

1. **Have the administrative services and compensation components been clearly defined?** It is vital that the arrangement addresses what type of services are being provided, the expectations and duties of each party, and how the administrative services provider is going to be paid for providing the services.

2. **Have appropriate adjustments been made to market-based typical management, billing, and collection fees?** If the service provider is providing additional or limited services compared to "the typical basket of services," a premium or discount should be applied to fees in the analysis.

3. **Has the cost to provide the administrative services been considered?** Analyzing the administrative services company's cost to provide the administrative services is of use to both the facility and the services provider. It allows the services provider to ensure the arrangement covers its cost plus a reasonable rate of return (consistent with FMV guidelines) and allows both parties to identify any absent or additional services distinct from typical services. This step also assists the parties in ensuring there are no duplicative services.

4. **Is the fee structure appropriate for the services and/or the referral relationship?** Particularly for arrangements between referring parties or for those involving physician-owned administrative services companies, a fixed fee is typically the preferred compensation structure as its value does not vary based on referral volume. Ultimately, healthcare entities should rely on counsel for best practices regarding the structure of proposed administrative arrangements.

5. **If the administrative services are provided by a physician, do the services require a physician?** If the administrative services require a physician and, specifically, require a physician specialized in a particular specialty, specialty-specific physician compensation data should be considered in the analysis. If the administrative services do not require a physician, then the cost of replicating similar services should be based on compensation data for non-physician personnel.

# On-Call Coverage 20

*Ben Ulrich, CVA*

*The OIG has outlined burden of call factors which need to be addressed in an FMV analysis*

From a financial, operational, and quality of care perspective, on-call coverage arrangements with physicians are essential in managing any emergency department. Though this fact has held true over the years, the on-call coverage environment has substantially shifted from its roots. Physicians have been increasingly more unwilling to provide this service without being compensated for it. As such, various forms of compensated on-call coverage arrangements have emerged and the increased regulatory focus on them have made ensuring fair market value (FMV) compliance vital.

In reviewing any compensated on-call coverage arrangement or assessing any independent valuator's opinion, there are key agreement structure, burden factors, and industry guidance to consider. These considerations and factors have all formed in light of the current reimbursement and marketplace reality presented to physicians today.

**199**

Physicians historically viewed on-call coverage as a job requirement as hospitals generally required and contractually mandated that physicians participate in call rotations in exchange for admitting privileges. However, today the market and coverage environment has shifted. Uncompensated on-call coverage has become a hot-button issue of contention for many physicians. One of the primary factors impacting this trend has been the growth in the nationwide population of uninsured individuals. Approximately 3.9 million more people became uninsured between 2007 and 2012, and more than one in six of the nonelderly population are currently uninsured.[1] Therefore, as the likelihood of providing care and not being able to collect professional fees is higher, more physicians are expecting to be compensated for providing the service.

The increasing demand and projected shortage in supply of physicians available to provide coverage has also contributed to the rise in on-call pay. According to the Association of American Medical Colleges, there could be a shortage of up to 130,000 physicians in the United States within the next 15 years.[2] Compounding the impact of this trend, recently it has also become more commonplace for tenured physicians to negotiate on-call opt-out clauses. With the need for coverage increasing and available physician supply being threatened, the pressure and demand for call coverage pay has intensified.

Other contributing factors include higher malpractice claim risk in emergency departments, physician quality of life considerations, and the relative time and expense incurred by physicians in providing coverage. For these reasons, health systems in many instances have been forced to compensate physicians in order to obtain adequate coverage.

## Compensated Call Coverage Fee Structures

The Sullivan, Cotter and Associates (SCA) *2014 Physician On-Call Pay Survey Report* states that 95 percent of the survey respondents

1. The Kaiser Commission on Medicaid and the Uninsured. "The Uninsured A Primer" October 2013, *available at* http://kaiserfamilyfoundation.files. wordpress.com/2013/10/7451-09-the-uninsured-a-primer-key-facts-about-health-insurance.pdf.

2. The Association of American Medical Colleges. "Physician Shortages to Worsen Without Increases in Residency Training," *available at* https://www. aamc.org/download/153160/data/physician_shortages_to_worsen_without_ increases_in_residency_tr.pdfl.

currently provide some method of compensation to nonemployed physicians for providing on-call coverage. Supporting this trend, SCA statistics show overall expenditures for call payments have been increasing exponentially since 2008. There are a variety of on-call payment models in the marketplace. Some common compensated call coverage models include:

## Unrestricted On-Call Coverage

A physician is compensated for being available within an emergent response time window to respond in-person to the contracting facility. These agreements are typically structured through a 24-hour or per-shift coverage rate. Commonly referred to as providing unrestricted call coverage or paying for the "burden of the beeper," these arrangements typically require a 30- to 45-minute in-person response time.

## Activation Fee Payments

A physician is paid per "activation" or emergent response into the facility. This can be in lieu of or in conjunction with a daily availability payment.

## Reimbursement Guarantees

This involves guaranteeing professional fees for providing care to uninsured patients or poor payors. Typically these are flat fees or guaranteed rates based on the Medicare Physician Fee Schedule. Guaranteeing professional fees is a means of shifting the payor mix risk from the physician to the contracting entity. This is typically seen in coverage arrangements involving a poorer payor mix.

## Excess Coverage Payments

This would typically be in the context of an employed arrangement although the terminology could be applied to contractors as well. The physician would have a required amount of coverage days each month that they would cover uncompensated and any coverage days beyond the requirement would be paid for excess services.

## WRVU-Based Payments

In certain PSA or employment arrangements with payment rates based on rates per work relative value unit (WRVU) performed, payment for call coverage services can be structured as a WRVU credit towards the individual compensation structure.

## Backup or Concurrent Coverage

In arrangements with a high likelihood of numerous emergent response, hospitals may contract with physicians to be on-call as a backup should the primary physician on-call already be in surgery or with a patient. Similarly, some physicians or practices are contracted to concurrently cover multiple facilities or sites in a given shift. Backup coverage is often a requirement in these situations to ensure consistent coverage is provided.

## Third-Party Locums Coverage

Generally this is a short-term last resort option where the hospital or contracting entity would keep the professional billings but would compensate third-party staffing companies at premium rates for coverage.

## Restricted On-Call Coverage

A physician is paid and required to be physically on-site at the facility should an emergent need occur (generally within a five-minute window). These arrangements are generally required in circumstances of acute need for immediate patient care. It is important to note the valuation method for restricted coverage is different from the methods outlined in this chapter. When data is available, the "hospital coverage valuation approach," as outlined in chapter 22 is preferred.

All of the above on-call payment models could be viable options for obtaining emergent coverage. Health systems utilize one or many different on-call models based on the employed physician mix, average emergent patient volumes, and budgetary considerations.

## *Valuation Drivers Impacting On-Call Compensation*

There have been Office of Inspector General (OIG) opinions addressing compensation for on-call coverage. As a result, it is extremely pertinent that the regulatory guidance noting what should be considered when assessing payments for on-call coverage be addressed in a valuation analysis. Specifically, the burden of call coverage and risk to the physician are the primary value drivers impacting the amount of on-call pay. The following are only guidelines, as both economic and noneconomic factors, as well as the facts and circumstances surrounding an arrangement, should be considered.

1. the physician's ability to collect or receive any guaranteed compensation,
2. the physician's relative payor mix risk,
3. the volume of expected emergent and telephonic responses,
4. average patient contact time,
5. procedure acuity and trauma designation, and
6. availability of other physicians within the particular specialty.

As an example, the higher the percentage of uninsured patients covered by the hospital, the less likely a physician will be able to collect professional fees when called into the facility. Therefore, this would increase the burden of providing these services on the physician. As such, the burden of call would be higher. As another example, in situations where the physician is receiving guaranteed reimbursement when called-in emergently, the hospital is incurring the risk of the uninsured payor mix and, thus, the burden of call would be lower.

## Key Considerations in Assessing On-Call Arrangement FMV Opinions

The analysis of on-call coverage should primarily rely upon the Cost Approach, or beeper rate. This analysis is meant to reflect the burden of call as described above. The Cost Approach applies a percentage to normal compensation for the physician in a particular specialty to be on-call, or "carry a beeper." This is common practice for nurse compensation. When on-call, they may receive $40 per hour for providing services during standard hours at a hospital, but paid $5 per hour to carry a beeper overnight, same concept. This is the preferred valuation approach among the valuation industry although on-call market compensation surveys do exist.

There are national on-call compensation surveys available in the market. Though having a range of compensation rates per specialty for on-call coverage can be helpful, the surveys include very little data related to the specific facts and circumstances of its respondents and provide no information related to the burden of call. Specifically, the reported rates for each specialty reflect a mix of employed and contractor respondents with various levels of reimbursement risk. Additionally, the volume of emergent responses, payor mix, case acuity, and physician supply and demand are not detailed in the surveys. Also, it could be argued that on-call survey data is tainted in that it reflects solely hospital-to-physician relationships. As the compensation rates include data from parties in a position to refer patient volume, many question whether the surveys can even be considered in a valuation. Given these factors, it is not recommended to rely solely on market on-call survey data.

The following is a list of questions to help clarify if an FMV analysis considered appropriate factors:

- **Have the call coverage services and compensation components been clearly defined?** It is vital that the arrangement addresses what type of coverage is being provided (i.e., restricted vs. unrestricted), what the coverage parameters are (including response time requirements), and how the physician is going to be paid for providing the service.

- **Is it clear which party to the agreement has the payor mix/ reimbursement risk?** The payment rate to the physician for providing coverage should appropriately account for the relative reimbursement risk being incurred.

- **Has the burden of coverage been documented in direct support of the call coverage payment?** Factors including payor mix risk, response volume, and the supply and demand of available physicians should be considered in deriving an appropriate call coverage rate.

- **In employment arrangements, have the stacked set of services and compensation been supported as FMV?** Employment is frequently a means of acquiring call coverage and commonly there is a requirement that a certain number of uncompensated days (consistent with staff bylaws or other physicians within that specialty) be provided prior to being paid for coverage. Specifically, some employed arrangements have established compensation based on an assumed call coverage schedule. Understand the agreement terms, medical staff bylaws, and the value of each service to ensure support for the aggregate payment to an employed physician.

# Telemedicine 21

Mary Fan, CVA, and Ben Ulrich, CVA

*In compensating physicians for telemedicine services considerations should include the relative potential reimbursement from third-party payors and patients associated with the service, along with the response burden incurred by the physicians in providing the coverage.*

Telemedicine is a key component amidst the healthcare industry's shift to value-based care. It provides a mutually beneficial relationship amongst healthcare providers, patients, and payors as a way to achieve the triple aim: reduce costs, improve patient satisfaction, and improve the health of populations. As different types of telemedicine arrangements constantly evolve in a highly fragmented reimbursement setting, the need to ensure they are consistent with regulatory guidance and fair market value (FMV) is challenging.

In general, telemedicine can be utilized through various modalities of care, primarily online, on site, or on a technologically compatible portable device (e.g., phone or tablet). Specifically, it can be classified as real time (synchronous telemedicine), store-and-forward (asynchronous telemedicine), or remote monitoring.[1] Synchronous telemedicine requires real-time communication amongst all parties, most often via videoconferencing, whereas asynchronous telemedicine involves the gathering and transmission of medical data, such as sending an image to a medical practitioner for interpretation. Remote monitoring consists of an external monitoring center for healthcare providers to monitor a patient remotely. Note that all of the aforementioned service are often used interchangeably with "telehealth," which represents the broader umbrella under which telemedicine resides.

The key benefits of telemedicine revolve around convenience, innovation, and efficacy. From healthcare providers' point of view, they are able to expand their patient reach and generate additional revenue with more flexibility and without incurring significant brick and mortar expenses. From patients' perspectives, traditional barriers, such as mobility, distance, and time constraints are less of a concern. The focus is on consumer choice, whereby patients can select their own healthcare practice, provider, and pharmacy. And for employers, telemedicine can help reduce the overall healthcare insurance costs, as well as work absenteeism.

A shortage of physicians and the growing consumer demand for more affordable and accessible care have helped fuel the growth of telemedicine. As of January 2016, more than half of all hospitals in the United States utilized some form of telemedicine.[2] REACH Health's *2015 U.S. Telemedicine Industry Benchmark Survey* indicates the telemedicine industry is quickly maturing, with nearly 60 percent of its respondents noting telemedicine as one of their top priorities in

---

1. "Telehealth Modalities," Center for Connected Health Policy: The National Telehealth Policy Resource Center, 2015, *available at* http://cchpca.org/what-is-telehealth.

2. "How Typical is Telemedicine?" American Telemedicine Association, 2016, *available at* http://www.americantelemed.org/about-telemedicine/faqs#.VpcRFLN7L8.

3. "Telemedicine in 2016: Consumerized and more highly utilized," BECKER'S HEALTH IT & CIO REVIEW, December 2015, *available at* http://www.beckershospitalreview.com/healthcare-information-technology/telemedicine-in-2016-consumerized-and-more-highly-utilized.html.

both high- and lower-acuity settings.[3] Nonetheless, a number of issues pose a challenge for telemedicine to function on a national platform, including those related to state licensing and credentialing, standard of care, technology, and, most notably, reimbursement.

## Telemedicine Compensation Structures

In reviewing any type of telemedicine arrangement, fundamental considerations include the parties involved, agreement structure, coverage burden factors, and industry guidance. It is important to understand the evolution of various payment models for telemedicine to continue to grow and, with new structures, there will be new FMV considerations. Currently, the most commonly observed telemedicine arrangements in the marketplace take place between the following parties (the list is not exhaustive):

### Independent Companies/Vendors and Physicians

For physicians who independently contract with independent telemedicine companies (e.g., Teladoc, American Well, MDLIVE), the general compensation structure is on a per-visit, per-member, or periodic flat-fee basis. These physicians typically treat this as a part-time job to generate additional revenue, with the flexibility of providing consultations on their own time.

### Between Facility and Healthcare Provider

For contractual arrangements between a hospital and a provider, the provider can either be employed or an independent contractor. If the provider is employed, the telemedicine service may be uncompensated either because it is part of the hospital's on-call provisions or it has been incorporated into the provider's employment agreement. Alternatively, the hospital may offer an internal payment model reimbursing the provider in a manner consistent with his or her existing compensation structure, such as paying a certain amount of work RVUs per telemedicine visit or consultation performed.

When the provider/provider group is acting as an independent contractor, the compensation structures may vary with consideration to expected consultation volume. If expected volume is low or uncertain (e.g., a pilot telemedicine program), a per-use/click or hourly fee may be preferred. However, oftentimes providers will request an availability fee, either daily or on a per-shift basis similar to traditional ED unrestricted call coverage, to guarantee the coverage required by the facility. Combinations of different payment structures have also been observed, such as guaranteeing the provider a certain number of consults per day equivalent to an availability payment, and then including a per consult payment for any consult in excess of contractually agreed upon number of consults.

## Between Hub Facility and Spoke Facility/Facilities

This involves a central hospital that is generally located in an urban area ("hub facility") providing services to one or more facilities either located in a rural area or in an urban setting lacking coverage in a particular specialty ("spoke facility"). The hub facility generally contracts with providers for coverage and is willing to sell this coverage out to spoke facilities in need of the service via telemedicine.

The hub facility generally will either charge or pass through the cost of the incremental physician coverage cost to the spoke facility. In some instances, the hub facility may lease the equipment or connectivity service to the spoke facilities as well, which are generally passed through at a marked-up rate to the spoke.

## Between Facility/Health System and Vendor (Enterprise-Level Arrangements)

Similar to an independent arrangement, independent telemedicine companies that possess the resources of software, infrastructure, and providers seek partnerships with stand-alone hospitals or large health systems to reach a broad client base. For the health systems, it may be an attractive option since all the services are provided: a virtual platform and consumer portal already prepared, with the potential of having independent providers as well to fill in as-needed gaps for their own physicians to ensure 24/7 coverage.

A bundle of services is typically included under these types of arrangements, including, but not limited to, one-time integration fees, annual software licenses, training and credentialing-related fees, and provider fees. For any telemedicine compensation model, it is not uncommon for implementation and/or management fees to be incorporated into telemedicine agreements. The costs of establishing and managing a pilot/new telemedicine program or service line can come as a one-time or monthly ongoing fee. Although a material start-up cost can be expected for the health systems, the general focus with these arrangements is to reduce costs and utilization. In addition to providing convenient visits and expanding the geographic reach, the systems are also able to control costs (e.g., ED visits) that can otherwise be avoided through the use of telemedicine.

With a multitude of feasible physician compensation and service options in obtaining telemedicine coverage, different valuation metrics and approaches must be considered in determining an appropriate payment for telemedicine services.

## *Valuation Drivers Impacting Telemedicine Compensation*

When valuing any type of physician coverage agreement, it is important that the availability burden on the physician be appropriately considered in addition to the value of the services rendered. Due to the virtual nature and continual access associated with telemedicine, a physician generally must be available to respond within a predefined time frame to any telemedicine request. The following are only guidelines, as both economic and noneconomic factors, as well as the facts and circumstances surrounding an arrangement, should be considered.

1. reimbursement risk (a provider's ability to collect or receive any guaranteed compensation);
2. consult volume (average number of telephonic and emergent telemedicine responses over the course of a week or month);
3. patient contact time (average time spent per telemedicine consultation);
4. response time requirement (stipulated/average response time per telemedicine consultation);
5. patient acuity (severity level of average patient according to a national standard in the subject specialty); and
6. existence of software, equipment, and/or technology platform.

For instance, a longer patient contact time on average would increase the availability burden due to more time spent per patient or consultation. In addition, due to the fragmented reimbursement setting, in many markets it may be difficult for either party to bill or retain professional collections for telemedicine services rendered from patients or third-party governmental/commercial payors.

## Key Considerations in Assessing Telemedicine Arrangements or FMV Opinions

A Cost and Market Approach can be applied to valuing telemedicine coverage arrangements. The Market Approach could consider time spent on a consult and/or the burden of being on-call. The Cost Approach would refer to market reimbursement for similar services. The following is a list of questions to help clarify if an FMV analysis considered appropriate factors:

- **Have the telemedicine coverage services and compensation components been clearly defined?** Ensure specialty (e.g., telestroke vs. teleneurology), provider type (e.g., physician vs. social worker), and compensation structure (e.g., per visit vs. per consult) of actual services being provided are appropriately reflected in the analysis. There may also be an equipment component related to software and connectivity usage.
- **Who has the right to bill and retain for telemedicine services performed?** Depending on which party is able to bill and collect (if any) and/or whether the provider receives guaranteed compensation, the reimbursement risk is a key factor of the analysis.
- **Have appropriate adjustments been made in light of the provider's professional status and/or infrastructure?** A telemedicine vendor cost premium may be warranted if the provider brings national recognition, a platform, and/or expertise to the subject program or service line.
- **Has the burden of coverage been documented in direct support of the telemedicine payment?** Factors including payor mix risk, volume, constant time, response time, and patient acuity should be considered in determining an appropriate availability burden. It is important to clarify the provider's available hours as stipulated under the agreement (e.g., if daily availability equals 12 or 24 hours).

# Hospital-Based Coverage (Subsidy) 22

*Ben Ulrich, CVA, Mary Fan, CVA, and Mallorie Holguin*

---

*The provider expense is generally the primary expense and should be analyzed to ensure reasonability based on the contracted coverage hours and expected productivity.*

---

Hospital-based coverage agreements stem from hospitals needing a supply of qualified provider's readily available to meet the patient demand within particular specialties. The idea is that the hospital is outsourcing the physician requirements to service the hospital versus employing, and that the professional collections earned by the physician services do not cover the market cost for those physician services. Many provider services may be included, such as clinical, medical directorships, and call coverage. These arrangements are sometimes referred to as "subsidies" when the hospital provides financial support to cover expenses exceeding professional collections, or "collections guarantee" when the professional collections guarantees and estimated expenses are reconciled.

Essentially, hospital-based coverage arrangements are typically formed to fill a gap in physician supply, improve patients' access to a specific specialty, and/or comply with the Emergency Medical Treament and Labor Act (EMTALA) and hospital bylaw guidelines. EMTALA was enacted to mitigate "patient dumping," or the refusal to treat patients due to insufficient insurance or inability to pay. Under EMTALA, a hospital is required to provide services that are routinely available, regardless of the probability that those services will generate revenue. In light of these considerations, hospital-based providers are unique in that they are less in control of volume, coverage, and payor mix. Referred to as coverage agreements, collections guarantees, and subsidies, these arrangements allow hospitals to compensate physicians for their time and availability, as well as other items, such as poor payor mix or unused capacity. Given the varying nature of these arrangements due to differences in payment structure, reimbursement patterns, and aggregate cost structure of the contracted practice, they should be evaluated closely to ensure the main driving factors align closely with the agreement.

These types of arrangements involving hospital-based specialties, such as anesthesiology, hospitalist, and emergency medicine typically consist of a hospital granting a practice group exclusive coverage of a specific service line in exchange for financial assistance. Hospitalist programs are key to ensuring the treatment of unassigned patients and continuity of patient care while improving quality.[1] They tend to branch out to further specialization among hospitalists, such as after-hours care (nocturnists), obstetrics (laborists), and neurology (neurohospitalist). For some specialties this may allow physicians of the same specialty to focus on more specialized services while tasking the hospitalist with pre- and post-treatment care.

Given that the financial viability of the groups providing this coverage depends fully on the payor mix of the hospital, many practices need financial assistance to help bridge the gap between actual

---

1. *6 Trends and Observations on Healthcare Transactions in 2011*, Becker's Hospital Review, August 2011, *available at* http://www.beckershospitalreview. com/hospital-transactions-and-valuation/6-trends-and-observations-on-healthcare-transactions-in-2011.html.

2. *Understanding Hospital-based Coverage Contracts*, Physicians Practice, September 2014, *available at* http://www.physicianspractice.com/blog/understanding-hospital-based-coverage-contracts.

professional collections and the costs to provide the coverage.[2] Since such agreements are frequently structured in advance around the group's estimated or actual productivity, it is imperative that the compensation being paid accurately reflects the services being provided and is set at fair market value (FMV).

## Compensation Structures

These arrangements may be formed directly through professional services agreements (PSAs) with an individual independent physician, or at the group level through larger service agreements whereby a comprehensive set of services is provided. Under such arrangements, services may consist of clinical, administrative, and/or on-call coverage. Financial assistance provided by a hospital to a practice group is typically structured in the form of a collections guarantee or a coverage amount (subsidy). This section will compare these two types of compensation structures in terms of how they vary.

## Collections Guarantee

This is a professional collections guarantee model, whereby the hospital makes up the difference if actual collections fall short of the predefined costs incurred by the provider(s) in servicing the arrangement. Under this arrangement, the providers would bill and collect for professional services rendered, and report those collections to the hospital. In turn, the hospital would cover the shortfall based on actual collections compared to the predetermined estimated costs.

## Coverage Agreement (Subsidy)

Similar to a collections guarantee in services and concept, the contractual amount is determined in advance by calculating the difference between estimated professional collections and operating expenses. Both parties are assuming financial risk that collections and expenses may be greater or less than expected.[3]

---

3. *Contracting with Hospital-Based Physician Groups*, Healthcare Financial Management Association–Georgia Chapter, *available at* http://www.georgiahfma.org/HFMAMembers/SharedFiles/Wednesday_ContractingWithHospitalBased PhysicianGroups.pdf.

Under either type of arrangement, periodic documentation and review of the group's volume, operating expenses, and payor mix are crucial in maintaining an FMV arrangement.

## Valuation Drivers Impacting Hospital Coverage Compensation

In determining the FMV of compensation payable to the providers, it is important that the following factors be appropriately considered: volume, production, and costs. The following are only guidelines, as both economic and noneconomic factors, as well as the facts and circumstances surrounding an arrangement, should be considered.

1. *Revenue*—Professional revenue retained by the practice is a key value driver in subsidy arrangements. Understanding the expected professional reimbursement generated by the service line is important and must be considered when deriving an FMV fee for a coverage arrangement.

2. *Volume*—This can be assessed through procedural volume and/ or based on the group's coverage schedule. There are a number of production metrics that can be utilized in the FMV process, namely professional collections, work RVUs (WRVUs) or ASA units, and sometimes patient encounter volume. Coverage hours is also a key driving factor of compensation since the group's coverage availability directly impacts required provider hours. For instance, covering 24-hour shifts versus 12-hour shifts would require fewer annual provider hours and therefore lower costs.

3. *Compensation of providers*—Provider compensation should be properly aligned with coverage hours and expected production. Specifically, the full-time equivalent (FTE) status of each provider should be carefully considered in order to appropriately reflect the contracted coverage. In deriving the cost build-up, actual salary data (if available) or market salary data based on national surveys could be utilized. Benefit, malpractice insurance, and continuing medical education expenses should also be considered as part of the aggregate costs if the

hospital is contracting with an independent contractor group that is responsible for these costs.

4. *Operating expenses*—If additional costs directly benefit the hospital and are incurred by the providers, they may be considered in the FMV analysis. These costs may include, but are not limited to, support staff, billing and collection, and management costs.

## Key Considerations in Assessing Hospital-Based Coverage Arrangements

The typical approach to value a hospital based coverage agreement is "the cost to recreate the services." Therefore, the valuation should provide a build-up of the costs the hospital would incur if it elected to employ and manage the services. The following is a list of questions to help clarify if an FMV analysis considered appropriate factors.

- **Have the revenues associated with the arrangement been accurately represented?** Historical professional collections are typically relied upon to begin the forecast. If this information is not available, expected figures may be deduced from productivity estimates and market data. This is one of the most integral and complex components and an important part of the analysis.
- **Have the coverage services been clearly defined?** This includes outlining the specialty, services, and coverage schedule (on-call or on-site) associated with the arrangement. The number and type of providers (e.g., 1.0 FTE physician and 2.0 FTE NPs) should also be clearly identified.
- **Have the operating expenses been appropriately identified and deemed to be reasonable?** A review and approval by both parties (when possible) to the agreement of any operating expenses to ensure the expenses are for the sole benefit of the hospital-based services is key.
- **Is the provider compensation set at FMV?** Confirming that salaries are consistent with the market utilizing multiple surveys is an important step in any compensation valuation.

# Professional Interpretation/ Read Fees

# 23

*Ben Ulrich, CVA, and James Tekippe*

*Professional fee arrangements should establish fees based on the relative case/ scan mix at the site of service in relation to how governmental and non-governmental payors are reimbursing for similar services.*

The billing and collecting process for healthcare services typically occurs in one of two ways: as two bills, with a distinct professional and technical component for a certain procedure, or as a global bill, which combines professional and technical components into a single reimbursement rate. This practice of having only one billing party can create several benefits, including simplicity for the patient, who will receive only one bill, but it can create confusion between the parties who must then properly allocate revenue amongst one another. When multiple parties are involved in the performance of certain medical procedures, and the bill is global, the question of how to appropriately allocate reimbursement arises. Al-

**217**

though these issues can become complex, understanding a few key points surrounding the process of split billing can help ensure that compensation agreements are consistent with fair market value (FMV).

For each possible medical procedure performed by a healthcare provider, CMS has established a five-digit identifier known as a current procedural terminology (CPT)® code. CPT codes provide the basis by which healthcare facilities bill and collect from Medicare, Medicaid, and third-party payors for the performance of medical services. The physician consultation and/or the interpretation of a procedure result is considered the professional component, as it represents reimbursement for the physician's time and expertise. The technical fee component represents reimbursement for the provision of equipment, supplies, and additional non-provider support necessary for the physician to perform the professional services. When performing a split bill, billing personnel will add the professional modifier, 26, or the technical modifier, TC, to the specific CPT code to indicate that separate parties have performed each component (Dolby). Note that the economics of the arrangement, site or location where the service is rendered, or relationship of the parties may prevent a split bill from being possible.

When a CPT code is billed globally, the billing party receives the entire payment as reimbursement for procedures performed. Common specialties affected by the need for split bills include radiology, radiation oncology, and pathology. Within these specialties, imaging services utilizing MRIs, CT scans, and ultrasounds comprise the majority of services requiring split bills (Dolby). This discussion will focus particularly on radiology imaging services in order to illustrate the major questions related to splitting professional and technical reimbursement that has been originally billed globally.

## Compensation Structures

### Split Bill Payments

In this scenario, each party is separately responsible for billing and collecting for that party's portion of the medical procedure performed. The agreement between the parties should clearly denote that each party is separately responsible for billing and collecting.

### Global Bill Payments

In this scenario, there is one bill for both the professional and technical component, and professional reimbursement is typically paid by the facility and stated as either a percentage of total collections or paid as a flat fee per procedure.

## *Valuation Drivers Impacting Professional Interpretation Compensation*

When reviewing professional and technical split arrangements to be paid on a fee as a percentage of collections (or per-procedure payment), it is critical to understand the expected services to be provided. In addition, when determining the FMV of compensation for the professional fee, the procedure mix and payor mix need to be considered. The following are only guidelines, as both economic and noneconomic factors, as well as the facts and circumstances surrounding an arrangement, should be considered.

1. *Procedure mix*—The relative mix of each procedure within the context of the greater business is necessary in determining an appropriate aggregate percentage payment. For example, radiology imaging services can range from CT scans to fluoroscopy procedures to ultrasound imaging. These various procedures can have vastly different expected reimbursement as well as professional and technical splits of an overall global reimbursement when viewed on a percentage basis.

2. *Payor mix*—In addition to understanding the expected procedure mix, it is also necessary to consider the expected payor mix. For example, CMS has spearheaded a reduction in the technical portion payment for many imaging services, resulting in the professional component comprising a larger percentage of the total global payment for many CPT procedures. However, in some markets it has been observed that commercial payors have been slower to adopt these price reductions, resulting in lower professional fee payments as a percentage of total collections when compared to Medicare. Thus, the relative mix between governmental and commercial payors should

be a consideration when determining whether the proposed professional payment is consistent with FMV.

3. *Specialty and time required*—A valuation approach to professional fee reimbursement may also consider what it would cost to compensate a physician based on the required specialty and time spent on the service.

## Key Considerations in Assessing Professional Interpretation Compensation

The following is a list of questions to help clarify if an FMV analysis considered appropriate factors:

- **Was the payor mix and procedure mix considered?** Payor mix and procedure mix both directly impact the appropriate professional fee and should be outlined in the FMV assessment.
- **Which party is billing and collecting?** It is important to understand which party bills and collects in order to properly allocate any meaningful costs associated with billing and collecting between the parties.
- **Is the physician group supervising and interpreting the scans?** For certain imaging procedures, CMS groups both the supervision of the procedure and the subsequent interpretation of the results of that supervised procedure under a single CPT code. This policy can result in two healthcare providers performing a portion of one professional component, adding an additional layer of complexity. Understanding the supervision requirements for a specific CPT code and keeping proper documentation of the parties and the performed services will help to mitigate any problems that may arise in the billing and collecting process and will help to ensure that compensation is appropriate.

## Conclusion

As the Affordable Care Act (ACA) continues to change the healthcare landscape, the focus on cost reduction and value-based care has become paramount for the Centers for Medicare and Medicaid Services

(CMS) and many third-party payors. According to a Neiman Policy Institute study, since its peak in 2006, annual spending on diagnostic imaging procedures dropped 21 percent by 2010 (Duszak). In addition, David Levin, MD, radiology professor at Jefferson Medical College and Thomas Jefferson University Hospital, has indicated that this reduction trend has not been reversed since the publishing of the Neiman study. Levin states that, "There's no question that reimbursement is going down when you look at Medicare dollars paid for noninvasive diagnostic imaging" (Howell). As the market continues to be reshaped, maintaining an understanding of the basic concepts of split billing and the necessary considerations when reviewing these agreements will be crucial for ensuring that compensation remains within the bounds of FMV.

*Sources*
1. Dolby, Ruth. "Learn When to Bill for the Professional or Technical Component." *HeathLeaders News*, Sept. 9, 2007.
2. Duszak, Richard. "Medical Imaging: Is the Growth Boom Over?" *Harvey L. Neiman Health Policy Institute* (2012). Available at http://www.acr.org/~/media/ACR/Documents/PDF/Research/Brief%2001/PolicyBriefHPI092012.pdf.
3. Howell, Whitney. "Imaging Utilization Trends and Reimbursement," *Diagnostic Imaging*, July 24, 2014.
4. Kauffman, Lena. "Radiology Managers Fight Private Payor Adoption of MPPR," *Diagnostic Imaging*, Jan. 1, 2016.

# Pay for Performance (Quality and Cost Savings)

# 24

*Alexandra Higgins*

*P4P compensation varies widely in services and fee structures. It is important to consider the financial risk and responsibility of the parties prior to determining how to allocate these payments.*

Due to the changing reimbursement environment in healthcare, both hospitals and physicians are seeking to align with each other in preparation for the transition from fee-for-service to value-based purchasing. Due to the need for integration and potentially high infrastructure costs, hospitals and physicians must work together to improve quality and cost savings for specific service lines, cases, or even across the entire continuum of care.

Since the early 2000s, there have been numerous governmental and third-party payor programs that have paid for quality and cost savings. The following are just a few examples of pay-for-performance (P4P) programs implemented by CMS to measure quality and cost savings and reward both hospitals and physicians for their efforts in achieving the goals in each program. For the healthcare executive, an understanding of governmental-approved programs serves as a solid foundation for reviewing P4P compensation agreements.

## Hospital Quality Incentive Demonstration Project

The Premier Hospital Quality Incentive Demonstration (HQID) recognized and provided financial rewards to hospitals that demonstrated high-quality performance in a number of acute care areas by increasing their payment for Medicare patients. The program began in 2003 and extended to 2009. During the six-year duration of the program, CMS awarded incentive payments of more than $60 million to participating hospitals.[1]

## Medicare Gainsharing Demonstration Project

The Medicare Gainsharing Demonstration was implemented to evaluate arrangements between hospitals and physicians whereby inpatient hospital resources were monitored for efficient use while focusing on quality and efficiency of care. The program began in 2008 and ended in 2011, with two hospitals as its participants. By the end of the program, approximately $750,000 in incentive payments were paid to the physician participants at the two hospitals. It is important to note that there where quality thresholds that were required in order to receive the gainsharing payments and that the gainsharing payments to the physicians were capped at 25 percent of the physician's affiliate Part B reimbursements.[2]

1. The Centers for Medicare and Medicaid Services. "Premier Hospital Quality Incentive Demonstration: Rewarding Superior Quality Care," December 2011, *available at* https://www.cms.gov/Medicare/Quality-Initiatives-Patient-Assessment-Instruments/HospitalQualityInits/Downloads/HospitalPremierPressRelease-FactSheet.pdf.

2. The Centers for Medicare and Medicaid Services. "Medicare Gainsharing Demonstration: Report to Congress on Quality Improvement and Savings," March 2011, *available at* https://innovation.cms.gov/Files/reports/DRA5007-Report-to-Congress.pdf.

## Medicare Shared Savings Program

The Medicare Shared Savings Program rewards accountable care organizations (ACOs) that lower their growth in healthcare costs while meeting performance standards on quality of care and putting patients first. In late 2011, CMS finalized new rules under the Affordable Care Act to help providers better coordinate care for Medicare patients through an ACO. [76 *Federal Register* (November 2, 2011), page 67802: "This final rule implements section 3022 of the Affordable Care Act which contains provisions relating to Medicare payments to providers of services and suppliers participating in Accountable Care Organizations (ACOs) under the Medicare Shared Savings Program. Under these provisions, providers of services and suppliers can continue to receive traditional Medicare fee-for-service (FFS) payments under Parts A and B, and be eligible for additional payments if they meet specified quality and savings requirements."][3]

## Bundled Payments for Care Improvement Initiative

The Bundled Payments for Care Improvement Initiative was designed by CMS to address fragmented care and reduce multiple payments to individual care providers for a single patient across an episode of care. In doing so, the program requires hospital and providers to coordinate care while lowering costs and improving quality of care. If these goals are achieved, Medicare may share achieved savings with the hospital and physicians.[4] It is important to note that the incentive opportunities to physician participants are capped at 150 percent of the Medicare Physician Fee Schedule.[5]

---

3. "Medicare 'Accountable Care Organizations' Shared Savings Program - New Section 1899 of Title XVIII, Preliminary Questions & Answers," the Centers for Medicare and Medicaid Services, *available at* https://www.aace.com/files/cmspremlimqa.pdf.

4. "Bundled Payments for Care Improvement Initiative (BPCI) Fact Sheet," August 2015, the Centers for Medicare and Medicaid Services, *available at* https://www.cms.gov/Newsroom/MediaReleaseDatabase/Fact-sheets/2015-Fact-sheets-items/2015-08-13-2.html.

5. "Bundled Payments for Care Improvement: Overview and Basic Parameters," March 2014, CMS Center for Medicare and Medicaid Innovation, *available at* https://innovation.cms.gov/Files/slides/BPCI-Overview2-4.pdf.

In addition to the governmental P4P programs previously described, commercial payors are engaging with hospitals and physicians in similar programs. In many cases, these programs are awarding additional reimbursement for superior performance related to both quality and cost metrics.

In response to the aforementioned programs, hospitals and physicians have developed several types of P4P programs, each with different service components, objectives, and payment structures. The more frequently observed types of P4P programs include co-management arrangements (most often focused on quality improvement, but may include cost savings for a specific hospital service line); gainsharing (focused on savings on a specific supply or device); shared savings (focused on quality and cost savings for a specific patient population across the entire continuum of care); bundled payments (focused on quality and cost savings for a specific episode of care); and hospital efficiency improvement programs (focused on the achievement of cost savings by improving specific quality indicators).

# Pay-for-Performance Compensation Models and Fee Structures

The following outlines five basic P4P payment models. There are currently variations in the market on each of these structures and new models will continue to evolve.

## Quality Payments

A fixed fee or percentage of compensation tied to quality has been observed in almost every type of physician arrangement, including clinical, administrative, and call-coverage arrangements.

## Co-Management

This model most commonly comprises two payment components: a fixed fee and a variable fee. The fixed fee is typically based on administrative services, such as committee meetings and/or time spent on the development of protocols and care pathways. This fixed fee may be stated as an hourly rate or a fixed annual stipend. The variable fee is based on performance related to predetermined quality metrics (and sometimes cost savings). Typically, there is payment for meeting target thresholds, as well as a stretch goal.

## Gainsharing

This model compensates physicians for their efforts in assisting a hospital to save money on a specific supply or initiative through product standardization or reduced waste. The payment is calculated based on historical cost and actual reduced cost. There are typically provisions in the agreement that prohibit reduction in patient care and quality, as well as other requirements that must be met (such as a third-party administrator monitor the programs).

## Shared Savings

This model is similar to gainsharing in that incentive payments are earned based on achieved savings. In this model, however, savings are typically related to a specific patient population and there is a focus on the continuum of care across all providers, including the hospital, primary care physicians, and specialists. The payment structure in this model is most often a flow of funds due to the fact that estimating or projecting savings for a patient population may be challenging. The various components of the flow of funds may include the amount of which the hospital should retain to recover infrastructure costs, the amount of savings the hospital should be paid for its efforts in achieving savings, and the amount of savings the physicians should be paid for their efforts in achieving savings. There is typically a minimum quality threshold that must be met for payments to be made to the physicians.

## Bundled Payments

This model allows for savings to be shared between a hospital and physicians for a specific episode of care, such as a knee replacement, from the onset of care to post-acute care. The payment model is typically an allocation of savings amongst the various participants based on effort. There is normally a quality threshold that must be met for payments to be made to the physicians.

## Hospital Efficiency Improvement Programs

This model typically includes most or all of the medical staff in an effort to generate internal cost savings for a hospital. Quality initiatives requiring coordination among many providers, and with material financial implications, such as sepsis treatment are common. The resulting compensation model aims to financially incentivize each of the providers driving the savings for their coordination and achievement of higher quality care.

Hospitals may choose to implement any of these payment models as an integration strategy with physicians to prepare for upcoming changes to reimbursement. Depending on the complexity of the hospital's infrastructure and needs of the patient population, one or all of these models may be beneficial.

## Value Drivers Impacting Pay-for-Performance Payments

When compensating physicians for quality outcomes or achieved cost savings, there are myriad factors and value drivers to consider. Some of these factors are related to the program itself, while others involve the market.

1.  *Funding source of P4P program*—It is important to understand whether the program is funded through a contract with a third-party payor or through a program that is self-funded by the hospital. If the program is funded by a third-party payor, then the hospital may have more latitude to share these additional dollars with the physicians based on their efforts, as the economics are there to support the payments. If the payments are self-funded by a hospital, then the hospital should determine if the payments are both fair market value (FMV) and reasonable from an economics perspective.
2.  *Market data on P4P*—How the market is compensating hospitals and physicians in similar P4P programs is critical to understanding FMV for P4P programs. For example, payments to hospitals warrant a different range of fees in the market than payments to physicians. Similarly, the types of quality metrics for hospital P4P programs may be different from practice-based P4P programs. Having a solid understanding of the market and payments must be considered.
3.  *Professional compensation risk*—If the participating physicians are at risk for professional reimbursement, either considered

independent contractors or, if employed, their professional compensation is based on productivity (i.e., $/work relative value unit model, as opposed to a fixed/guaranteed salary), support for quality payments may be greater.

4. *Quality metric strength*—When paying for quality, there are a number of value drivers to consider in determining a reasonable maximum quality incentive amount. Key value drivers may include, but are not limited to:

   a. *Physician responsibility*—The degree the physicians (versus the hospital's staff) are responsible for impacting the selected metrics.

   b. *Metric type*—The portion of the metrics that are outcomes-based (i.e., clinical outcomes, patient satisfaction, and/or efficiency metrics) versus process metrics (i.e., adherence/compliance to protocols, etc.).

   c. *Metric source*—The portion of the metrics that are nationally measured/supported by credible medical evidence (compared to metrics that were established internally or created to meet a hospital-specific objective).

   d. *Performance threshold for payout*—The portion of the metrics that require measurable superior performance (i.e., national/industry top decile performance).

   e. *Number of metrics*—Substantial number of meaningful metrics.

   f. *Likelihood of achieving maximum payout*—The portion of the metrics that are maintenance goals (i.e., metrics in which historical performance already meets a payout performance threshold benchmark) compared to hard-to-achieve goals.

## Key Considerations in Assessing P4P Compensation

The following is a list of questions to help clarify if an FMV analysis considered appropriate factors.

- **Have the services and compensation components been clearly defined?** It is first necessary to understand the services being provided under a P4P arrangement. Each service should be valued separately. The valuation should clearly tie to the services and the compensation structure in the agreement. For example, if the agreement encompasses hourly services and outcomes payments, there should likely be two valuation sections.

• **Who is responsible for the service and for driving the quality outcomes/cost savings?** There should be a clear understanding of who is providing each service and how responsible each party is for driving the quality outcomes/cost savings metrics. This should be considered in the valuation and may have a material impact on the value of the P4P payments.

• **Who is responsible for infrastructure or any other administrative resources?** If the hospital bears the cost of infrastructure or administrative services that facilitate the earning of the P4P payments, then these costs may need to be considered prior to payments to the physicians.

• **Have the economics of the service line or program been considered?** In self-funded programs, there may be circumstances where the FMV payments may be higher than what can be supported by the economics of the service line. From a commercial reasonableness perspective, the hospital may need to cap the payment so it is financially reasonable, or the hospital may need to justify why it is necessary to make the payments based on community need.

• **Has the compensation been considered on a per physician basis (cap)?** Although there is no bright line, it may be prudent in some circumstances to consider caps on payments to physicians for quality and cost savings. This is a safety measure to help ensure that payments do not appear excessive on a per-physician basis. In addition, governmental programs have utilized caps on payments to physicians in certain programs.

• **Are the physicians required to document time and services prior to receiving payment for administrative services associated with quality and cost initiatives?** P4P programs requiring physicians to submit time logs in order to receive administrative services payment is best practice from a compliance perspective.

# Life Sciences Physician Compensation

# 25

*Jen Johnson, CFA, and Kevin McDonough, CFA*

---

*The Sunshine Provision has brought physician payments to the forefront of regulatory scrutiny.*

---

Life sciences generally comprises the diverse yet related sub-industries of pharmaceuticals, biotechnology, medical devices, and medical technology. Today, there is an increasing number of academic medical centers working within the life sciences industry and its regulatory framework. Similar to many of the relationships within the healthcare industry, there exists a referral relationship between healthcare providers (HCPs) and life sciences companies. HCP is a standard term used and is often interchangeable with physician, but may also include advanced practitioners. HCP is the most commonly used term within the industry.

HCPs are in a unique position to both contribute value to the life sciences industry through advisory, consulting, and development services, as well as to contribute directly on the consumer side through the prescription of pharmaceuticals and the procurement and use of medical devices and other bio and medical technology. While such compliance risk is not novel to life sciences, the industry is increasingly facing new scrutiny and requirements as it relates to transparency. On March 23, 2010, President Obama signed the Patient Protection and Affordable Care Act (PPACA). Included within the PPACA are provisions promulgating the Physicians Payment Sunshine Act (Sunshine Act), with a goal of containing healthcare costs and increasing the transparency of relationships between HCPs and drug and device manufacturers. The Centers for Medicare and Medicaid Services (CMS) published the Sunshine Act Final Rule on February 1, 2013. The primary goal of the Sunshine Act is to increase transparency by making information about certain payments to physicians and academic medical centers available on a public, searchable website. These compensation arrangements may include payments to HCPs who provide advisory, consulting, development or clinical services, all of which must be set at fair market value (FMV).

In short, life sciences companies seek out the valuable expertise of HCPs, who are able to advance certain business goals by providing a myriad of consulting services. The business and economic relationships between life sciences companies and HCPs can potentially result in over-utilization of a product and/or in kickbacks paid to a HCP. As a result, the government has determined that compensation for HCP consulting services provided to life sciences companies must be set at FMV.

The advisory and consulting services provided by HCPs to life sciences companies come in different forms. Typical advisory and consulting services include:

- *research services*—review of or participation in clinical trials;
- *product education services*—speaking to HCP assemblies regarding a company's product;
- *business advisory services*—serving on a company advisory board or aiding in a company's strategic business planning;
- *development services*—leading or participating on a team involved with novel product development; and
- *conveyance of intellectual property (IP)*—participation on a development team may involve the transfer of intellectual property. Such a conveyance may warrant a unique compensation method, such as royalty fees.

# *Life Sciences Compensation Models and Fee Structures*

## Hourly Rate Structure

Most agreements are part-time in nature and therefore compensation is set based on an hourly rate. Many companies have tiered hourly rates based on various specialties, experience, skillset, and notoriety, as well as the expertise required per the agreement's services.

## Per Procedure

When the services are clinical in nature, HCPs may be compensated based on a certain procedure and associated fee schedule.

## Royalty Fee

In some cases, HCPs are instrumental to developing a product, drug, or device and may be eligible for royalty payments associated with the HCP's contribution to intellectual property. These arrangements are less common.

# *Value Drivers Impacting Life Sciences Payments*

1. *Market reimbursement*—If the services are clinical in nature, Medicare and commercial reimbursement for similar work should be considered as an indication of value.
2. *Expertise required*—If the services require a thought leader in a particular specialty, more experience is required and a higher hourly rate may be supported.
3. *Recognition*—HCPs with national versus local recognition could warrant a higher rate, assuming the services require a top-tier HCP.
4. *Time*—Since most agreements are based on hours worked, the more time, the higher the fee. It is important to note that travel time is not typically paid at the same hourly rate as services requiring the HCP's expertise.

## Key Considerations in Assessing Life Sciences Compensation

Multiple market data points, including surveys and outside research, should be considered when determining payments to HCPs. In addition, the following questions are closely tied to the FMV requirement and should be asked when reviewing a life sciences consulting arrangement:

- **Is there a legitimate need for the services, expertise, *and* number of HCPs engaged?** Essential to meet the commercially reasonable (CR) standard, these questions are common compliance concerns for these types of arrangements.
- **Is the HCP able to bill and collect for procedural work while earning the hourly rate or fee?** It is important that there is no double payment for the same hour of service.
- **Is there documentation that the services were actually provided?** Time logs demonstrate best practice and the services performed should tie to the agreement terms.
- **Is there appropriate documentation of the HCP's IP contribution?** If a royalty rate is stipulated, strong documentation related to the HCP's contribution is critical, and there is robust legal guidance on what constitutes IP.

# Part Four:
## Real Estate and Capital Asset Valuations

# Real Estate 26

*Victor H. McConnell, MAI, and John S. Trabold, MAI*

---

*Understanding true market comparables is important when determining the FMV for various types of healthcare facilities; a medical office building is very different from a radiation therapy center.*

---

Real estate appraisal has become increasingly important in the context of healthcare. This is in part due to the increased scrutiny associated with transactions, as well as physicians' growing involvement with investing in real estate. These transactions, whether a lease or a sale, require the same valuation due diligence as any other healthcare arrangement. Similar to a business valuation, it is critical to understand that the burden of establishing that the arrangement is commercially reasonable (CR) and established at fair market value (FMV) is the responsibility of the parties involved in the transaction. In addition, timeshare arrangements (further addressed in chapter 28) warrant a real estate valuation as part of adhering to FMV guidance.

## *Key Valuation Considerations*

In order to determine FMV for real estate, the area market must be analyzed, with consideration given to the demographic, economic, governmental, and environmental forces that have a direct or indirect influence on the property. A site visit is generally necessary in order to accurately assess the condition and overall quality of a property relative to its competitors. A site visit should also include thorough visual observation of the market area, and any proximately located competitive buildings. Public records, applicable zoning laws, and availability of utilities and other city services should also be evaluated.

After a space or property has been accurately and thoroughly identified, the appropriate date of value must be determined. The effective date of value should consider the condition of the premises as of that date and should clearly state if the value (or rent rate) relies upon any assumptions concerning completion of tenant improvements, renovations, or additions. If an existing lease is going to be renegotiated as a sublease, or if a new lease is to be signed, then the appraisal date should be current.

The Uniform Standards of Professional Appraisal Practice (USPAP) indicates that "current appraisal assignments are based on the effective date of the appraisal being contemporaneous with the date of the report."[1] However, appraisers may be requested to perform a retrospective analysis. In these instances, the appraiser should analyze the market conditions that existed on the effective date of the appraisal. The market conditions should reflect the physical condition of the improvements as of that specific date. Similarly, a date in the future may be appropriate in the case of prospective analyses involving proposed construction.

It is important to note that the specific locational adjustment cannot consider proximity to the referral source. However, in certain instances, such as the evaluation of on-campus medical office space versus off-campus medical office space, the appraiser must evaluate whether an adjustment is merited due to nonreferral-related amenities (including superior parking and amenities). When a building is located on campus, it is also essential that the appraiser adequately

---

1. USPAP 2016-2017 edition, the Appraisal Foundation, page 275.

evaluates the host hospital; depending on the health of the host hospital, a skybridge could be an amenity in one case (the contributory value of which could be reflected on a return-on-cost basis to the medical office building to which it connects) and a nonfactor in another case due to functional or economic obsolescence. Accordingly, while no carte blanche adjustment for on- or off-campus can be made, a careful analysis of each particular on-campus location should be made to determine if a rent rate premium exists.

After the application of a detailed adjustment process, the sales or rent indicators must be reconciled into a range (or single indication) of fair market value or fair market rent. As part of the real estate valuation process, similar to business valuation, there are three generally accepted real estate appraisal techniques used to determine value, which are referred to as: the Cost Approach, the Sales Comparison Approach (Market Approach), and the Income Capitalization Approach. While the three approaches to value are independent, they are in many ways interrelated.

## Cost Approach

The Cost Approach is based upon the proposition that the informed purchaser would pay no more than the cost of producing a substitute property with the same utility as the subject property. The Cost Approach is particularly applicable when the property being appraised involves relatively new improvements that represent the highest and best use of the land or when relatively unique or specialized improvements are located on the site and for which there exists no comparable properties in the marketplace. The Cost Approach can also be useful in allocating component values (between real property, personal property, and intangibles) within a transaction. In the healthcare setting, it is essential that the valuation professional has a thorough understanding of the unique construction components inherent to many specialized health facilities. Additionally, the valuation professional must have a thorough understanding of reimbursement trends within each given healthcare sector, as shifts in reimbursement can sometimes substantially impact real estate values.

## Sales Comparison Approach

The Sales Comparison Approach is based upon the principal that an informed purchaser would pay no more for a property than the cost of acquiring an existing property with the same utility. This approach is applicable when an active market provides sufficient quantities of reliable data that can be verified with authoritative sources. The Sales Comparison Approach is less reliable in an inactive market or in estimating the value of properties for which no real comparable sales data is available.

Market comparables utilized must be adjusted for elements of comparison, such as real property rights conveyed; financing terms; conditions of sale (lease); expenditures made after purchase (lease); market conditions (time); location; and physical characteristics (such as age/condition, finish out, building components, square-foot-to-bed ratio, and others). Paramount is an understanding of the term comparability. The data analyzed should represent properties that are similar physically and in terms of location. Any differences should be adjusted for in accordance with generally accepted appraisal practices.

## Income Approach

The Income Approach is a procedure in appraisal analysis that converts the anticipated benefits (dollar income or amenities) to be derived from the ownership of property into a value estimate. The Income Approach is widely applied in appraising income-producing properties. In this approach, an estimate of potential income for the subject property is first projected. From this amount, deductions are made for typically incurred costs involved with ownership of the property, resulting in a net operating income estimate. An appropriate capitalization rate is then applied to the net operating income to derive an indication of value.

# *Fair Market Value Rent/Lease Payments*

In the determination of FMV for a rental agreement, FMV (rent) is generally synonymous with market rent. A generally accepted definition of market rent is: "The most probable rent that a property should bring in a competitive and open market reflecting the conditions and restrictions of a specific lease agreement, including the rental adjustment and revaluation, permitted uses, use restrictions, expense obligations, term, concessions, renewal and purchase options, and tenant improvements (TIs)."[2]

Similar to the previous discussion, there are generally three approaches for estimating a FMV (rent). One of these approaches, a return-on-depreciated-cost analysis, consists of performing a Cost Approach analysis and then estimating a market-derived return of and on the subject's depreciated improvement cost and land value using a capital return methodology. This methodology is often applied on de novo real estate projects (new construction) and specialized healthcare properties. Return-on-cost rates fluctuate over time in the market, with changes in perceived risk dependent on factors such as current cost of capital; property type; location; and tenant credit associated with the proposed build-to-suit lease. A review of survey data, recent projects, and interviews with developers active in the market is critical to accurately model current return-on-cost rates.

Another method, called a market rent comparables approach, consists of analyzing the rental rates of actual leases and/or listings of comparable healthcare facilities. This method mimics the aforementioned Sales Comparison Approach to value. This method is the most common method of determining FMV (rent) for typical medical office space, though it can sometimes be less applicable to certain specialized medical properties.

A rental rate can also be developed through an analysis of a property's financial operations. This method is a variation of the Income Approach in that historical normalized financial statements are reviewed and analyzed. Earnings before interest, taxes, depreciation, amortization, and rent (EBITDAR) are estimated, and a rent coverage ratio that indicates how much rent can be supported by the financial operation is selected. This method of analysis is often applied in the analysis of healthcare space involved in higher levels of acuity.

The seemingly simple step of identifying the property to be valued can be quite problematic in some instances. Stark law states that the lease must clearly specify the premises. For instance, a lease of space within a hospital must appropriately account for common areas

---

2. THE DICTIONARY OF REAL ESTATE APPRAISAL, 6th ed., the Appraisal Institute, page 140.

and other nonexclusive portions of the host building that are used by the tenant. An accurate measurement of the tenant's space, the host building, and the common areas is essential. These measurements are typically performed in accordance with Building Owner and Management Association standards and are provided to the third-party appraiser who is providing the FMV opinion.

Parties involved in lease negotiations need to understand the various elements of lease terms and their effect on FMV, as well as other basic elements of appraisal theory for a lease or sale arrangement associated with real estate. For instance, a landlord who is a provider cannot provide abated or below market rent, or above market tenant improvements. Other elements of a lease transaction that should be supported by market evidence include escalations, renewal terms, tenant improvements concessions, and expense structure. Use of a third-party opinion can ensure that each element of a lease negotiation is within market parameters while maintaining that the opinion is perceived as being objective. When an acquisition is being made, all leases in place at the time of acquisition should be reviewed to ensure compliance with Stark law.

A commonly used Stark exception involves the rental of office space. The exception allows payments for the use of office space made by a tenant to a landlord if the leasing arrangement meets the following requirements:

1. The agreement is in writing, signed by the parties, and specifies the premises.
2. The term of the agreement is at least one year. To meet this requirement, if the agreement is terminated during the term with or without cause, the parties may not enter into a new agreement during the first year of the original term of the agreement.
3. The space rented or leased does not exceed that which is reasonable and necessary for the legitimate business purposes of the lease or rental and is used exclusively by the lessee when being used by the lessee (and is not shared with or used by the lessor or any person or entity related to the lessor), except that the lessee may make payments for the use of space consisting of common areas if the payments do not exceed the lessee's pro rata share of expenses for the space based upon the ratio

of the space used exclusively by the lessee to the total amount of space (other than common areas) occupied by all persons using the common areas.

4. The rental charges over the term of the agreement are set in advance and are consistent with FMV.

5. The rental charge over the term of the agreement is not determined in a manner that: (a) takes into account the volume or value of referrals or other business generated between the parties or (b) uses a formula based on the revenue raised, earned, billed, collected, or otherwise attributable to the services performed or business generated in the premises, or per unit of service rental charges (to the extent that such charges reflect services provided to patients referred by the lessor to the lessee).

6. The agreement would be commercially reasonable even if no referrals were made between the landlord and tenant.

In the case of a lease of space, this value may not be adjusted to reflect the additional value the prospective lessee or lessor would attribute to the proximity or convenience to the lessor when the lessor is a potential source of patient referrals to the lessee. For purposes of this definition, a rental payment does not take into account intended use if it takes into account costs incurred by the lessor in developing or upgrading the property or maintaining the property or its improvements.

## *Important Tips When Reviewing a Real Estate FMV Analysis*

For health systems, attorneys, and other professionals, an understanding of answers to the following questions will provide guidance in reviewing a real estate FMV analysis.

### *Who provided the opinion?*

A review of an independent opinion of FMV (rent) should always begin with the author of the opinion. Is the author an appraiser or other real estate professional? Appraisers are governed by the Uniform Standards of Professional Appraisal Practice (USPAP), as well as by state-mandated certification laws. A professional appraiser's inappropriate actions have recourse to the general public. In case of an appraiser's inappropriate action, the individual can be turned into either the licensing state or the appraiser's professional organization for discipline. Real estate appraisers are required to be informed of the requirements set forth in developing and reporting real property appraisals (Standards 1 and 2), which are readily identified in the document. USPAP is intended to "promote and maintain a high level of public trust in appraisal practice by establishing requirements for appraisers. It is essential that appraisers develop and communicate their analyses, opinions, and conclusions to intended users of their services in a manner that is meaningful and not misleading."

Aside from appraisers, other professionals, including brokers, property managers, and accountants, may offer opinions of FMV, but the scope applied by these individuals varies widely, as does their familiarity with valuation theory. Additionally, other professionals often have some form of vested interest in the property, which could be perceived as a conflict in expressing an independent unbiased opinion. Lastly, other professionals are not governed by USPAP, so there is no assurance that generally accepted appraisal practices were employed in their analysis.

### Is a competent individual providing the opinion?

Healthcare real estate is a specialty within the real estate world, due both to the complexity of healthcare businesses, as well as the specialized nature of the associated facilities. Thus, an individual providing an FMV opinion must have adequate experience to account for the unique attributes of the property in question. If a cancer center is being valued, does the individual have an understanding of linac vault costs, as well as the associated rental rates in the marketplace? If an ambulatory surgery center is being valued, does the individual understand operating room classifications, as well as the building specifications required by each?

Does the individual have a general understanding of Stark law, the Anti-Kickback Statute, commercial reasonableness, and the False Claims Act?

### Are the comparables comparable?

The selection and analysis of comparable properties is a key component of many real estate valuations. An appraiser must understand how to analyze building type, construction components, location, reimbursement trends, and variances in state law that impact profitability and/or highest and best use (e.g., certificate of need laws). A frequent error is the use of medical office buildings as comparables for specialty properties, such as cancer clinics, ambulatory surgery centers, and specialty hospitals. This often occurs when an appraiser lacks the experience (or the data) to select appropriate comparables.

Geographical proximity can sometimes be the most important element of comparability (in the case of small medical offices, for instance). In other cases, geographical proximity can be a secondary consideration, with physical similarity of the building more significant.

Due to the complexity of many healthcare transactions, a thorough understanding of each comparable is essential. Was there a referral relationship between lessor and lessee? Was the lease executed as part of a sale/leaseback, and, if so, was the lease rate reflective of solely real estate value? Was the building impaired by economic or functional obsolescence?

### Were assumptions relied upon reasonable?

Opinions of FMV incorporate a variety of assumptions as part of the valuation process. These assumptions must be reasonable in the light of available market evidence and the methodologies employed. For instance, if construction or renovations are proposed, have these been appropriately and reasonably accounted for, given the effective date of value? An appraiser may rely upon "extraordinary assumptions" or "hypothetical conditions" within a report. The impact of these on the opinion of FMV must be carefully considered and understood.

### Was the opinion of FMV expressed as a range, and did it include all appropriate elements?

Typically, FMV opinions are expressed as a range to reflect the reality that no single point is solely representative of FMV. However, it should be noted that point estimates are required in some instances. The final indication of FMV (rent) should also report other considerations normally associated with a lease rate, including:

- length of lease term;
- operating expense treatment;
- concessions;

- escalations; and
- tenant improvements.

If the opinion involves a value rather than a lease rate, it should be made clear what property interest the value represents (such as fee simple, leased fee, or leasehold estate).

## Were the following common lease-related issues considered?

The intricacies of Stark law present a mine field of potential violations for health systems to navigate. The following represent common violations observed in the marketplace with regard to lease-related violations:

- an unsigned lease is relied upon;
- an expired lease is relied upon;
- the premises are not adequately defined in the lease;
- the lease rate is outside of a reasonable range of FMV;
- expenses are either not passed through as specified in the lease or are passed through incorrectly (or incompletely);
- services are provided by the landlord yet are not included in the lease; or
- common area is allocated incorrectly.

Some of these items are relatively simple to address (such as assuring a lease is signed), while others require either in-house or third-party expertise (such as ensuring a lease rate is within a reasonable range of FMV). A structured leasing program or third-party ownership (via a sale/leaseback) can also address some of these issues. Overall, the current climate requires providers to understand basic appraisal procedures and methodologies, as well as the nuances of Stark law, in order to ensure compliance.

# Capital Assets (Fixed Assets) 27

*Nick Shannon, ASA, and Kevin M. Florenz, ASA*

---

*There are many different definitions of value associated with Capital Asset valuation and correctly understanding the scope, methodology, and analysis will assist the reader in understanding the analysis.*

---

Capital assets (personal property) is defined as, "A type of property, which, in its most general definition, can include any asset other than real estate. The distinguishing factor between personal property and real estate is that personal property is movable. That is, the asset is not fixed permanently to one location as with real property such as land or buildings."[1]

Capital assets exist in nearly every healthcare transaction, from a single physician practice to an ambulatory surgery center (ASC), imaging center, radiation oncology center, or hospital.

---

1. http://www.investopedia.com/terms/p/personalproperty.asp.

The role of capital assets within the healthcare business increases along with the size of the organizations involved in the transaction. Based on Stark law requirements of transacting at fair market value (FMV), nearly all, if not all, acquisitions should adhere to the FMV standard and be commercially reasonable (CR). In addition, most leasing agreements and timeshare arrangements (further addressed in chapter 28) require a capital asset valuation as part of adhering to FMV guidance.

## Key Valuation Considerations

The American Society of Appraisers (ASA), which is the recognized source in capital asset appraisal training (referred by the ASA as Machinery and Technical Specialties), has several FMV definitions to reflect specific sets of circumstances, including going-concerns or installation considerations.

Of most important note to the healthcare attorney is that the standard definition of FMV excluding the aforementioned factors is considered a more conservative definition to be applied to most arrangements. The definition allows the appraiser to determine the value of the asset only to any third-party acquirer and excludes synergies and/or going-concerns that may or may not change over time, which synchronizes directly with Stark law compliance.[2]

The scope of a capital asset analysis is determined by the intended use of the appraisal, facility, or entity being acquired, and whether there are external reporting requirements beyond Stark law. Specifi-

---

2. Comparing and contrasting the FMV definitions from ASA and Stark law has led to questions, interpretations, and, ultimately, confusion for appraisers regarding the appropriate value to be applied to a transaction. Some valuation experts have argued that FMV in continued use is the appropriate definition to use, since many buyers would acquire a business or practice and continue to operate the practice in its current location going forward. For example, in a physician practice acquisition, FMV in continued use would be correct if an appraiser could accurately understand the factors involved with the practice. Pertinent questions would include: Does the physician own or lease the facility and, if leased, what are the terms? Does the acquiring system intend to continue to have the acquired physician remain in his or her current location or does the system have a medical office building to which the physician would be moved?

cally, an acquisition of a hospital or ASC may have financial reporting implications beyond the traditional Stark law, and therefore may require a different scope and analysis, including supporting documentation and information required by an external auditor.

It is important to note that there are several alternative representations of value that are mistakenly assumed to reasonably represent FMV of capital assets. Historical cost or net book value (financial or tax reporting) are inappropriate representations of FMV for capital assets. Historical cost of an asset will overvalue the individual assets because it excludes depreciation that may have accrued since acquisition. Similarly, tax net book value can be misleading since it likely undervalues the assets based on statutory depreciation policies.[3] Please see the key terms at the end of this chapter for capital asset appraisal terms including various definitions of value.

Physician practice acquisitions that fall under the domain of Stark law provide a specific set of requirements. Requirements may include developing a detailed inventory list of assets that may not directly reconcile to the fixed asset ledger to clearly and accurately identify the assets that are being acquired.

There are three basic appraisal methods that are used to derive an indication of value for capital asset: the Cost Approach, the Sales Comparison (or Market) Approach, and the Income Approach. An appraiser is required to consider all three approaches to value and the appropriate approach(es) based upon the property under consideration, data available for analysis, and other relevant factors. The following section outlines the three approaches to value in the context of capital assets.

---

3.  To illustrate, the depreciable life of capital assets is dictated by the IRS, under the modified accelerated cost recovery system (MACRS) to provide a taxpayer accelerated depreciation for income tax purposes. The tax lives typically range from five to seven years for most personal property asset categories and 15 years for leasehold improvements. Additionally, from 2008 through 2014 the physician was provided "super bonus depreciation" under the tax code. Super bonus depreciation allowed an acquirer of an asset to depreciate 50 percent of the asset immediately in the early stages of this tax treatment. In the latter stages, depending on the cost of the capital asset, the purchaser may have been able to write off 100 percent of tax net book value.

## Sales Comparison (Market) Approach

The Sales Comparison Approach (Market) Approach estimates value by comparing the price of similar assets recently sold or the buying/asking prices of similar items to the subject asset being valued. Using similar units of comparison, adjustments are made to the comparable assets for various factors, including condition, capacity, age, etc., to correlate to the subject asset. It is assumed that market transactions are conducted between willing buyers and willing sellers in an arm's-length transaction.

In applying the Sales Comparison Approach, an appraiser will research secondary market information to obtain transaction or asking prices of similar assets. When a number of sales of similar properties occur, a pattern of definable prices is established. Once the appraiser obtains sales comparable information, the appraiser makes certain adjustments to the comparable sales to correlate to the subject assets. Adjustments typically made will be based on asset characteristics, such as condition and age.

When there is sufficient comparable sales information available in the secondary market, the Sales Comparison Approach should be used, particularly as it relates to certain capital assets found in the following categories: medical equipment, office furniture, office equipment, communications equipment, computer equipment, and other equipment.

## Cost Approach

The Cost Approach incorporates the economic principle of substitution that states:[4] a prudent investor would pay no more for a property than the cost of acquiring an equally desirable substitute in the market. The Cost Approach takes into consideration the replacement cost new of a property less all forms of depreciation and obsolescence.

The Cost Approach can be performed using two different methods to estimate current cost new. The first approach is to estimate the "direct" replacement cost new by researching current cost information provided by equipment manufacturers, dealers, and various online resources. The direct replacement cost analysis should include all of

---

4. VALUING MACHINERY AND EQUIPMENT: THE FUNDAMENTALS OF APPRAISING MACHINERY AND TECHNICAL ASSETS, 3d ed. (Washington, D.C.: American Society of Appraisers, 2011).

the direct costs associated with the cost of acquiring the capital asset (i.e., the cost new of the equipment and the costs associated with freight and tax). If the facts and circumstances of the appraisal require a premise of FMV in continued use, the appraiser would consider the cost to install the capital asset as well. This is typically more relevant for major equipment assets, such as linear accelerators, MRIs, CTs, nuclear cameras, etc.

The second approach to estimate current cost new is to estimate an "indirect" reproduction cost new. Reproduction cost new is estimated by applying equipment-specific cost indices to the historical cost of the asset. Appropriate resources include information published by the Bureau of Labor Statistics and Marshall Valuation Services. There are limitations when estimating reproduction cost new due to the reliability of applying cost indices to older assets subject to rapid changes in technology.

Once appraisers determine current cost new, they then apply depreciation to reflect physical, functional, and economic obsolescence. To estimate physical depreciation, an appraiser will estimate the expected normal useful life of the capital assets and consider the respective effective age. As part of that consideration, other factors may include physical condition, current and historical utilization (where appropriate), preventive maintenance programs, and expected future utilization. The appraiser will then develop a retirement relationship to the age of the capital assets and estimate physical depreciation using a variety of techniques. Many capital assets physically deteriorate or decline from a physical usefulness perspective on a consistent basis, so straight line depreciation is frequently considered. Other elements of depreciation associated with functional and economic obsolescence create variable depreciation on a year-by-year basis.

After applying physical depreciation, an appraiser should consider functional obsolescence. Functional obsolescence, defined at the end of this chapter, is typically found when the capital assets experience excess operating cost, excess construction or capital cost, overcapacity, inadequacy, lack of utility, or similar conditions. To the extent that a capital asset is not considered state-of-the-art, or is unable to perform at a comparable level to the new peer assets, functional obsolescence likely exists.

After considering functional obsolescence, an appraiser considers economic obsolescence. There are a variety of methods to estimate economic obsolescence but, without a definable secondary market, most appraisers will rely on business enterprise analysis provided by a business valuation expert. The theory is that the value of the business is required to generate cash flow to support the value of the capital assets. If the business does not generate sufficient income to support the assets, a deduction for economic obsolescence must be considered. If a business is dramatically underperforming, applying economic obsolescence may drive the value below what the asset could be realistically liquidated for. Clearly, the Cost Approach has some limitations and may not necessarily reflect a reasonable FMV for the assets.

Key terms to be considered under the Cost Approach are outlined in the following sections and formally defined at the end of this chapter.

## Income Approach

The Income Approach estimates value by analyzing the historical financial information in order to estimate the future level of cash flows generated by assets, securities, or services. The present value of these future cash flows represents value to an investor. Once the appropriate rate of return is estimated, the cash flow stream is then discounted (capitalized) back to present value using the investor's appropriate rate of return.

The Income Approach is typically excluded as a methodology because the capital assets generally do not generate a specific and identifiable income stream related to only that isolated asset. Given that there are other assets that contribute to the overall value of the business, isolating an income stream to an exam table, as an example, is problematic. Portions of the Income Approach may be considered in the course of developing a lease payment related to a contemplated lease between two parties, or in the instance of a timeshare lease arrangement, but that is usually the extent of the use of the Income Approach.

## Reconciliation

It is important to note that most, if not all, valuation analyses for capital assets will rely on the Cost and Sales Comparison Approaches. The selection of the approach is driven by the availability of secondary market data, which is a critical requirement to perform the Sales Comparison Approach. If there is an active secondary market, emphasis should be placed on the Sales Comparison Approach because comparable sales information (price of similar property recently sold or buying/asking prices of similar property) reflect all forms of obsolescence.

Use of the Cost Approach is applied when there is a lack of sufficient sales comparable information in the secondary market. The Cost Approach is an acceptable approach to value in all situations, but caution should be taken when reviewing an analysis exclusively based on the Cost Approach, since identifying the functional and economic obsolescence inherent in the capital asset is difficult to quantify without market data or a business enterprise valuation overlay. The appraiser should be aware that there are a number of external factors beyond physical depreciation that may impact value, such as increasing competition in the medical equipment industry, healthcare reform, changes in industry regulations and reimbursements, static capital spending, and rapid changes in technology.

## *Fair Market Value Lease Arrangements*

Leasing arrangements for capital assets are becoming increasingly popular between a health system and a physician/physician group due in large part to providing both parties time flexibility in assessing the potential for a long-term relationship without a significant capital expenditure at the outset of an employment agreement. However, with increased flexibility comes the possibility of increased scrutiny and consideration of whether the arrangements comply with Stark Section § 411.357 exceptions to the referral prohibition related to compensation arrangements subset (b) Rental of Equipment, stated as:

1. A rental or lease agreement is set out in writing, is signed by the parties, and specifies the equipment it covers.
2. The equipment rented or leased does not exceed that which is reasonable and necessary for the legitimate business purposes of the lease or rental and is used exclusively by the lessee when being used by the lessee and is not shared with or used by the lessor or any person or entity related to the lessor.

3.  The agreement provides for a term of rental or lease of at least one year. To meet this requirement, if the agreement is terminated during the term with or without cause, the parties may not enter into a new agreement during the first year of the original term of the agreement
4.  The rental charges over the term of the agreement are set in advance, are consistent with fair market value, and are not determined by taking into account volume or any reference of referrals or business.

Based on the above, it is clear that any leasing arrangement should attempt to mirror the terms of a disinterested third party. Examples of disinterested third parties are banks, leasing companies, and other financial institutions that provide asset-based financing through a variety of financing vehicles to assist borrowers. The structure of the transaction has a significant impact on the requirements that the appraiser must follow.

Questions to ask if the leasing arrangement is intended to be an operating lease:

*   What is the intended lease term?
*   Does the lease term reasonably reflect a lease term that a third-party financial institution would consider?
*   What processes or considerations would a financial institution include in developing the appropriate interest rate applicable to the transaction given the credit risk of the potential lessee (could be either a health system or a physician/physician group)?
*   What is a reasonable process to estimate the residual value and what support can be provided to reasonably estimate the future FMV residual at lease termination?
*   Does the contract explicitly state that one of the end-of-lease options for the lessee is to purchase the equipment for the then FMV?

Questions to ask if the leasing arrangement is intended to be a capital lease:

*   Do both parties understand that the title will transfer at lease termination?

- What processes or considerations would a financial institution include in developing the appropriate interest rate applicable to the transaction given the credit risk of the potential lessee (could be either a health system or a physician/physician group)?

Defining the type of lease and providing a copy of the sample language to be included in the lease agreement assists the appraiser in determining the approaches required to opine on the FMV lease rate applicable to the potential transaction.

In addition to the economic considerations for leasing arrangements, it is important to remember Stark law and the Medicare Anti-Kickback Statute also require that each equipment rental arrangement to be "commercially reasonable." Under the equipment rental safe harbor, the office of inspector general (OIG) defines a "commercially reasonable business purpose" as one "that must be reasonably calculated to further the business of the lessee or purchaser. In other words, the rental or the purchase must be of space, equipment, or services that the lessee or purchaser needs, intends to utilize, and does utilize in furtherance of its commercially reasonable business objectives."

## *Important Tips When Reviewing a Capital Asset FMV Analysis*

For health system personnel, attorneys, and others who engage appraisers, an understanding of answers to the following questions will provide guidance in reviewing a capital asset FMV analysis.

*Were the appraiser's qualifications considered?*
It is important that an opinion of value be developed by an appraiser who is both competent and experienced with the subject capital assets. A lack of competency and industry experience can result in flawed appraisal methodology and assumptions that can lead to an understatement in value, or worse, an overstatement in value. There are several organizations that govern best appraisal practices and include, but are not limited to, American Society of Appraisers, as discussed previously, and the Uniform Standards of Professional Appraisal Practice (USPAP).

*Was the appraisal purpose and intended use defined?*
It is important that a reviewer be informed and understand the purpose
and intended use of the appraisal. The intended use of the appraisal
may determine the appropriate value premise to be applied, as discussed under ASA value definitions.

*Was the project scope defined and agreed upon?*
In general, capital asset appraisals can be performed under various
levels of project scope, which can range from a "limited" desktop
scope to a complete physical inspection and inventory of the subject
assets. A desktop scope is considered "limited" in nature because an
appraiser develops an opinion of value based strictly on provided information and does not physically inspect the capital assets. In contrast, a project scope including a physical inspection allows the appraiser
to gather additional information that may be necessary to develop a
credible and accurate opinion of value. A reviewer should consider
the circumstances of the appraisal and whether the project scope is
appropriate from a support and compliance perspective.

*Were the appraisal methodology and assumptions carefully reviewed?*
A reviewer should understand the appraisal methodology and assumptions applied to develop an opinion of value. For example, if the subject assets include major medical equipment with an active secondary
market, was the Market Approach considered in deriving a value conclusion? In addition, what are the underlying appraisal assumptions
and how do they affect value? In every appraisal and opinion of value,
there are qualifying assumptions that may materially impact a conclusion of value.

*Is the arrangement commercially reasonable?*
There are limited case law rulings in regard to the acquisition of capital assets. However, there has been increased scrutiny on acquisitions
and leasing arrangements that appear to lack any bona fide justifica-
tion for the transaction other than securing potential patient referrals.
For example, in the *Bradford* case summarized in chapter 2, the court
found that the hospital violated Stark law and the Medicare Anti-Kickback Statute by "subleasing" a nuclear camera from a physician-owned
entity and concluded that the purpose of the sublease arrangement

"was not simply to acquire a piece of equipment." Rather, according to the court, BRMC's CEO George Leonhardt, "expected BRMC would get substantial referrals from Drs. Vaccaro and Saleh as a result of the sublease," and stated, "that he would not have entered into the sublease arrangement if he knew that BRMC would not receive any referrals from Drs. Vaccaro and Saleh." Indeed, the court indicated that "BRMC did not believe that the GE camera was suited to its long-term needs, and knew that it would shortly replace the GE camera with another camera. In fact, the nuclear camera was never even relocated to the hospital, but remained in V&S's office, and was not used for nuclear imaging tests after a few months."[5])

## *Terms Related to the Valuation of Capital Assets*

The following outlines the various standards of value related to the appraisal of capital assets.

- *Fair market value*—An opinion, expressed in terms of money, at which the property would change hands between a willing buyer and a willing seller, neither being under any compulsion to buy or to sell and both having reasonable knowledge of relevant facts, as of a specific date.
- *Fair market value in continued use with assumed earnings*—An opinion, expressed in terms of money, at which the property would change hands between a willing buyer and a willing seller, neither being under any compulsion to buy or to sell and both having reasonable knowledge of relevant facts, as of a specific date and assuming that the business earnings support the value reported, without verification.
- *Fair market value in continued use with an earnings analysis*—An opinion, expressed in terms of money, at which the property would change hands between a willing buyer and a willing seller, neither being under any compulsion to buy or to sell and both having reasonable knowledge of relevant facts, as of a specific date and supported by the earnings of the business.

---

5. http://www.prnewswire.com/news-releases/court-finds-bradford-regional-medical-center-violated-federal-law-107560298.html.

- *Fair market value installed*—An opinion, expressed in terms of money, at which the property would change hands between a willing buyer and a willing seller, neither being under any compulsion to buy or to sell and both having reasonable knowledge of relevant facts, considering market conditions for the asset being valued, independent of earnings generated by the business in which the property is or will be installed, as of a specific date.

- *Fair market value removal*—An opinion, expressed in terms of money, at which the property would change hands between a willing buyer and a willing seller, neither being under any compulsion to buy or to sell and both having reasonable knowledge of relevant facts, considering removal of the property to another location, as of a specific date.

The following definitions and terms are to be considered during the Cost Approach for the appraisal of capital assets.

- *Reproduction cost new*—The cost of reproducing a new replica of a property on the basis of current prices with the same or closely similar materials, as of a specific date.

- *Replacement cost new (RCN)*—The current cost of a similar new property having the nearest equivalent utility as the property being appraised, as of a specific date.

- *Depreciation (appraisal)*—The actual loss in value or worth of a property from all causes, including those resulting from physical deterioration, functional obsolescence, and economic obsolescence.

- *Physical depreciation/deterioration*—A form of depreciation where the loss in value or usefulness of a property is due to the using up or expiration of its useful life caused by wear and tear, deterioration, exposure to various elements, physical stresses, and similar factors.

- *Functional obsolescence*—A form of depreciation in which the loss in value or usefulness of a property is caused by inefficiencies or inadequacies of the property itself, when compared to a more efficient or less costly replacement property that new technology and changes in design, materials, or process that result in inadequacy, overcapacity, excess construction, lack of functional utility, excess operating costs, etc., has developed. Symptoms suggesting the presence of functional obsolescence are excess operating cost, excess construction or capital cost, overcapacity, inadequacy, lack of utility, or similar conditions.

- *Economic obsolescence*—A form of depreciation or loss in value or usefulness of a property caused by factors external to the property. These may include such things as the economics of the industry; availability of financing; loss of material and/ or labor sources; passage of new legislations; changes in ordinances; increased cost of raw materials, labor, or utilities (without an offsetting increase in product price); reduced demand for the product; increased competition, inflation, or high interest rates; or similar factors

- *Normal useful life*—The physical life, usually in terms of years, that a new property will actually be used before it is retired from service. A property's normal useful life relates to how long similar properties actually tend to be used, as opposed to the more theoretical economic life calculation of how long a property can profitably be used.

- *Economic useful life*—The estimated period of time that a new property may be profitably used for the purpose for which it was intended. Stated another way, economic life is the estimated number of years that a new property can be used before it would pay the owner to replace it with the most economical replacement property that could perform an equivalent service.

- *Effective age*—The apparent age of a property in comparison with a new property of like kind; that is, the age indicated by the actual condition of a property.

- *Remaining useful life*—The estimated period during which a property of a certain effective age is expected to actually be used before it is retired from service.

# Medical Office Timeshares 28

*Britt Martin, CVA*

---

*Timeshare valuations should consider all the terms, services, and space outlined in the agreement.*

---

Medical office timeshares (MOTs) refer to part-time medical office space lease arrangements between a licensor and a licensee. MOTs have become more prevalent as this type of arrangement provides a cost-effective way for medical providers to serve surrounding markets. In the *Proposed Policy, Payment, and Quality Provisions Changes to the Medicare Physician Fee Schedule for Calendar Year 2016* the Centers for Medicare and Medicaid Services (CMS) established a new exception (411.357(y)) to permit timeshare arrangements for the use of office space, equipment, personnel items, supplies, and other services.[1] In its most basic form, a MOT is generally structured as a combined lease of some or all of the following:

---

1. 80 FR 70885 issued Nov. 16, 2015, *available at* https://federalregister.gov/a/2015-28005.

**261**

1. medical office space,
2. medical and office equipment,
3. clinical and non-clinical staff,
4. medical and office supplies, and
5. other items and services.[2]

MOTs typically utilize partial space, are part-time in nature, and are frequently structured as leases of specified blocks of time.

## MOT Fee Structures

The two most common payment structures for MOT arrangements are a fixed monthly payment and a variable payment.

### Fixed Monthly Payment

A common structure for a MOT payment is fixed monthly payment dictated by the amount of time the tenant will utilize the MOT as stated in the agreement. The fixed monthly payment is based on predetermined days and times the tenant will utilize the MOT throughout the month.

### Variable Payment

Another common structure is a variable payment, which allows the tenant to utilize the MOT on an as-needed basis. The licensor and licensee agree on a flat fair market value (FMV) payment per block of time (set in advance), which is usually a payment per four-hour or eight-hour block, and the licensee's monthly payment will be variable, based on the number of blocks utilized during the month.

## Value Drivers Impacting MOT Payments

There are a few key value drivers that may assist management with the selection of an appropriate MOT payment amount. The following are only guidelines, as both economic and non-economic factors, as well as the facts and circumstances surrounding an arrangement, should be considered:

---

2. May include items such as telephone services, cable television, and beverage services.

1. *Facility space:* Reflects one of the most fundamental components of a MOT, yet it is often the most difficult to define. Since MOTs are often part-time leases for partial space, it is crucial that the utilized space be clearly defined. Generally, the licensee will have access to both exclusive space and common area space. Exclusive space reflects areas that are designated solely for the subject provider's use during the leased block of time.[3] Common area space reflects areas that are shared with other providers on-site. An appropriate allocation of the common area space the licensee shares with other occupants during the MOT should be included in the defined space. Examples of common area space include waiting rooms, nursing stations, breakrooms, restrooms, and hallways. In addition, if the medical office space is located within a larger medical office building, a common area factor for the building should be allocated to the licensee as well.

   Once the space has been defined, an FMV appraisal of the lease rate per square foot should be obtained and applied to the defined square footage. It is noted that most facility rental rates within MOTs are stipulated on a gross basis so that the licensor bears all expense incurred in the real estate ownership. This means if a market typically leases space on a triple net basis (licensee pays pro-rata share of real estate operating costs), then this rate must be grossed up. Please see chapter 26 for further detail on what to look for in a real estate appraisal.

2. *Equipment:* Another essential component of a MOT arrangement is the medical and office equipment provided to the licensee. Equipment generally reflects the assets that are included in the exclusive and common area space being leased. Examples of standard equipment in a MOT may include exam tables, exam stools, patient scale, waiting room furniture, and computers, among numerous others. Even though the licensee may not use the equipment provided during the MOT, if it is made available to the licensee and the licensee's patients, and included under the lease arrangement, then the equipment should be included in the FMV analysis of the MOT. Valuators

---

3. For example, the provider may have exclusive access to three exam rooms during the leased block of time.

and parties to the agreement alike can confuse this interpretation of equipment usage and, as such, the parties should be cognizant of use versus availability.

Once the equipment has been defined, an FMV appraisal of the equipment lease rate should be obtained for the defined medical and office equipment. Please see chapter 27 for further detail on what to look for in a capital asset appraisal.

3. *Staff and supplies:* Staffing, supplies, and other services are commonly included in MOT arrangements, but not always expressly outlined in the agreement and, therefore, may not be accounted for in the lease or valuation. Typical staff in a MOT arrangement may include administrative staff (such as receptionists and medical records clerks) and clinical staff (such as medical assistants and registered nurses). Staffing arrangements should be clearly defined in the agreement and reflected accordingly in the FMV analysis.

   In addition to the staff, certain supplies/services, such as office supplies, medical supplies, telephone, cable television, and beverage services, should be accounted for if they will be utilized under the MOT arrangement. Although these services can be a nominal amount in the scheme of the entire arrangement, it is important to consider these costs in the FMV analysis.

4. *Amount of time leased*: The amount of time the licensee utilizes the MOT directly impacts the amount of the payment. The time utilization should be clearly outlined in the arrangement and tied directly to the FMV MOT payment.

5. *Timeshare premium*: A primary consideration in the analysis of a MOT arrangement is the premium that is recognized in the marketplace for MOT arrangements. The premium should account for the risk factors assumed by the licensor under a MOT arrangement, which may include:
   a. utilization risk;
   b. vacancy risk; and
   c. the additional burden of marketing and legal costs associated with numerous partial lease arrangements.

The timeshare premium should be reflective of the risk factors noted above. For example, there may be less risk to a licensor if a licensee is leasing three full days per week as opposed to a licensee leasing one four-hour block per month. As such, the degree of the part-time nature of the arrangement, amongst other risk factors, should be carefully considered in the FMV.

## *Key Considerations in Assessing MOT FMV Opinions*

The valuation analysis of MOT payments considers both the Cost Approach and the Market Approach. Under the Cost Approach, the costs of the underlying services are considered, plus a reasonable rate of return.[4] The development of market costs for facility and equipment usage often require a separate fair market rent study and fair market equipment lease rate analysis. Please see chapter 26 for key considerations in assessing a real estate appraisal and chapter 27 for key considerations in assessing a capital asset appraisal. For staffing and services, if actual or historical cost data is unavailable, the valuation professional may be required to use market research and available market data to develop reasonable costs.[5]

Under the Market Approach, payment rates for similar MOT arrangements in the marketplace are considered. One of the major challenges with use of the Market Approach is identifying available information on existing MOT arrangements and, specifically, information for MOTs that are similar to the subject arrangement.[6] Another obstacle with the use of the Market Approach is identifying untainted MOT comparables that do not reflect hospital-physician relationships.[7] Although the Market Approach may be used as a reasonableness check on the results of the Cost Approach, it is typically not utilized as the sole basis for FMV of a MOT.

---

4. Includes both a normal rate of return and part-time premium.

5. As an example, if the costs for staffing are not available, the valuation professional may be required to rely on independently published compensation survey data to develop reasonable costs for the support staff.

6. The scope of specific services with timeshares will often vary. Without a detailed agreement or build-up of the comparable rate, it is difficult to ensure that the identified timeshares are truly comparable to the subject.

7. The argument being that the market MOT arrangements may include payment rates that are not at FMV due to referral relationship between the parties.

The following is a list of questions to help clarify if an FMV analysis has considered appropriate factors:

- **Have all components of the MOT arrangement (i.e., space, equipment, staff, and services) been clearly defined in the agreement?** The agreement should clearly define the services being provided and should encompass all space, equipment, staff, and other services the licensee will utilize during the MOT. The valuation should clearly reflect the terms of the agreement and account for all services described.

- **Does the valuation analysis rely solely on MOT market comparables that reflect hospital-physician relationships?** Since existing MOTs between hospitals and physicians may reflect payment rates that are tainted with referral relationships, it is prudent that the valuation professional rely on additional or alternative approaches in establishing the FMV of the MOT.

- **Have the unique aspects of the space or the licensee's needs been considered as part of the valuation?** There may be other components of a MOT that are unique to the specific arrangement, such as storage space and specialized medical equipment, that may be overlooked in the process of constructing and valuing the overall arrangement. These unique services should be specifically identified and included in the FMV analysis.

- **Has the degree of the part-time nature of the services been considered?** As stated previously, the part-time premium applied is correlated to the amount of time the licensee will occupy the space. The part-time premium should be applied/adjusted based on the licensee's occupancy and documented appropriately in the FMV analysis.

# Appendix:
# Checklist for Reviewing
# an FMV Opinion

*Jen Johnson, CFA, Colin M. McDermott, CFA, CPA/ABV,*
*and Bridget Triepke, CPA*

The chapters of this book outline important value drivers and key considerations when assessing a fair market value (FMV) analysis for almost every type of healthcare transaction and compensation arrangement. The following checklist has been provided to illustrate a broad set of points to be considered when reviewing any FMV analysis. Adherence to this list, along with an understanding of the specific chapters, will assist in ensuring the analysis is thorough and defensible.

## General Checklist

✓ Confirm that the arrangement (transaction or compensation agreement) has documentation supporting that it is commercially reasonable (CR) absent the consideration of referrals. See chapter 2 for additional guidance on CR.

✓ Ensure the transaction or compensation terms are clearly outlined, set in advance, and agreed upon in writing.

✓ Ensure that the valuation analysis reflects and matches the agreed-upon terms.

✓ Determine that the appraiser engaged to provide the analysis has the appropriate credentials? See chapter 3 for additional guidance.

## Business Valuation Questions

✓ Did the appraiser consider all three generally accepted valuation methods (Income, Market, and Cost Approaches) and adequately describe why certain method(s) were relied upon over others?

✓ Does the appraisal contain a definitive opinion or just a series of observations?

✓ Is the appraisal consistent with the level of value being acquired (control versus minority)?

✓ Were there any qualifying assumptions or scope of restrictions based on data availability or timing that should be discussed further? Do these qualifications and limitations impact the ability of the appraisal to withstand regulatory scrutiny?

✓ Did the appraiser have discussions with management of the subject entity to discuss any anticipated changes in the following:

- payor mix,
- case mix,
- volume,
- staffing,
- capital expenditure requirements,
- service area demographics, and
- competitive factors?

✓ Is the FMV indication consistent with the assets that are being acquired? For example:

- Net working capital:
  o Are all components of net working capital being acquired or only certain components? Often cash is retained by the seller and accounts receivable are excluded due to liability and/or calculability issues.
  o If net working capital is acquired, is it based on a normalized or target amount? Will there be any purchase adjustments for net working capital excess/deficiencies?
- Non-operating assets: Will assets such as excess land and investments be acquired? If so, are the values of these assets reflected in the FMV indication?

✓ Did the appraiser make normalizing adjustments to exclude one-time events and nonrecurring revenue or expenses?

✓ If the appraiser utilized a discounted cash flow method, were the cash flows forecasted until the point at which the subject business had reached a stabilized state?

✓ If the subject business being valued is a department of a health system or other larger organization, were adjustments made to adjust the cost structure to that of a freestanding business? Adjustments could include (but are not limited to) the removal of corporate overhead allocations that the department does not directly benefit from and/or the addition of staff that the department is utilizing from the health system.

✓ If the facility is owned by a related party to the subject business, was consideration given to performing a fair market rental rate analysis?

## Compensation Arrangement Questions

✓ Did the appropriate party representatives to the arrangement review understand and verify the assumptions and value drivers relied upon in the analysis?

✓ If there are multiple services provided, does each have a defensible valuation methodology outlined?

✓ Have multiple, objective market surveys (when available) been considered as part of the analysis? If only one survey is utilized, it is important that the valuation provide sufficient reasoning to explain the departure from use of multiple surveys.

✓ If comparable arrangements are relied upon, are they truly comparable?

✓ Does the valuation address whether it is an employed or independent contractor arrangement?

✓ If the services are billable, is it clear which party is retaining collections and are they considered in the analysis?

✓ If physician compensation data was considered, is a physician required based on the services outlined?

✓ Are the physicians required to document time and services prior to receiving payment for the services? Requiring physicians to submit time logs in order to receive payment is a best practice from a compliance perspective.

✓ Commercially reasonable questions (see chapter 2 for additional guidance):

- Do the services being provided overlap with what the hospital or health system's staff is providing?
- Was the physician chosen based on his or her expertise in a particular specialty?
- Are there an excessive number of physicians engaged?

# Index